Discworld and Philosophy

Popular Culture and Philosophy® Series Editor: George A. Reisch

Volume 1 *Seinfeld and Philosophy: A Book about Everything and Nothing* (2000)

Volume 2 *The Simpsons and Philosophy: The D'oh! of Homer* (2001)

Volume 3 *The Matrix and Philosophy: Welcome to the Desert of the Real* (2002)

Volume 4 *Buffy the Vampire Slayer and Philosophy: Fear and Trembling in Sunnydale* (2003)

Volume 9 *Harry Potter and Philosophy: If Aristotle Ran Hogwarts* (2004)

Volume 12 *Star Wars and Philosophy: More Powerful than You Can Possibly Imagine* (2005)

Volume 13 *Superheroes and Philosophy: Truth, Justice, and the Socratic Way* (2005)

Volume 19 *Monty Python and Philosophy: Nudge Nudge, Think Think!* (2006)

Volume 25 *The Beatles and Philosophy: Nothing You Can Think that Can't Be Thunk* (2006)

Volume 30 *Pink Floyd and Philosophy: Careful with that Axiom, Eugene!* (2007)

Volume 35 *Star Trek and Philosophy: The Wrath of Kant* (2008)

Volume 36 *The Legend of Zelda and Philosophy: I Link Therefore I Am* (2008)

Volume 39 *Jimmy Buffett and Philosophy: The Porpoise Driven Life* (2009) Edited by Erin McKenna and Scott L. Pratt

Volume 42 *Supervillains and Philosophy: Sometimes Evil Is Its Own Reward* (2009)

Volume 45 *World of Warcraft and Philosophy: Wrath of the Philosopher King* (2009) Edited by Luke Cuddy and John Nordlinger

Volume 46 *Mr. Monk and Philosophy: The Curious Case of the Defective Detective* (2010) Edited by D.E. Wittkower

Volume 47 *Anime and Philosophy: Wide Eyed Wonder* (2010) Edited by Josef Steiff and Tristan D. Tamplin

Volume 48 *The Red Sox and Philosophy: Green Monster Meditations* (2010) Edited by Michael Macomber

Volume 49 *Zombies, Vampires, and Philosophy: New Life for the Undead* (2010) Edited by Richard Greene and K. Silem Mohammad

Volume 51 *Soccer and Philosophy: Beautiful Thoughts on the Beautiful Game* (2010) Edited by Ted Richards

Volume 52 *Manga and Philosophy: Fullmetal Metaphysician* (2010) Edited by Josef Steiff and Adam Barkman

Volume 53 *Martial Arts and Philosophy: Beating and Nothingness* (2010) Edited by Graham Priest and Damon Young

Volume 54 *The Onion and Philosophy: Fake News Story True, Alleges Indignant Area Professor* (2010) Edited by Sharon M. Kaye

Volume 55 *Doctor Who and Philosophy: Bigger on the Inside* (2010) Edited by Courtland Lewis and Paula Smithka

Volume 57 *Rush and Philosophy: Heart and Mind United* (2011) Edited by Jim Berti and Durrell Bowman

Volume 58 *Dexter and Philosophy: Mind over Spatter* (2011) Edited by Richard Greene, George A. Reisch, and Rachel Robison-Greene

Volume 60 *SpongeBob SquarePants and Philosophy: Soaking Up Secrets Under the Sea!* (2011) Edited by Joseph J. Foy

Volume 61 *Sherlock Holmes and Philosophy: The Footprints of a Gigantic Mind* (2011) Edited by Josef Steiff

Volume 62 *Inception and Philosophy: Ideas to Die For* (2011) Edited by Thorsten Botz-Bornstein

Volume 63 *Philip K. Dick and Philosophy: Do Androids Have Kindred Spirits?* (2011) Edited by D.E. Wittkower

Volume 64 *The Rolling Stones and Philosophy: It's Just a Thought Away* (2012) Edited by Luke Dick and George A. Reisch

Volume 67 *Breaking Bad and Philosophy: Badder Living through Chemistry* (2012) Edited by David R. Koepsell and Robert Arp

Volume 68 *The Walking Dead and Philosophy: Zombie Apocalypse Now* (2012) Edited by Wayne Yuen

Volume 69 *Curb Your Enthusiasm and Philosophy: Awaken the Social Assassin Within* (2012) Edited by Mark Ralkowski

Volume 71 *The Catcher in the Rye and Philosophy: A Book for Bastards, Morons, and Madmen* (2012) Edited by Keith Dromm and Heather Salter

Volume 72 *Jeopardy! and Philosophy: What Is Knowledge in the Form of a Question?* (2012) Edited by Shaun P. Young

Volume 73 *The Wire and Philosophy: This America, Man* (2013) Edited by David Bzdak, Joanna Crosby, and Seth Vannatta

Volume 74 *Planet of the Apes and Philosophy: Great Apes Think Alike* (2013) Edited by John Huss

Volume 75 *Psych and Philosophy: Some Dark Juju-Magumbo* (2013) Edited by Robert Arp

Volume 79 *Frankenstein and Philosophy: The Shocking Truth* (2013) Edited by Nicolas Michaud

Volume 80 *Ender's Game and Philosophy: Genocide Is Child's Play* (2013) Edited by D.E. Wittkower and Lucinda Rush

Volume 81 *How I Met Your Mother and Philosophy: Being and Awesomeness* (2014) Edited by Lorenzo von Matterhorn

Volume 82 *Jurassic Park and Philosophy: The Truth Is Terrifying* (2014) Edited by Nicolas Michaud

Volume 83 *The Devil and Philosophy: The Nature of His Game* (2014) Edited by Robert Arp

Volume 84 *Leonard Cohn and Philosophy: Various Positions* (2014) Edited by Jason Holt

Volume 85 *Homeland and Philosophy: For Your Minds Only* (2014) Edited by Robert Arp

Volume 86 *Girls and Philosophy: For Your Minds Only* (2014) Edited by Richa Greene and Rachel Robison-Greene

Volume 87 *Adventure Time and Philosophy: The Handbook for Heroes* (2015) Edited by Nicolas Michaud

Volume 88 *Justified and Philosophy: Shoot First, Think Later* (2015) Edited b Rod Carveth and Robert Arp

Volume 89 *Steve Jobs and Philosophy: For Those Who Think Different* (2015) Edited by Shawn E. Klein

Volume 90 *Dracula and Philosophy: Dying to Know* (2015) Edited by Nicolas Michaud and Janelle Pötzsch

Volume 91 *It's Always Sunny and Philosophy: The Gang Gets Analyzed* (2015) Edited by Roger Hunt and Robert Arp

Volume 92 *Orange Is the New Black and Philosophy: Last Exit from Litchfield* (2015) Edited by Richard Greene and Rachel Robison-Greene

Volume 93 *More Doctor Who and Philosophy: Regeneration Time* (2015) Edited by Courtland Lewis and Paula Smithka

Volume 94 *Divergent and Philosophy: The Factions of Life* (2016) Edited by Courtland Lewis

Volume 95 *Downton Abbey and Philosophy: Thinking in That Manor* (2016) Edited by Adam Barkman and Robert Arp

Volume 96 *Hannibal Lecter and Philosophy: The Heart of the Matter* (2016) Edited by Joseph Westfall

Volume 97 *The Ultimate Walking Dead and Philosophy: Hungry for More* (2016) Edited by Wayne Yuen

Volume 98 *The Princess Bride and Philosophy: Inconceivable!* (2016) Edited by Richard Greene and Rachel Robison-Greene

Volume 99 *Louis C.K. and Philosophy: You Don't Get to Be Bored* (2016) Edited by Mark Ralkowski

Volume 100 *Batman, Superman, and Philosophy: Badass or Boyscout?* (2016) Edited by Nicolas Michaud

Volume 101 *Discworld and Philosophy: Reality Is Not What It Seems* (2016) Edited by Nicolas Michaud

In Preparation:

Orphan Black and Philosophy (2016) Edited by Richard Greene and Rachel Robison-Greene

David Bowie and Philosophy (2016) Edited by Theodore G. Ammon

The Ultimate Game of Thrones and Philosophy (2016) Edited by Eric J. Silverman and Robert Arp

Deadpool and Philosophy (2016) Edited by Nicolas Michaud

Peanuts and Philosophy (2016) Edited by Richard Greene and Rachel Robison-Greene

Red Rising and Philosophy (2016) Edited by Courtland Lewis and Kevin McCain

Jimi Hendrix and Philosophy (2017) Edited by Theodore G. Ammon

For full details of all Popular Culture and Philosophy® books, visit www.opencourtbooks.com.

Popular Culture and Philosophy®

Discworld and Philosophy

Reality Is Not What It Seems

Edited by

NICOLAS MICHAUD

OPEN COURT
Chicago

Volume 101 in the series, Popular Culture and Philosophy®, edited by George A. Reisch

To find out more about Open Court books, call toll-free 1-800-815-2280, or visit our website at www.opencourtbooks.com.

Open Court Publishing Company is a division of Carus Publishing Company, dba Cricket Media.

First printing 2016

Printed and bound in the United States of America.

ISBN: 978-0-8126-9919-7

This book is also available as an e-book.

Library of Congress Control Number: 2016937735

Contents

* Ephebian translation: Where's my towel!?

** True not all Ephebians are philosophers, but we assure you, every great mind here was deeply in need of a towel by the end of the their chapter.

In memory of Sir Terry Pratchett

Eureka!?

Hello!

Let's be honest, if you are reading this it is because you love Discworld. You already know that Terry Pratchett's creation is one of the most magnificent, brilliant, and funny contributions any one person has made to the world. The Disc is a vibrant, magical, and dangerous place full of insight, truth, and dangerous ideas. The experience of Discworld, I imagine, would be much like holding a werewolf by the ears, you know eventually it is going to end, tragically, but it is a hell of a ride.

The authors collected here are philosophers, but more importantly, like you, they love Discworld and they love Terry Pratchett. Speaking for myself, as the editor of the book, I can honestly say that Sir Terry's gift to the world brought me some of my most cherished moments. I remember the first person to recommend the first Discworld book I ever read. Since then, I have reread the series multiple times and have found continuing joy in sharing Pratchett's gift with others.

Discworld is where I met my first philosophers. When I read *Small Gods*, I had no idea I would become a philosopher, but I know now that Pratchett's picture of philosophy, and philosophers, has forever colored my own perception of myself and my career. I will always think of philosophers as first, and foremost, people who are smart, but not smart enough to pack spare towels around the neighborhood for when they shout "Eureka!" and jump out of the tub to write the idea down. To me, this perspective on philosophy is important, because it means I don't take myself too seriously, because, the fact of the matter is that there are things far more serious than whatever silly idea I come up with, like family and illness.

Another important lesson I learned from Sir Terry early on was about death. Death himself appears in every Discworld book, and he will appear in every chapter here. I am reminded, by that ever-looming shadow, that I have limited time and have no clue what, if anything, comes next. I am reminded that I should try to do some real good like Sir Terry, and reminded about the things that really matter like being a good person who is willing to grow and change like my heroes on the Disc, Vimes and von Lipwig. I never had the honor to meet Sir Terry, and I hesitate to call such a giant anything other than "Sir." But, nevertheless, I do owe him, and I am sad that I will never have a chance to thank him. So now is my best chance, and so, I say to him, "Thank you." I will donate any personal profit I receive from this book to Alzheimer's research, as my small contribution to Sir Terry's legacy.

Well, enough with all of the serious philosopher prattle. Let's have some fun exploring some of the most profound ideas Sir Terry has presented us with. Questions like, how absurd is the Luggage, really? Is Rincewind a hero? And how did Death help us come to terms with death? We could write untold chapters on the thousands of brilliant questions that Discworld brings us, but these are some of the most fun, most challenging, and most Ephebian. So grab a barstool next to the Librarian at the Mended Drum and a mug of something likely to melt through the bar when spilt, and enjoy!

Welcome to *Discworld and Philosophy!*

I

Rewriting Your Chem

1
More Golems around Than You Might Think

VANESSA FRÖHLICH

Golems just creep the living hell out of people. And even in the huge melting pot of a city like Ankh-Morpork, with its many different species like humans, trolls, dwarfs, or werewolves,[1] people don't quite know what to make of them. And can we blame them?

Just imagine yourself, peacefully walking home through the dark alleys of Ankh-Morpork after your nightly volunteer shift at the Sunshine Sanctuary for Sick Dragons. You're not too worried—after all, there has been a good deal less murder and mayhem in the streets with old Sam in charge of the City Watch. Also, you've already had your fill of run-ins with the Guild of Thieves this month, and you carry the receipts to prove it. But suddenly you hear heavy, thumping footsteps. You look up, and, outlined against the lantern-lit Ankh-Morpork fog, you see a huge, misshapen figure with two glowing red embers for eyes slowly lumbering in your general direction. It's a golem—one of the giant, person-like "machines" made of clay that are used everywhere around the city for all the hard or dangerous jobs nobody else wants to do. You try to stop the chill running down your spine by being reasonable. It's probably on its way back from some job and won't hurt you. Technically, it isn't even alive; it's only a machine kept going by a *chem* (a piece of parchment with religious instructions) that rests inside its hollow head. And you've also heard something about their not being allowed to hurt humans because the words in

[1] And for that matter, *whatever* Nobby Nobbs is.

their head tell them not to. Or have you? Suddenly, you're not at all sure as that gigantic shape slowly drags its weight towards you. You hear all kinds of things about golems suddenly going berserk . . .

This is more or less how most people in Ankh-Morpork feel about golems—being so *different* from everybody else, they just make people feel uneasy. Cheery Littlebottom of the City Watch, for example, has some serious issues with them, even with her colleague Angua trying to calm her down.

> "Sorry, look," said Cheery. "Are you telling me this . . . thing is powered by words? [. . .]"
>
> "Why not? Words *do* have power. Everyone knows that," said Angua. "There are more golems around than you might think." (Pratchett, *Feet of Clay*, 113)

And Angua is right. There really are a lot of golems around—you're one, for example. And there's no need to be insulted, here. I'm one too. Actually, we all are. Now, before you decide that I'm completely off my rocker, let me clarify. I'm not claiming that you have a hollow skull containing a piece of parchment filled with written instructions.[2] What I am claiming is that your life and your behavior are determined by texts, by the words in your head, just like the lives and behavior of the golems and all the people on the Discworld.[3]

Don't believe me? Then let's have a look at *Feet of Clay* and at the golem Dorfl, the chief suspect in two of the murder cases that Sam Vimes and the Ankh-Morpork City Watch have to solve in this novel. Dorfl and his fellow golems suffer from their situation, so they have created themselves a king golem to lead them to freedom. Sadly, they have made one huge mistake: they put too many words inside its head, so it went insane and started murdering people, creating a whole lot of trouble for the Watch. In the end, Dorfl saves the day and becomes a Watchman, but only after he has learned that he can choose his own words, words in his heart, and that he can follow these words rather than the words in his head.

---

[2] If you do, you should probably not be reading this but seeing a doctor about it, right about now.

[3] DETERMINED BY TEXTS BOOKENDED BY ME.

Beware of the Words in Your Head . . .

The best Discworld character to turn to if you want to understand why we're all not so unlike Dorfl the golem has little to do with Ankh-Morpork and probably wouldn't hold with golems at all: It's Granny Weatherwax. Granny and her coven have to journey to the far-off city of Genua to stop a girl from marrying a prince in a storyline that sounds suspiciously like *Cinderella*. This does not seem too difficult, at first. Things get a lot more complicated when Granny's long-lost sister Lily enters the picture. Lily is terrorizing the entire kingdom by forcing its inhabitants to live according to fairy tale plots. Her main interest is, of course, to marry Ella, the daughter of Genua's former ruler, to a frog that she has turned into a prince. This way, Lily would become the one truly in control of the city. In a final confrontation, this is what Granny tells her sister: "Things have come to an end, see [. . .]. That's how it works when you turn the world into stories. You should never have done that. You shouldn't turn the world into stories. You shouldn't treat people like they was *characters,* like they was *things.* But if you *do,* then you've got to know when the story ends" (Pratchett, *Witches Abroad*, 270). Knowing when the story ends sounds like it's quite simple. Granny herself would probably tell you that reality is really real, while stories aren't. Modelling life on fairy tales and failing to acknowledge the real world has barely done anyone good. While this approach works quite well for our pragmatic witch, a bunch of other people wouldn't think that it was all that easy. They call themselves "postmodernists."[4]

Postmodern philosophy is very interested in language and what it does—its "functions." One of the most important functions of language is of course that it allows us to communicate. This means that the definition of a *text* is much wider for postmodernists than you would think. For a postmodernist, not only are words written down on a piece of paper, on a parchment, or

[4] Postmodernism has unfortunately nothing to do with Moist von Lipwig and his reform of Ankh-Morpork's postal system, but is all about a bunch of philosophers thinking that they have some revolutionary new ideas that will succeed the thoughts of modernism, and which are therefore a lot better. There's a whole lot of arguing going on about whether this is true. Or about whether their ideas are new at all. Philosophers are just as competitive as the next person and a good deal more awkward at parties.

on a screen texts, but also everything that fulfills a communicative function is considered a text. A movie can be a text. So can a painting.[5] An idea that is accepted by everybody in a society can also be a text—for example, the idea that all dwarfs must look and act male, no matter their actual sex. The dwarfish language on the Disc does not even have female pronouns. The words we use say a lot about the way we see the world, and the other way round, too.

Postmodernists believe that our culture is dominated by lots and lots of contradictory texts, which constantly compete for our attention. If any text is successful, it is not so much because it tells us what is really real, but rather because a large number of people would *like* to believe that what it tells them is real. Unless Lily Weatherwax happens to be around, young women could wait for a prince on a white horse to come by and whisk them off to a life of luxury until their heads fell off and it still wouldn't happen, but it's nice to *believe* it will if you're just patient and nice and humble enough, isn't it? It sounds so much easier than, say, studying and working hard to earn a life of luxury all by yourself. Also, if you're patient and nice and humble enough, your evil stepsisters will apparently end up losing their toes in a bloody mess. That's always a plus.

Culturally promoted ideas like this are what the postmodern philosopher Jean-François Lyotard[6] (1924–1998) calls *metanarratives*. He describes metanarratives as culturally accepted texts that people use to justify certain ways of thinking and acting, often without even noticing it. Examples of metanarratives that postmodernists love to use are political systems (capitalism, communism, fascism, Vetinari-ism), religious beliefs, gender, and race, but there are many more. If it tells you how to behave or what to believe because "you belong in this or that group and that's just what we do," you're probably dealing with a metanarrative.

Postmodernism is not only defined by its fascination with texts but most importantly by its belief that there's definitely something fishy about metanarratives. This rejection is basically founded in the assumption that most of the information

---

[5] Even if there are no urns or fat babies with wings in it.

[6] Not to be confused with Jean-Marie Jules Léotard, the inventor of the popular sports garment. (This is actually true. Funny things, words!)

we receive on a daily basis[7] is manipulated by people who have the power to do so and want to feed us certain "texts"—world views, value systems, beliefs—without our noticing it. This begins with those people in charge of commercials telling us that we absolutely need their product for our happiness and can end with politicians telling us that we need to go to war against this or that nation because we have always hated them, those evildoers. Postmodernists tend to reject the totalizing explanations that metanarratives want to offer us and instead side with those who do not "fit" into these narratives, those who are left out of them or who are regarded as inferior in them. What right do random children wandering through the woods have not only to eat other people's houses but also to brutally murder old ladies? For that matter, can golems really be nothing but mindless machines if they want their own king to lead them to freedom? In thinking like this, postmodernists turn against the Lily Weatherwaxes of this world—those people who have the power to manipulate narratives and to put words into our heads to achieve their own ends.

. . . and of the Buggers Who Put Them There

So, if the reality that we all live in is mostly based on texts that are put in our heads by the people in power, what does this mean for our everyday lives?

For one thing, it means that reality as we see it is not really real, but rather is based on stories, and that these stories can be manipulated by those people in power. Lily Weatherwax, who sees other people as characters in fairy tales and forces them to live by them, is one example for such a manipulative person. Or think of Dragon King of Arms in *Feet of Clay,* who pretends to be a simple herald, but who actually manipulates Nobby's family tree to make him the Earl of Ankh and finally the new king. King Nobby would of course be much easier to

---

[7] And we receive *lots* of information, what with our constant exposure to the media. We are a long way from the days when we could get married, buy a farm, and diaper our first child by the time we get a letter back from our cousin Clem telling us, "I really don't trust that gurl you fancy; you should find yerself a new one else before she cons you into buyin' Old Man Dotson's farm." Information moves a mite speedier these days, Pardner.

control than Lord Vetinari, or say, King Carrot. The power to change texts gives Dragon the power to control people.

So, evil people manipulate the words in our heads to make us believe in those stories that play into their hands. It's not quite as simple as that, of course. People don't live according to stories because other people force them to do so, but mostly because they like it. I think it's safe to say that most of us prefer neat and easily comprehensible patterns to chaos in our lives. Stories offer just that: neat, comprehensible patterns to structure our lives on, so that its whole complexity seems less confusing. It's exactly this urge to believe in stories that can make humans so easy to manipulate.

Terry Pratchett doesn't like this human tendency to fall for stories one bit, and his plots and characters show this dislike. Two characters who strongly share it with him are Granny Weatherwax and Sam Vimes. Vimes, for example, may not know a thing about postmodernism, and he wouldn't recognize a metanarrative if it hit him in the face,[8] but he instinctively understands a lot about the power that stories can have over people. He is furious at those people who are weak or stupid enough to completely model their lives on stories without questioning them. The people of Ankh-Morpork, for example, still believe that, some day, their long-lost king will return to rule over them all.

Just like Granny, Vimes deeply hates anything that degrades people and makes them unequal. As he puts it when accusing Dragon King of Arms of having manipulated Nobby's family tree: "I don't like to see people treated like cattle. [. . .] And of course that's what you've always done, isn't it? These are the stock books of Ankh-Morpork" (*Feet of Clay*, 330).

This is also the reason Vimes burns down the archives containing Dragon's "stock books." In a social system controlled by stories and the people who manipulate them, he sees it as his

---

[8] That would not stop him, however, from using his pair of "perfectly legal" brass knuckles to pummel it into submission, arrest it, and throw it in the Tanty for "Being a word that causes Nobby Nobbs to wink knowingly at ladies passing by."* (*This charge is kind of like "Impeding an Officer of The Law" . . . Nobby can reduce *any* word to four letters and make even a lamppost blush.**) (**Immediately after which the lamppost would look at the almost-human face of Nobby Nobbs and run away . . . quickly.)

duty as a policeman to protect all who suffer from the injustice of it. This is also why he insists that Dorfl be given a voice at the end of the novel. With his own voice and the ability not only to reject the words that are put in his head by others, but also to choose his own words, Dorfl finally gets a chance to be free.

How Would You Like Your Texts?

Now, Lily's manipulation of fairy tales and Dragon's messing with Nobby's family tree will already have given you a clue: The interesting thing about texts is that they are not unchangeable. They develop and they evolve, often based on what society would like them to be like, or on the intentions of the one who is narrating them. The history of Ankh-Morpork as Dragon is writing it has little to do with the actual historical facts, but much more with his own political aims. Just like Lily, Dragon likes to think of himself as an author who is writing a story, and of other people as characters in that story, which he can manipulate as he likes. Granny Weatherwax would tell you that evil begins with seeing people as things. This is just what Lily and Dragon do.

A good example for a whole society that modifies a text to fit its own needs are the people of Ankh-Morpork, who are rather fond of the story of Vimes's famous ancestor Old Stoneface, and how he killed their last king—but who are not so fond of the actual historical facts. At the three-hundred-year anniversary of the revolution, Nobby gets to play the king and is allowed to wear nice clothes and ride around on a white horse. But nobody wants to play Old Stoneface, "on account of him being on the losing side" (*Feet of Clay*, 81). When Vimes points out that the king was a vicious tyrant, and that Old Stoneface did rule the city for six months after killing him, Nobby explains to him how everybody in the Historical Society thinks that he shouldn't have. After all, he was outnumbered, and he was a bit of a bastard, chopping a king's head off and all (*Feet of Clay*, 81). Also, he was apparently not the most handsome guy around.[9]

This way of thinking is not so much evil as it is stupid, but it is still alarming. Thinking in orderly but extremely simple patterns like this not only keeps people from seeing the bigger

---

9 This coming from Nobby should be counted as an insult all in itself.

picture, it also makes them easy to manipulate for others, who have a feeling for what the masses want to hear and who can change texts to fit those needs.

Words in Our Heads, Heads up Our Bums

Now, if the way we see the world is controlled by the words in our heads, and if these words can be manipulated and changed, where does this leave us, morally speaking? Well, first things first, it means that questions of morality and ethics are a lot more complicated than it seems, because their answers depend a lot on our individual point of view—and we can't even be sure that this point of view is really our own.

Dorfl and his fellow golems are only alive because of their chems, the rolls of parchment with religious words on them inside their heads. They are also controlled by these words and must follow their rules, and where the words don't control them, they are slaves to the will of their owners. All across Ankh-Morpork, people use them as working machines and think of them as things, without feelings or rights. That the golems do have feelings, and that they suffer from their situation, is clear. After all, they built themselves a king to lead them to freedom. Even golems seem to think that kings are a great idea.

Still, the only one who sympathizes with the golems and believes that they have thoughts and feelings is Carrot. After he buys Dorfl from his owner, the butcher Mr. Sock, he puts the receipt inside the golem's head to give him to himself. The idea of freedom is pretty overwhelming for poor Dorfl at first, but slowly he begins to understand that he does not need to follow the words that others prescribe to him but that he can choose his own words to follow instead.

Meanwhile, everybody but Carrot still sticks to the view that golems are not thinking and feeling creatures, but things. Even when Dorfl comes to their aid to fight the golem king and is smashed up, Angua still insists that this is not murder,[10] because Dorfl was never alive (*Feet of Clay*, 314). And just when you think that Carrot is all about treating people equally and

---

[10] And she, as a werewolf who gets her fair share of discrimination in Ankh-Morpork every day, would have to know better.

without prejudice, look at his reaction when Cheery begins to look and act more like a girl. After he delivers a lengthy rant about how she should have the decency to keep her femininity to herself instead of drawing attention to it, Angua has to inform him that he probably has his head stuck up his bum (*Feet of Clay*, 228).

The problem with Carrot's head is not so much that he has it stuck up his bum, but rather the words he has inside it. Carrot was raised as a dwarf, and thinks of himself as one, which means that the words in *his* head are pretty much those that his dwarf parents and dwarf society have put in there. While it's maybe not morally right, it's still almost natural for him to be irritated by Cheery's behavior. This only shows how difficult it is for us to break out of the moral systems that our peers teach us, and how hard it can be to tell "right" apart from "wrong" because of this.

In the end, we all have a more or less big collection of words in our heads that tell us what to do and how to behave. This is actually alright, as long as we do not let them trick us into judging people because they don't seem to fit into the world drawn up by these words. Just like we believe the words in our heads to be the right ones, other people think the same thing about the words in their heads. If we don't want to end up with our heads up our bums, we should stop to think about this from time to time.

Freedom Is Like Having the Top of Your Head Opened Up

What Terry Pratchett is telling us here is that "right" and "wrong" are not quite so simple. Nobody should come along and hand us a manual on what is right and what is wrong. Instead, the values that we follow should depend on our own choices. We have to choose what we believe is right and act according to it. It's choices like this that make us really free. Golems like Dorfl cannot be free before they reject the words in their heads and choose their own. Similarly, the people of Ankh-Morpork are so easy to manipulate because they like to believe in texts, like the old, romantic stories of ancient kings, and model their world views and behavior on them. Cheery Littlebottom cannot be truly free before she rejects her society's belief that she is not allowed to act and look female. In a way, this is what we're all like. We as free persons are not controlled by metanarratives, the words that are put in our heads by the Lilys and Dragons around us, but choose our own stories to believe in because they seem right.

Still, letting go of the words in our heads is not all that easy, and the freedom that comes with it can be extremely confusing and scary, which is why a lot of people shy away from it. No longer blindly believing in the words in your head means having to think and act for yourself, having to make all of your decisions by yourself, and taking full responsibility for your actions. This is hard, especially because you can never really be sure if you are making the right choices until you see how they turn out. Dorfl recognizes this when he tries to free the animals from the slaughterhouse and his fellow golems by smashing their stalls and working places and releasing them into the streets.

> "I Smashed The Treadmill But The Golems Repaired It. Why? And I Let the Animals Go But They Just Milled Around Stupidly. Some Of Them Even Went Back To The Slaughter Pens. Why?"
>
> "Welcome to the world, Constable Dorfl."
>
> "Is It Frightening To Be Free?"
>
> "You said it."
>
> "You Say To People 'Throw Off Your Chains' And They Make New Chains For Themselves?"
>
> "Seems to be a major human activity, yes."
>
> Dorfl rumbled as he thought about this. "Yes," he said eventually. "I Can See Why. Freedom Is Like Having The Top Of Your Head Opened Up." (*Feet of Clay*, 349)

Dorfl has to realize that simply setting the animals and his fellow golems "free" will never work as long as they don't choose freedom by themselves and are actually scared of it—and, what's even more important, he doesn't blame them for being scared of freedom, probably because he remembers how painful it was when he had to let go of the words in his head. So, instead of trying to force freedom on his fellow golems again, he decides to save his wages from his new job as a Watchman to buy more golems and give them to themselves, like Carrot did for him.

Now, what can we learn from that? Well, for example, that even if we are machines driven by texts, and if everybody else around us is just another machine, driven by another set of words, that doesn't mean that we should let our fellow humans suffer for it. Not because their words are different from ours and not because we think they're stupid for not realizing what's going on. Much like Dorfl does, we should realize that we're all in the same boat together and try to encourage others to see make their own words.

Words in the Heart Cannot Be Taken

So, we're all not so unlike Dorfl and his fellow golems at all. We're all controlled by the words that others put in our heads and there's nothing we can do about it. It's also extremely hard to reject this influence, because once you get rid of one story bouncing around inside your skull, the next one already comes along to replace it and manipulate you. Well, that's just too bad! Let's just sit down and lament the fact, but let's not try and change anything, because those darn words are too powerful for us, anyhow.

Believe it or not, this is actually what your typical postmodernist would have to say about the matter.[11] Radical postmodernists not only think that metanarratives are basically everywhere around us, but also that they are all-powerful and we can never escape their influence. Well, knowing Terry Pratchett, we know that he would beg to differ.

Of course we are controlled by the words in our heads. Of course we are faced with huge numbers of different stories competing for our attention every day. Of course the Lilys and Dragons around us are trying to put their words into our heads to manipulate us into following their aims. And of course it is next to impossible to get out of this mess.

The important thing is to notice what is going on. The next time we see a dwarf wearing a skirt and lipstick in public,[12] before becoming all upset about it, let's all think about *why* it

---

[11] Give them a few drinks however and you will have a small army of philosophers charging the gates of the university demanding change, and a small raise.

[12] Alright, not so likely. How about a man wearing a skirt and lipstick?

upsets us. What words are at work in our heads just now? Who put them there? Do we agree with them? Or wouldn't it be better to think them over, reject them maybe, and choose another set of words, which we personally like better? Every single one of us can choose the words they want inside their heads—and kick out those nasty little buggers that make us see the world too narrowly, treat other people unfairly, or that make us do things we don't actually want to do. If we do this, the words become our own. They become words in our hearts, rather than words in our heads. And, as Dorfl knows in the end, these can never be taken from you.

2

Golem Morality in the Modern World

MATTHEW SKENE

You're on your way to your favorite band's music with rocks in concert. You go past the River Ankh, and you see a small child gradually descending into the water. You could easily walk across the crust of the river and save the child, but then you would have to go home and bathe for several hours, and you would miss your concert. Should you save the child and miss your concert, or go to the concert and let the child eventually drown? According to pretty much everyone, you should save the child. After all, the child's life is more important than your attendance at the concert, and it would be wrong to sacrifice something more important in order to do something less important. A morality so undemanding as to let you get away with letting kids drown is clearly not up to snuff.

On the other hand, the kids on Cockbill Street often don't have enough to eat. In at least some cases, a lack of food for an extra few days could be just as eventually fatal as being unable to swim while sinking into the River Ankh. Having enough food to eat is also more important than going to the concert. And you could have used the money you spent on the ticket to buy food for them instead. So, in buying the ticket haven't you already decided to privilege something less important over something more important? If it was wrong to think attending the concert justified letting the kid drown, why isn't it equally bad to let the kids on Cockbill Street starve so you can go to the concert?[1]

---

[1] TAKE IT FROM ME. FEEDING THEM ANKH-MORPORK FOOD MAY BE JUST AS DANGEROUS AS LETTING THEM STARVE.

What Does Morality Demand of You? Perhaps It's "Give Me All Your Money!"

The problem just presented is, more or less, the same one raised by Peter Singer in his paper, "Famine, Affluence, and Morality." According to Singer, there is no real difference between these cases. Whenever we decide to spend money on something like concerts, or movies, or *Discworld and Philosophy* books rather than giving it to those in need, we are effectively choosing to let children needlessly die.[2] Singer's moral system is very demanding. It would require you to forgo almost all of your desires and ambitions (not to mention all your Discworld books) in order to help those in need. There is something that makes us suspicious of the view. For instance, why doesn't that guy on the dust jacket look like he's wearing clothes from the Shonky Shop and living off of boiled cabbage and sausages sold at cut-throat rates?[3] Singer himself gives away a lot of money, but he certainly doesn't sacrifice everything less important than a child's life in order to help those in need. Singer also doesn't strike me as the sort of person who could live with himself if he really thought he was murdering children by the thousands. Yet he seems to get through each day without suffering a mental breakdown.[4] The idea that going about our daily lives amounts to killing children is overstating things (I hope). Although we may not be ending their hunger, at least we aren't causing it. So how demanding should a moral system be? I think the proper balance might be found in the moral system of the golems, especially as described in *Going Postal*.

Old-Fashioned Values from Old, Fashioned Beings

Golems are artifacts created to do various jobs. They are intelligent, but they have no free will and usually no voice prior to

---

[2] On the other hand, perhaps the *Discworld and Philosophy* book will help motivate you to help others more in the long run. I'd say it's worth the risk.

[3] Singer is known for caring very deeply about animals, and would normally never eat a sausage. But given that an Ankh-Morpork sausage sold by Dibbler might contain only something that has been *near* a pig or even just within *earshot* of a pig, that's not really an issue here. (For details on such things as Dibbler's sausages, see Pratchett and Briggs, *Turtle Recall*.)

[4] At least as nearly as this can be ascertained for a philosopher.

being set free. As tools in the hands of others, they have a clear sense of the jobs people want done, and are often asked to participate in questionable activities. Perhaps because they don't have it, the focus of golem morality rests in freedom. German philosopher Immanuel Kant also believed that our free choices were the foundation of morality. He thought that our ability to make choices made moral evaluation possible. Despite focusing on freedom, neither Kant nor the golems thought that freedom involved freedom to do anything one desired.[5] Instead, Kant and golems both understand that "Freedom Without Limits Is Just A Word" (Pratchett, *Feet of Clay*, 347), and that with freedom we must also have responsibility. Neither Kant nor the golems go light on responsibility. They think our responsibility includes an obligation to reason through our choices in ways that respect and don't wrongly make use of others, or demonstrate an indifference to their will or their choices. Unlike Kant, who focuses only on the reasons for our choices, golems also think we should focus on the consequences of our actions. As beings who would wait until the world comes around again to deliver a package, they have little forgiveness for ignoring the long-term effects of our actions.

The golems possessed a sense of justice and morality even in the absence of their own freedom. Their efforts to make a king to free them included a desire to instill justice and morality into it, and its crimes created such deep shame and sorrow that they drove most of its creators to suicide. Despite feeling the wrongness of their actions, owned golems must follow the orders they are given. While shamed by the consequences of creating their king, in their work lives[6] they can't be blamed for their actions. They lack the ability to refuse orders, and sometimes are used in immoral ways. This perhaps helps explain why they can see the consequences of immoral choices so clearly. Like guns, golems don't kill people, people kill people. But your Luger can't feel remorse at what will happen when the bullet leaves the barrel or understand what it has done. The golems can, and it pains them.

---

[5] Kant was so unmoved by his own desires that if he would've had a golem's anatomical structure, it probably wouldn't have hindered his life in the slightest.

[6] That is to say, their lives.

The first free golem was Dorfl. Dorfl began his free life by forming a moral code of his own. Despite being made by priests and brought to life by holy words in his head, Dorfl is an atheist by choice who devises and freely abides by his own moral beliefs. The core of his moral code is freedom. Freedom and the responsibility that comes with it are new and vibrant for golems; they are passionate about and awed by the responsibility of freedom. Freedom is "Like Having The Top Of Your Head Opened Up" (Pratchett, *Feet of Clay*, 349), and comes with freedom to take the consequences, which is what gives it its value.

A clear example of the demands of a golem moral system is found in the character of Pump 19. Mr. Pump calls the never-violent Moist von Lipwig a murderer for his life as a con man. Pump 19 claims Moist has killed 2.338 people. How?

> You Have Stolen, Embezzled, Defrauded, And Swindled Without Discrimination, Mr. Lipvig. You Have Ruined Businesses And Destroyed Jobs. When Banks Fail, It Is Seldom Bankers Who Starve. Your Actions Have Taken Away From Those Who Had Little Enough To Begin With. In A Myriad Small Ways You Have Hastened The Deaths Of Many. (Pratchett, *Going Postal*, 100)

Pump 19 doesn't go as far as Singer does. Singer claims that if you fail to help those in need when you could have done so, you are responsible for their deaths. Pump 19 only claims that if you engage in wrongful actions that hasten the deaths of others, then you are responsible for their loss of life. Yet the moral theory is still quite demanding. Casual actions that fail to take into account probable long-term effects aren't forgiven. In addition, the wrongness of an act isn't limited to consideration of the act itself, but is also a form of killing by the inch, a far greater crime to be responsible for.

Moist protests against this idea at first. He thinks it can't be right to call him a killer. The idea seems to press on him, though. When he discovers that he cost Adora Belle Dearheart her job in a bank, he begins to feel some of that responsibility hit home, exclaiming to himself "Gods damn Mr. Pump and his actuarial concept of murder!" (*Going Postal*, 310). Through the eyes of the golems, Moist begins to question his own life, and to stop seeing his actions as quite so innocent. His defense that he was not actually violent in his efforts to enrich and entertain himself at the expense of others starts to ring hollow. Finally seeing the extent of his crimes, Moist acquires a strong desire to prove to himself that at the very least he isn't Reacher Gilt. Moist always enjoyed the freedom his intelligence and skill gave him to get by in life on trickery. But in the stare of the unmoving eyes and unbending morality of Pump 19, he finds a need to redeem himself. Freedom for Moist begins to involve consequences, and accepting them makes Moist more capable of understanding himself as he finds himself falling into good ways.

Golem Morality in Politics

The leaders of Ankh-Morpork throughout most of its history were evil and corrupt. From the rule of the last King Lorenzo the Kind[7] through the patricians before Vetinari, nearly every ruler turned to torture and insanity by the end of their reign. In addition to direct harms, leaders promoted disastrous policies like weapons laws that made every day Hogswatch for criminals, and tax policies that bled the city dry. "Royalty pollutes people's minds," says Sam Vimes. Vimes also recalls "a line full of leeches that'd make Vetinari seem like a breath of clean air" (Pratchett, *Night Watch*, 209). Vetinari maintains some of the elements of a tyrant, with scorpion pits for the deserving,[8] but he also ensures that the city is better off because of him. The greatness of Lord Vetinari rests primarily in his ability to make the city run smoothly. He can ensure, often simply by not getting in the way, that the city prospers. He opens his door to the world, inviting in the ingenuity and the prosperity that comes with life in a multi-vital society, and finds a way to keep everything functioning smoothly. Vetinari's skill is rare, and his temperament and insight into human nature rarer still. In contrast, most governments create needless suffering through their policies, explaining the tenor of Pratchett's views on government throughout his works.

Pratchett's condemnation of government in his books is full of anger and passion. From the golem's perspective, it is easy to see why. The only place where actuarial murder is applied in

---

[7] Abuser of children and owner of torture pits too gruesome to imagine.

[8] Mimes and other undesirables.

real life is in evaluating the comparative evils of government. Perhaps this is because it is in government where the connection between a leader's decisions and effects on innocent parties is clearest. Chairman Mao, for example, is probably the greatest murderer in history. The state directly killed plenty of people in his time, with estimates in the millions. But most of the deaths at his hands were not caused by execution, they were caused by unpardonable indifference to the effects of his policies. Mao instituted agricultural policies that directly led to widespread famine, which are agreed to have killed tens of millions of people (Dikötter, *Mao's Great Famine*). He was convinced by pseudo-scientists whose ideas had failed elsewhere that things like growing crops closer together would be a good idea. After all, farmers must grow them farther apart because they're stupid or lazy or like less food, and not because history had taught them that it worked more efficiently. Mao not only maintained these disastrous agricultural policies in the presence of their failure, but also insisted that people make backyard steel smelting a routine part of life. With strict quotas in place, this led to a life with fewer pots, pans, and farming tools, but plenty of useless, fragile clumps of metal sitting around. Like aspiring comrade Reg Shoe, if there wasn't already a famine, Mao could certainly arrange one. When we see that it is proper to judge rulers by the effects of their decisions, it is harder to see why we shouldn't bring the same judgments to bear on ourselves when we choose to act without consideration for the harms our choices cause.

Golem Morality in Daily Life

The essence of golem morality is the idea that those who make decisions that will affect others have an obligation to care about those effects. It's not too much to ask that we care about the consequences of our choices. If we decide to take on the task of making decisions that impact the lives of others, we should take our obligation to avoid harming them seriously. The demands of golem morality find a good balance between sacrificing ourselves to help those in need and avoiding all responsibility for their lives. The effects you have on others in your daily life are most directly brought on friends and family. Fortunately, we tend to have an easier time concerning ourselves with their futures. But we also make decisions in other areas that impact the lives of people, like the jury box or the voting booth. A willingness to vote carelessly or decide on a verdict without concern for the effects on the accused could violate the obligations laid out by the golems.

Another part of our lives where we place ourselves in positions to decide things that affect others is in our careers. Positions where we can be responsible for the success or failure of business that others depend on for employment, or for the reliable provision of important goods can influence the length and quality of a number of lives. The more responsibility we take on, the greater our need to ensure we are acting for reasons that don't ignore such consequences. The most obvious way to make decisions that affect others is to become involved in politics. But in our global economy there are an increasing number of jobs that can lead you to make decisions that influence the lives of others. This fact was powerfully and painfully demonstrated by the banking crisis of 2008.

Golem Morality and the Banking Crisis

Reacher Gilt was guilty of a number of crimes in his time as chairman of the Grand Trunk. Playing the "find the lady trick" with whole banks, he managed to take Moist's game to a whole new level. He killed a number of people in more direct ways, but by the application of the golem standard or morality, he killed even more people through the indirect harms his practices caused to the city. The Grand Trunk under Gilt has been legally stolen from its creators and become so costly and inefficient that most people can no longer rely on it as a means of communication. The Trunk is reviled by everyone in Ankh-Morpork. Despite doing all the mucky jobs, Miss Dearheart won't even let the golems at the Golem Trust work there, explaining, "There's some shit not even a golem should work in . . . They are moral creatures" (*Going Postal*, 170).

One might wonder at first glance why the Trunk is so passionately reviled. People don't like inconvenience, but why is a return to the difficulties of communication faced a few years ago justification for such outrage? As Vetinari explains, though, the clacks is "the lifeblood of trade, and commerce, and diplomacy" in Ankh-Morpork. People depend on the Trunk for information about where to sell and buy goods, whether or not their goods have safely arrived, and what opportunities and risks can be found in new areas. Just as the internet opened markets to the world and made commerce vastly more productive and easier, the clacks is the key to an expansion of employment and business. Like banks failing, communication failing usually doesn't harm those who run the Trunk. The collusion, price fixing, and maintenance of a monopoly have crippled the effectiveness of those communications while cutting almost everyone off from the rest of the world. Like Moist's crimes, this hastened the deaths of those who don't have enough to begin with.

The only groups who have historically been in a position to drastically effect large groups of people have been governments, or other forms of official authority. With the growth of certain industries, however, businesses have started to have the ability to drastically affect the lives of millions. The last banking crisis was a drastic example of the long-term effects of these decisions. Published four years before the banking scandal, Mr. Pump's recognition that when banks fail it isn't the bankers who starve seems almost prophetic in hindsight. Exact numbers are hard to come by, but it is likely that tens if not hundreds of thousands of premature deaths were caused worldwide by the financial crisis in 2008. According to UNICEF, as many as 27 thousand children may have died prematurely as a result of these decisions in sub-Saharan Africa alone (see UNICEF in References). This isn't as bad as Mao's "Great Leap Forward," but it is still mass murder by the standards of golems. Many people are outraged by the lack of punishment for those responsible for the collapse. In light of these consequences, the outrage is rather understated.

Golems and Singer's Morality

Golems are first described as making people very uncomfortable. Everyone is ready to believe stories that a golem went mad somewhere and killed people, and Vimes points out that "Given how we use them, maybe we're scared because we know we deserve it" (*Feet of Clay*, 141). The suspicion that we aren't really acting as we should is common in human life. Vimes, who watches himself with an ironclad morality all his own, still feels uncomfortable in the stare of the golems. "Those expressionless eyes watch us, those big faces turn to follow us, and doesn't it just look as though they are making notes and taking names?" (*Feet of Clay*, 140–41). Eyes staring at us, especially expressionless ones, set us into reflection about our own moral status. A Newcastle University study showed that the presence of a photocopy of eyes makes people far more likely to pay the honesty box for drinks and food left for sale in the canteen. When we are unreflective, we often assume we are doing enough. But something about blank eyes of creatures like golems unnerves us, and makes us feel the need to do more.

I have demonstrated great sympathy for the golems and suggested that in contrast Singer is too extreme. Yet some days I worry that a defense of the golem standard of morality really isn't enough. Maybe I am vainly fighting like Moist to reject the responsibility that really does belong to me when I reject Singer's higher standard. I worry that one day it will hit home like it did for Moist when he learned of how he hurt the woman he was coming to love. People look away from the TV and even express rage at having to see ads showing suffering around the globe. We resent efforts to make us feel inadequate in response to morality's demands. It is hard to look into those children's eyes and not feel judged. Humans are very good in daily life at exempting themselves from morality's demands. We tell ourselves, as Reacher Gilt tells others, that we haven't done anything wrong, and that "bad things had happened by spontaneous generation in some weird, chilly, geometrical other world, and 'were to be regretted'" (*Going Postal*, 307). But unless we're faced directly with the suffering, we usually don't think tragedies require any real change to how we live. Perhaps part of the reason golems are so often described as old-fashioned in their morality is that they don't try to obfuscate and justify themselves as we have learned to do so well.

I wonder to myself, having written all this, whether or not a golem would endorse Singer's views. The golems started a volunteer fire brigade and don't let harm come to others if they can avoid it. They work tirelessly once freed to free other golems, rather than simply enjoying their own freedom. They obviously care about the harms that come to the innocent and seek to avoid them. They would certainly walk along the river[9] to save the child, and already do give away what they have to help others. If such moral creatures would be happy to embrace Singer's view, then perhaps we shouldn't be so quick to dismiss it after all.

[9] Or more likely, on it's bottom.

3
We Willna Be Fooled Again! Wee Free Anarchists!

MICHAEL KUGLER

Tiffany, the little girl of Terry Pratchett's *The Wee Free Men*, learns her brother has been kidnapped. A talking toad tells her of the Nac Mac Feegle, pictsies whose specialty is breaking in and thievery. Desperate to recruit them to help her find him, she lures them out with some very smelly sheep liniment—the very drink the Feegles love. Instantly hundreds emerge, six-inch tall blue-skinned men with orange hair and faces "like a hatful of knuckles." All wear kilts, some wear helmets made from rodent skulls, and each is armed with a sword. "We are a famously stealin' folk," one says. "Aren't we, lads? Whut's it we're famous for?" Together the Feegles shout: "Stealin'!" "Fightin'!" and "Drinkin'!" When their leader asks, "And what else?" they cry out "Drinkin' and fightin'!" Anything else? "Stealin' an' drinkin' an' fightin'!" Tiffany is shocked, but desperate enough that the Wee Free Men become the best hope she has to return her brother home.

This story, like others from Pratchett's Discworld, does what great art should do for us as moral creatures. It prods us into feeling strongly and then reflecting on such fiction as "what if?" possibilities about our world. *The Wee Free Men* tests, among other things, our convictions about what we must do to protect the dignity and freedom of creatures, human or not, often powerless against the authorities, and how they might defend themselves and others. Pratchett must have cared a great deal about these characters, if only because they are so much fun; he would write four more books about them. And Pratchett, through those characters, seems to suggest that we have laws and government *only* so people can flourish. Flourishing requires individual freedom—the kind of freedom the Wee Free Men enjoy.

If You Didn't Find Some Way of Stopping It, People Would Go on Asking Questions

The individual freedoms that allow flourishing are another way to describe their *rights.* When government acts for its own sake, it wrestles with people for authority over their lives. Political philosophers typically distinguish the moral law—what our conscience tells most of us is right—from the written or positive law. Anarchists argue that in creating and enforcing written law states must violate the moral law and integrity of individual freedom. No state however minimal can protect liberty without also violating it. Anarchism usually gets discussed along with libertarianism, where the only morally defensible state is the minimum necessary to insure the maximum necessary individual liberty. In *The Problem of Political Authority,* Michael Huemer begins with a defense of the libertarian state to challenge the foundations of political authority. He argues in favor of anarchism, suggesting that libertarianism has an anarchist streak. In his classic book *Anarchy, State, and Utopia*, Robert Nozick carefully discusses anarchism before defending the libertarian state. In this way anarchists seem useful in their ability to expose specific examples of the gross over-reach of government into individual liberty, while arguing that no anarchist community could actually work.[1] The anarchist's intense skepticism of formal authority is like a watchman on the community's walls, wide awake in case the authorities violate the rights or integrity of their fellow citizens. Though Pratchett's imagined world of *The Wee Free Men* is ruled like a medieval kingdom, it inspires reflection about the proper role of anarchy in a just state. Are his main characters anarchists?

---

[1] Anarchists function like the Roto-Rooter woman: we need her to help dig through a theoretical mess, but we probably won't invite her back for our Christmas party.

Have You Ever Heard the Saying, *The Land Finds Its Witch*?

A little girl, Tiffany, grows up on her parent's farm with her irritating but loveable little brother. She's stubborn, smart, and tough; she does her chores. She's also compassionate. Her Grandmother Aching was the gentle woman who taught her to read, to be kind to animals and people. After her grandmother's death, Tiffany discovers she was a local witch with a reputation for courage and integrity, but also with contempt for the authorities, particularly the Baron. He is more interested in processions and ceremonies than serving the real needs of his people, especially the poor. Tiffany's life flips upside down when she catches a group of fairies stealing eggs from her barn. Sharp-eyed and quick, she meets the Nac Mac Feegle. Think of tiny Braveheart troops led by Groundskeeper Willie. They are drunk whenever possible and often violently beating each other. They are an Englishman's stereotype of the Scots, apparently all thieves from Glasgow. They are only loyal to one another, and to their queen or "kelda." The one law they recognize is their heartfelt commitment to one another if threatened by someone outside the clan.

Tiffany can't believe that her grandmother respected and worked with the Wee Frees, any more than she can imagine befriending them. That changes when an evil Fairy Queen kidnaps Tiffany's little brother. In desperation, Tiffany has to get help from this utterly undependable band of bruised brawlers. Soon Tiffany learns that this isn't the first time the Queen has abducted a child. The Fairy Queen is cruelly selfish and can't tell the difference between what she wants and what others need. She is powerful and takes what she wants, and in this way she's like the Baron. In fact, Tiffany, Grandmother Aching, and certainly the Wee Frees also often ignore the law, but the difference is their reasons for doing so.

The Feegles come to trust Tiffany, so they bring her to their home under a hill. She meets their dying kelda, whose last act is to appoint Tiffany as her temporary successor. The Feegles enthusiastically agree.[2] In return they follow her to the

---

[2] The Wee Free swear to guard their new kelda at every moment, but they promise not to peek at her when she, ahem, has to answer "a wee call o' nature."

Queen's realm. "Why won't you do what I say?" the Queen demands. "Everyone could be so happy if only they'd do what I say!" Tiffany defeats the Queen and rescues her brother as well as the Baron's son, kidnapped years before. "*Someone has to care,*" Tiffany realizes. "*Sometimes they have to fight. Someone has to speak for that which has no voice . . .* My dreams! My brother! My family! My land! My world! . . . *I have a duty!*" (*Wee Free Men*, 232–33). In this adventure Tiffany realizes she's inherited her grandmother's magic powers. But her power has its roots in the chalk lands of her birth, and is woven into her moral capacities, her sympathy and sense of justice, as well as mercy.

Tiffany: Rebels? Against who? Toad: Everyone. Anything.

The Feegles embody a basic contempt for authority. Once the Queen's henchmen, they fled from her because she enlisted them against the poor and defenseless. They had learned to their horror that she exploited their shared contempt for law, but was willing to assault and exploit even those far weaker than herself. The Feegles' creed says it all: "Nae quin! Nae king! Nae laird! Nae master! We willna be fooled again!" (70). Lawyers were the worst.[3] The poor, often poorly educated, are at the mercy of lawyers who write and interpret the law.

Rulers like the Baron and their advisors twist the law to unjust purposes, earning Granny Aching's contempt. She tells Tiffany the tale of the Baron's valuable hunting dog caught killing sheep. Law requires the dog be killed. Through his servants the Baron tries to hire the witch to save it. Aching concocts a humorous but stern compromise: release the dog into a barn full of aggressive rams, which pound him. This saves the dog's life and teaches it to leave sheep alone.[4]

Later, fighting the Fairy Queen, Tiffany recalls the trial of a simple woman, Miss Robinson, also caught kidnapping a child. Though the law demands severe punishment, the commoners and the Baron realize that this woman was so lonely that kidnapping a child seemed, madly, her only hope. The child was

---

[3] Lawyers are the professional Orcs of Discworld—a Feegle's sword glows blue when lawyers are nearby.

[4] REST ASSURED THE DOG DID EVENTUALLY DIE.

returned unharmed, and the Baron decides that even though their written law demands a harsh penalty, the spirit of that law would be better served by the entire community vowing in the future to care far better for Robinson. The story asserts that we hurt others often because we've been badly hurt. Understanding why they hurt someone might make it possible to save them. Since every person is so valuable, it is at least worth a try. All creatures are frail in some way, and the weak deserve understanding. Understanding requires intimacy. Intimacy is born of the face-to-face relationship, provoking sympathy out of which morals are born. Pratchett's Discworld advances the wisdom of people who know the laws, but realize that no law, however carefully written, covers all the possible challenges of our lives together. "It's just the rules, and they didn't know what to do about them," Tiffany concludes. "There must be a way around it" (133).

To get around rules, you typically need lawyers. But they do it for payment, for powerful folk who can afford their cunning. They are the Sophists of Pratchett's world, ancient Greece's hired clever men paid to be indifferent to moral justice. In Pratchett's books we see that there is a wrong way, and a right way, around the law. The right way requires at least knowing someone well, belonging to a community where together you try to balance their frailty and needs to those of everyone else. In *Anarchy, State, and Utopia* Nozick argued for the smallest and least intrusive possible civic authority. A basic claim of any government is its assertion of the right to exclusive use of violence to protect the rights of citizens. Throughout the first half of the book Nozick pushes aside the various ways citizens concede to government greater and greater intervention over their daily lives ("People tend to forget the possibilities of acting independently of the state," 14). Yet modern government permits no rivals to its claim to use violence to enforce its will. At one point he argues that it is reasonable for citizens to form spontaneous associations to protect themselves. The Feegles, a clan of relatives, would no longer serve as the Fairy Queen's henchmen for her cruel and wicked assaults on the poor and defenseless. Rob Anybody tells Tiffany:

> "We used tae live in the Quin's country, ye ken, but we rebelled against her evil rule—"

"And we did that, an' then she threw us ooout on account o' bein' drunk and' stealin' and fightin' a' the time," said Daft Wullie. (142)

Nozick probably didn't imagine clans of drunken Scottish robbers as an example of spontaneously-formed citizen alliances. But if they are (mostly) sober, he concedes that under some circumstances an extra-governmental group might have the right to act as a state within a limited area. The Feegles, Aching, and Tiffany seem to share traits with Nozick's idea of small local authorities initiated on the spot by groups of citizens.

The Wee Free Men are "the way around the rules" embodied. They refuse allegiance to anyone, respect no law for its own sake, and regularly violate a slew of codes of behavior and propriety. Their drunkenness, fighting, and thievery are the stuff of legends. They enjoy the good times, the adventure of it all. Their wee kilts tell you everything—anyone going commando 24/7 has no use for any rules. But they follow a moral code. They rob, for example, but only from those who have some to spare, never from the poor. Tiffany discovers that they had robbed her grandmother many times, and is shocked to learn that Aching knew and tolerated it. Shepherds left tobacco in the fields for her, but the Feegles stole it. The shepherds shared their tobacco because they respected the old woman; the Feegles watched her sheep because they too respected her. Stealing tobacco was a just desert for their kindness and Aching understood that. In the beginning Tiffany believed that their thievery meant disrespect for her grandmother, but it eventually makes sense.

"Ye're nae gonna get nasty aboot it?" said Rob Nobody.

"No. It all . . . works."

The Wee Free enjoyed a relationship with the old woman, meaning for Pratchett a bond between people formed from a history of trust, reasonable forgiveness of slights, and flexibility about enforcing such agreements. There is no written law here and even the moral law is hard to define. Aching and the Nac Mac Feegle understood intuitively the nature of their relationship; one party's *affection* for the other guided them intuitively to know what could be demanded, where advantage could be taken, and what it meant to abuse the relationship.

Stealing the tobacco the old woman left outside for the shepherds, for instance, the Feegles in return watched out for sheep lost or lambs strayed and returned them to their folds. The Baron's authority and his agents have no role here. This tightly-knit community operates as a state unto itself. Without them, some needs would go unmet and some injustices unchallenged. The authorities can't or won't intervene in every assault on its citizens. It seems some victims only find justice with the help of opponents of government.

The Baron Pushed the Law Book Aside and Said: Perhaps We Should Do This a Different Way

Granny Aching figures out how to save the Baron's dog and teach it to protect sheep. In a moment of moral clarity the Baron leads his community to save a kidnapper and probably prevent her harming anyone again. The Feegles shamelessly steal from shepherds and from Granny Aching, but as part of a mutual understanding about looking after one another's interests. Pratchett suggested therefore that we should treat the law as merely a guideline for moral behavior. As such it must be considered flexible depending upon circumstances. The law punishing dogs for killing sheep helps prevents the loss of valuable property and loved animals; the law punishing kidnapping of children needs no defense. But in each case the well-being of creatures, animals, and people, mean there are possible exceptions to the harshness of the penalty. Since the Baron engaged Granny Aching to save his dog, the witch takes advantage of this to scold him about his tendency to see the law as the mere expression of his own will and rights as ruler. "Things were a lot easier after that. The bailiff was a little less unpleasant when rents were late, the Baron was a little more polite to people . . . and the Baron had been shown what happens when sheep rise up . . ." (77). Typically the Baron and his court seek more than that; they want deference, honor, their persons and their office revered as if they were made of something sacred. Aching's treatment of the Baron and his lackeys suggests that authorities deserve as much respect as they earn protecting citizens.

Tiffany's grandmother helped the Baron understand that the laws in fact define his relationships with his people as much as they do with them among themselves. Later, facing the kidnapping case which seems even less morally ambiguous, the Baron and his subjects, who know the woman charged, understand her as a young woman wrecked by brutal loneliness who in the end did not really harm the child. What could Pratchett suggest if even a positive law like punishment for kidnapping can in this situation be set aside? The law is not overlooked or distorted; that is what the Baron had attempted by bribing Granny Aching to save his dog. That is what bad lawyers do. They exploit ambiguous legal language to serve the masters who can afford their cleverness at the expense of the poor, weak or voiceless. Saving Robinson, the kidnapper, is different. Had she harmed the child, her neighbors would not have been merciful. Each situation is distinctive and requires, for the sake of compassion and the duty, that neighbors care about one another. They bend the law even slightly for the sake of the well-being of criminals who themselves were victims. Did this decision leave Robinson's neighbors content? No. "It wasn't perfect, and not everyone was happy, but it worked" (196). Such actions honor the moral complexity of our lives in a way strict adherence to the law cannot.

Aching helps Tiffany understand that her sorcery is powered by her compassion and moral integrity, strangely nourished by the chalky lands they call home. Law, properly observed, represents moral balance among people, reflecting Aching's conviction about balance between human needs and those of the land itself—the soil, forests and animals. But Tiffany can't defeat the evil Queen without the Wee Free Men. Their power is a joyous affection and care for one another, their obsessive rejoicing in breaking laws and challenging authorities. The Feegles do this instinctively. They "take the piss" from every boss and chief. United with Tiffany they act without care or respect for any other authority than their own moral consciences. The Feegles have no half-measures—their unconquerable joy at insulting and beating each other, at stealing and getting drunk, is matched by their all-out service to Tiffany's quest.

The anarchist argues that freedom and moral integrity are not possible under even the smallest intervention from political authority. In *The Problem of Political Authority,* Huemer encourages the individualism of ad hoc anarcho-capitalist groups to spontaneously carry out government-like functions, protecting rights and resolving disputes as citizens contract with them, but without coercive power. Pratchett's characters share a similarly basic distrust of authority. Granny Aching and the Feegles came to trust and care for one another. The Wee Free Men loved and respected the old witch, so they joined up with her when she asked for their help. Meeting Tiffany and learning that the same convictions, a similar heart, and sources of magical power were as strong in her, they offered her their friendship too. As their kelda they obey her only because they respect her. From her deep affection for her grandmother, and knowing of incidents like the trial of Miss Robinson, Tiffany refused a reverence for the authorities and the literal trustworthiness of the law. The Feegles explode into her life, challenging and confusing her, but she quickly learns to love and admire their courage and loyalty. Despite their predictable unpredictability they are a powerful force for caring for the weak and defenseless. Their fistfights and stealing are small prices to pay for their affection and courageous care. The poor and vulnerable seem to pay a much greater price for the Baron's commitment to the letter of the law, which he and his lawyers of course interpret as it suits them. As she develops her powers to confront the authoritarian Queen of Fairyland, Tiffany reinforces this skepticism of rulers and the instruments of their power.

By the book's end, Pratchett seems to suggest that the moral law is rooted in a basic intuition, our love for one another. "What is loving?" may require disobeying the positive law—even on occasion the moral law. Laws might not, likely don't, embody love. The Baron's laws, especially as he interprets them, often serve his selfish convictions and sense of honor. The evil Queen is also a source of law, but arbitrary, selfish, and cruel. Saving and protecting those too weak to defend themselves, might well require skirting if not violating such law. Tiffany becomes a far more dangerous opponent than the Queen imagined, and to defeat her she has only one weapon. She must tempt the girl to save herself. She attacks Tiffany's trust in her love of others, which leads her to doubt her sorcery. Tiffany's battle with the Queen will result in defeat or victory based largely on the girl's secret fear that she too acts from selfishness, or if she is confident that she does so from love and duty.

Ye Must Love Your Wee Brother to Face a' These Monsters for Him

With such anti-authoritarian characters Pratchett test drives a vision of anarchism fueled by a strong instinct of affectionate duty to other people, to the land and its creatures.[5] The force behind this is outrage over injustice and cruelty. As Tiffany leads the Wee Free Men to liberate her brother she learns that any decent community must encourage citizens with the creativity to imagine more virtuous associations as well as the means to combat injustice. Such outrage and creativity are rooted in knowledge of the land, its natural sources of power, ancient traditions and the many, many lives which came before her and to whom she is responsible. Chalk lands are formed across many millions of years by the bones of billions of tiny creatures. They remind Tiffany of the many, many lives which long before hers made her life possible. So, she is duty-bound to act on behalf of others. Inheriting her grandmother's sense of duty, Tiffany cooperates with the Wee Free Men out of love and respect, even when they act outrageously. They cannot abide any authority beyond their own autonomy. Yet they don't imagine overthrowing the Baron for a rule more just, democratic, or constitutional. Their creed—"We willna be fooled again!"—recalls the other line from The Who song: "Meet the new boss; same as the old boss." Pratchett's characters accept their duties to others without imaging themselves better "bosses." They live within the existing system of authority, maintain a watch over the dignity and welfare of the people and the land, and look for opportunities to exploit the system for the sake of creativity, liberty, dignity, and compassion.

The joyful wildness of the Wee Free Men makes anarchism attractive; Grandma Aching and Tiffany act as moral free agents with indifference to the Baron's rule, often with open contempt if not opposition to his authority. A child and these anarchic fairies are moved by fierce love and loyalty for others. They will do nearly anything to care for them. As such, the moral problems presented by risking themselves for those they

---

[5] Interestingly, this "law of love" combined with contempt for all forms of state authority perhaps sounds most like the Christian anarchism of the French sociologist Jacques Ellul (1912–1994).

love seems to them simply the right thing to do. Further, they don't care enough about their material possessions that the risk of losing them hinders their dangerous actions. These characters in Pratchett's story narrate key elements of legitimate challenges to the authority of the state suggested by Nozick in *Anarchy, State and Utopia* and Huemer in *The Problem of Political Authority.* The charisma of the Wee Free Men wins our hearts, but some rule, even if only a leader who knows when to challenge the authorities and when to stay out of their way, necessarily guides the joyful force of nature that are the Nac Mac Feegle.

Concentrating on the winning qualities of the Wee Free Men helps us recognize the romantic attractiveness of anarchism. To a person of a certain temperament anarchism is quite seductive. It not only promises freedom to do as you please and freedom from interference by the state, but also presents a picture of courage, imaginative creativity, of zeal for the fullest possible expression of human potential. Epicurus's adage, "Nothing human is foreign to me," implies the necessary condition of the freest conceivable circumstances in which curiosity and creativity flourish. While Nozick tries to argue that it would be most reasonable and best for the anarchist to join the libertarian's minimal state, Huemen defends an anarchism Nozick considered pretty unlikely. But in the last analysis these political positions seem different than what Pratchett narrates with so much zest. In a story the anarchists are far more charismatic than the rational, obedient citizens of the minimal state or the philosophical anarchists; they win your heart, not your mind. Most of us are not anarchists, but we clearly love reading about their zany exploits. That should make us think.

In Fairyland Words Really Do Have Power

In *The Wee Free Men* characters exercise an unusual power, the Three Sights, which I have come to understand in the following way: The First is to see the world as it truly is; the Second is to see oneself truly; and the Third is to see the truth through dreams that inspire you to act in compassion for someone else. First, Tiffany sees through the Queen's manipulation of dreams to confuse everyone in Fairyland. Second, she is next honest about her powers and how she can't defeat the Queen without the Wee Frees. Finally, she can defeat the Queen only if she remembers and imagines the ancient history of her chalky home and her duty to her family and neighbors.

> *There's always been someone watching the borders. They didn't decide to. It was decided for them. Someone has to care. Sometimes they have to fight. Someone has to speak for that which has no voice.*

Tiffany's obedience to the three Sights suggests both a kind of moral discipline as well as a way of life. Be honest about the world and yourself, then you can dream of a better world, imagine the most loving and just circumstances, and then act to bring it about. Yet never act upon the last in a way that violates the first two. Courageous, even audacious acts to care for others begin in the imagination. In her fight with Tiffany, the Queen tells her that humans are weak because they are great dreamers; they dream of a better world where each one is the hero of their own tale. But Tiffany learns that even if tempted by selfishness, anyone has the capacity to care for others. We don't need to be really smart or brave; we have to pay close attention to our compassion, and to act on it. Our dreams, and in them our compassion, is where we are freest. The one undisputed realm of anarchy is in our imagination. As a writer, Pratchett knew very well that the imagination is where we can narrate a better world.

In the great stories, our imagination liberates our sympathies to join our moral outrage, to inspire serving others, especially those too weak to care for themselves. This is especially true when we stand before the bosses who have the law, the lawyers, the emblems of office, the moral sanctions, and the ruthlessness to bend all that to their purposes. The chalk lands of *The Wee Free Men* might have been orderly and quiet had the Baron ruled just as he wished, if the lawyers were never interrupted in their work, if kidnappers and thieves were strictly punished *except* when they were rich and powerful. The authorities have deeply vested interests in maintaining their own power, and they pour their creative energies into protecting it. Burdened by reverence for the authorities, burdened by dependence upon them to take care of everyone, the average person can't move from outrage and anger at injustice to acting to care for them. Pratchett's characters see through ceremony and civic decorum, they know their duty and how to recruit others to join up, and they figure out how to obey that duty. Any decent society, Pratchett's work suggested, required a minimum of creative anarchists and malcontents to speak out against the likely injustices or abuses of human dignity and rights by agents and authorities of the state. Reform starts with the creative distrust of political power and of the law found in the anarchist impulse. Imagine a Wee Free Man in a kilt, standing on his head. Shocking, eh? What if it is also inspirational? We clearly enjoy and have great affection for such characters, these anarchists of heart and imagination. We should consider carefully why that is so.

4
The Liberating Power of Nanny Ogg's Bouncing Bosom

VANESSA FRÖHLICH

Let's talk about bosoms! [1]

Now that I have your attention . . . let's actually talk about bosoms![2] About Nanny Ogg's bosom, to be more specific.

Now, you may wonder: Why, with the wide selection of bosoms available on the Disc, would I want to talk about Nanny Ogg's? Well, if you think about it for a minute, it actually makes a lot of sense. More sense, at least, than talking about Granny Weatherwax's bosom. While we're all fairly certain that she must have one under all these layers of black clothing, thinking and talking about it doesn't come all that easy. Probably because we're somewhat afraid to suddenly find her looming behind us, ready to deal out dire retribution.[3] Nanny on the other hand, wouldn't mind you talking about hers at all—in fact, she's always ready to get it out and into action, for example for balls[4]:

> What Granny could achieve with two pounds of hobnailed syncopation Nanny Ogg could achieve merely with her bosom.
>
> It was a large and experienced bosom, and not one that was subject to restraint. As Nanny Ogg bounced down, it went up; when she gyrated right, it hadn't finished twirling left. [. . .] The total effect obliged her partner to dance several feet away, and many surrounding couples

---

[1] I'D LIKE TO SUGGEST THEY ARE OVERRATED.

[2] Bet you didn't see that coming!

[3] I'm in fact anxiously looking over my shoulder as I'm typing this.

[4] As in dance parties. Sheesh!

> to stop dancing just to watch in fascination, in case the build-up of harmonic vibrations dropped her into the chandeliers. (Pratchett, *Witches Abroad*, 229–30)

Nanny definitely knows how to get all the fun she can out of her bosom—and the rest of her body for that matter. Whether or not twirling and bouncing bosoms are appropriate at fancy dance parties doesn't really doesn't really matter to her all that much. This character trait not only makes her way better at parties than Granny—some people would even argue that it gives her the power to attack entire social systems.

Fun with Body Fluids

One of these people is the Russian literary scientist Mikhail Bakhtin (1895–1975). During World War II, he published a study on the functions of comedy, carnival, and the grotesque.[5] The study was named *Rabelais and His World,* and it was mainly about the famous French Renaissance writer François Rabelais and his works, but also about medieval and Renaissance feasts and humor in general. Now, what has some medieval French bloke got to do with Nanny Ogg's bosom? The answer is: quite a lot!

The most important distinction that Bakhtin makes is the one between "high" culture and "low" culture. While high culture includes all those elements of a culture that are generally considered valuable and somewhat posh, low culture is—well, the exact opposite. It includes all facets of a culture that may be fun, but do not have much intellectual value—popular TV shows, gossip magazines, the hedgehog song, and the like. Now, the riff between the two is as old as human culture itself. And all the while, high culture is sneering down on low culture and feeling so much better and posher. Bakhtin, in fact, explains that the official feasts of medieval and Renaissance times basically served only one purpose: to showcase high culture and the hierarchies in society. During these feasts, everybody knew where to stand, what to wear, and what to say, and all this represented their specific place in society. While those on the lower

---

[5] Which probably makes sense at this point in world history, in a twisted kind of way.

ranks of the social ladder did not get to join the "fun" at all, or were reduced to mere spectators, the high and mighty apparently took this quite seriously. There are actually reports about fistfights between priests and university professors over who got to stand in the most prestigious spot. Religion and science don't seem to get along in any world—anybody who knows the Ridcully brothers will be able to tell you that much.

Judging by these official feasts alone, you could surely say that medieval folks had some serious deficits in the party department. Luckily, there was still the carnival. While other feasts were all about status, the carnival was all about chaos. Bakhtin describes it as a short time where, once a year, people could throw all the rules and norms dictated by high culture over board. Hierarchies didn't matter anymore, and everybody could stand where they wanted and wear what they liked. There was also drink. Lots of it. It was loud, and unstructured and chaotic, but that was exactly what was so great about it. It allowed a freedom that was unthinkable on all other days of the year. A great deal of this liberation was achieved by what Bakhtin calls grotesque elements. While the word *grotesque* already calls certain images to mind, and while Nobby Nobbs is probably one of the first to pop up,[6] when Bakhtin is talking about the grotesque, he is talking about something very specific: namely about the human body, with all its functions. And by all, he means the whole set: sex, eating, drinking—and also the bit that happens when the food and drink have run their natural course, and the various fluids and substances that are involved in this. For Bakhtin, all these things are nothing to be ashamed of, but something positive, something that we all have in common, no matter who we are and what our place in society is. With carnival and the grotesque, the body becomes a symbol for all that is fun in human life—because admit it, who doesn't like doing all this stuff?

When carnival and the grotesque meet high culture, they can bring it down to earth and question its boundaries. What is high culture? Why exactly is it so much better than low cul-

---

[6] Which can admittedly be a bit distracting as even just the image of Nobby is likely to hang around for a while eating leftovers, propping his feet up on the good furniture, and scratching himself unashamedly as might a smelly in-law with a face like a car accident.

ture? Who says so anyhow and why should be believe them? If you really think about it, no element of any culture is automatically better than others; it is only thought of as better because a lot of smart and posh people claim that it is. But when it is paired with elements of the carnival and the grotesque, high culture transforms into something more fun and more relatable. Even Lord Vetinari, if we were to imagine him in the privy,[7] would suddenly seem somewhat less threatening and awe-inducing. Bakhtin, being a big fan of medieval and Renaissance art and literature, thought that modern forms of humor didn't possess this transforming and liberating power anymore. We, as fans of Terry Pratchett's writing, know that he was wrong about that, of course.

Bugger the Ball—It's the Carnival

Witches Abroad, for example, is a novel that is all about the opposition between high and low culture, and about the role of the carnival and the grotesque in mixing up the boundaries between the two. In the kingdom of Genua, Granny Weatherwax's older sister Lily, self-proclaimed fairy godmother and secret ruler of the city, is hosting a ball at the palace. Now, if this ball, with its noble guests and their fancy clothes does not represent high culture, what else could? But even more importantly, the ball also serves one very special purpose: Lily plans for her goddaughter Ella, the rightful heir to Genua's throne, to meet her straw man the Duc at the ball, and to have them get married. Ella doesn't love the Duc, in fact she despises him—and who would blame her? He is a frog-turned-human.[8] But for Lily, this is of minor importance. If Ella, as the city's rightful ruler, would marry her puppet, nobody could accuse her reign of being illegitimate anymore. Fairy godmothers aren't all that good, sometimes.

While the ball takes place at the palace, the common people in the streets of Genua celebrate the feast that Ella would much rather go to: the annual carnival. From the way Sir Terry describes the Genua city carnival, it seems like he sure knew

---

[7] Surely, he has to use it sometimes, right? Right?! I imagine it is where he does his best work on the *Times* crossword puzzle.

[8] This would probably make conversations in that marriage kind of difficult.

his Bakhtin.[9] For both Bakhtin and Terry Pratchett, the carnival is the feast for the common people, and it allows them to chuck the rules and norms of society aside for a while. For the people of Genua, this means that, for one day, they can behave as something other than fairy tale characters without having to face the wrath of Lily Weatherwax. And they sure know how to put their one free day to good use. They like their carnival as loud and chaotic and with as much booze as possible. The whole thing is right up Nanny Ogg's alley of course, and she joins in the fun as soon and as much as she can. And the similarities between Bakhtin and Terry Pratchett don't stop here. They both stress the carnival's power for challenging the power structures and hierarchies in society. If you believe the notes left to the witches by Ella's other, deceased, godmother Desiderata,[10] they will only be able to defeat Lily while the carnival lasts:

> "But no-one can stop Mardi Gras," [Granny] read. "If anything canne be done it be on Samedi Nuit Morte, the last night of carnivale, the night halfway between the Living and the Dead, when magic flows in the streets. If L. is vooneruble it is then, for carnivale is everything she hates . . ." (Pratchett, *Witches Abroad*, 97)

In Genua, Lily's fairy tale reign represents high culture—a high culture that is extremely tyrannical at that, and does not allow room for changes or for anybody doing anything out of the norm. The carnival on the other hand, is the night "halfway between the Living and the Dead," and represents change and the shaking up of norms and boundaries, allowing people to behave outside of the rules for a short time. And naturally, it is everything that Lily hates, because she would like people to believe that her fairy tale reign is eternal and unchangeable. In the end, she has to learn that it is anything but that.

Nanny Ogg Knows How to Party

Thankfully, Lily doesn't get her way. Instead, the carnival and the grotesque sneak into her precious ball and mess with it

---

[9] And knowing him, he probably did.

[10] Once you have deciphered them, that is. Desiderata saw spelling rules as more of a loose guideline.

until high and low culture can no longer be told apart, shattering the hierarchies and power structures that Lily has taken so many pains to build.

Now, you cannot possibly talk about grotesque features in *Witches Abroad* without talking about Nanny Ogg.[11] As you have probably heard, a coven of witches traditionally consists of three women, who all fulfill different roles: they are typically called the maiden, the mother, and the crone.[12] In our favorite coven of witches, it is Nanny who fulfills the role of the mother,[13] who traditionally stands for fertility, abundance, growth, and all other sexual aspects of womanhood. When Nanny was younger, she was an immensely attractive woman with a fair share of lovers. Now, that she has outlived several husbands and is the matriarch of a huge family, half the population of Lancre is probably of Oggish descent. You can accuse Nanny of a lot of things—but being infertile is most certainly not one of them. Even though she likes to eat and drink a lot and has the body to prove it, this does not keep her from enjoying her sexuality—and that of others, for that matter—to the fullest. Unlike both Magrat, the Lancre coven's resident maiden, and Granny, the . . . erm . . . well, the *other one*, Nanny draws tremendous fun from flirting with men, from saucy jokes, and from folk songs of a certain class.[14]

As we have seen before, the grotesque as Bakhtin describes it is all about having fun with your body, high culture be damned—and you cannot possibly have any more fun with your body than Nanny Ogg! In fact, with her easy-going, extroverted nature and her immense love for food, drink, and anything sexual, she shows us exactly how much fun the human body can be, if you just use it properly. Her tremendous bouncing bosom may not be pretty, or elegant, or even remotely appropriate at Lily's posh ball, but it's *her* bosom, bugger it, and she will be damned if she doesn't get the maximum amount of fun it can offer out of it.

---

[11] Bakhtin would have loved Nanny Ogg, in fact.

[12] Though we, of course, call her "the other one," if we don't want to face the everlasting grudge of Granny Weatherwax. And when we say "everlasting" let's be honest, it'll last for a very long time. Granny would not let something like the end of the time get someone off the hook.

[13] Or she does most of the time. Terry Pratchett isn't too fond of fixed roles.

[14] A wizard's staff has a knob on its end, anybody?

Dead Man Walking

While Nanny certainly shakes things up at the ball, the event that completely ends Lily's reign is the arrival of the zombie Saturday—who is actually Ella's father and the former ruler of the city, who was conveniently killed off by Lily so that the Duc could take his place.

To defeat Lily, the voodoo witch Mrs. Gogol—who also happens to be Ella's mother—has given Saturday the power of the swamp, that bubbly, mushy piece of landscape that surrounds the beautiful, clean city of Genua. The swamp in itself resists all attempts to define it, tame it, and put it into categories. Is it a body of water or is it land? Why are things moving around all the time, and where the bloody hell do all the alligators come from? Thanks to the power of this chaotic strip of landscape, Saturday is at the peak of his power when he arrives at the ball, and Terry Pratchett fittingly calls him "Baron Saturday" in this scene, which is his proper title. But this is not all. His name and his appearance as a skeletal figure with a top hat and a silver cane are also a dead ringer for a certain "Baron Samedi." That guy is the gatekeeper of death in voodoo mythology, and known to be a charming, but rather obscene, fellow who especially likes his rum and his tobacco. In voodoo lore, only Baron Samedi can accept a person into the underworld after they have died—but he is also able to heal people who are close to death, and is often called by mortals to do this.

Much like his mythological namesake, Baron Saturday does not take the boundaries between life and death all too seriously. For one thing, he's a zombie, walking about and ready for action in spite of being technically very, very dead. He also has the power of the swamp; it follows him around and even invades Lily's precious sparkly ballroom along with him. And unlike everything that Lily likes, the swamp cannot be tamed and structured—structures and rules are against its very nature. It is a whole lot like the grotesque and the carnival that way. This is why Baron Saturday messes up Lily's ball—not only literally by getting swamp all over it, but also by smashing up the social system that she has created and by helping his daughter Ella into power.

Why Should the Carnival Only Be Once a Year?

Just like Bakhtin describes carnival, the Genua city carnival is a short time during which the people can forget all about hierarchies—only to have the nasty buggers sneak back up on them again once the party is over. This is true for Lily's Genua, and certainly also for the one that Mrs. Gogol and Baron Saturday are planning. Once they get rid of Lily, they want to place Ella officially in power, but Mrs. Gogol would still be the one to pull the strings in the background.

Well, Granny Weatherwax can't have that sort of thing at all. She convinces Mrs. Gogol to drop those plans and puts Ella, the girl who desperately wanted to go the carnival, in full charge of the city, finally giving Genua a true chance at change and a democratic government.

For Bakhtin, in the end, the carnival is nothing but another means for those in power to keep their reign up and running. The lowly and oppressed people are allowed to blow off steam for a short time and then return to their miserable lives. In the end, this never leads to any changes. But Granny and Nanny Ogg's bosom break the never-ending circle of regular life and carnival. This may turn out to be very chaotic for the kingdom of Genua, but at least the people have gained a chance of leading more self-determined, and also much more fun, lives in the future. And that's worth a lot, isn't it?

5
The Truth Shall Make Ye Fret

JAMIE CARLIN WATSON

A lie can run round the world before the truth has got its boots on.

— LORD DE WORDE in *The Truth* by Terry Pratchett

When people are allowed to say anything they want, there's bound to be trouble. They are able to spread fantastical rumors and malicious lies. Worse yet, they can tell the truth. And when a society built on . . . not-quite-truths, begins to hear bits of . . . well, something like the truth, figuring out just who to believe suddenly becomes everyone's problem. In Pratchett's *The Truth*, wordsmith William de Worde inadvertently invents the newspaper industry and stumbles onto a plot to replace the Machiavellian Patrician Lord Vetinari with a more agreeable lookalike. But to get that bit of truth into print, he has to compete against those printing their own version of the truth and those who are trying to stamp it out altogether. In Ankh-Morpork, telling the truth is dangerous, and most people are more interested in lies. The Discworld's turbulent reaction to a free press highlights all the pitfalls of letting people say just anything they want while reminding us why it's so necessary.

Express Yourself . . . Modestly

Lord Vetinari, venerable tyrant and sometime sage, is uncomfortable with his citizens' having too much freedom. Most people have nasty ideas and, therefore, require guidance of a particularly strong-armed sort. Samuel Vimes, Commander of the City Watch, is not especially comfortable with freedom, either. When people start taking liberties, they rarely know when to stop. Until recently, citizens were pretty easy to control—a little collusion with the Assassins' Guild, a little coercive diplomacy, and Ankh-Morpork would keep a stable rate of nefarious activity. But when William de Worde, ostracized son of the aristocratic Lord de Worde, got the clever idea of combining his passion for—tongue fully in cheek—*words* with the dwarfish facility in moveable type, the number of ideas spreading through the city increased at a dizzying rate, and along with it, the potential for nastiness. Vetinari might say that most dank dungeons are too good for people like de Worde

The idea that nastiness accompanies free speech has a long history. Some claim that the most famous example of state censorship occurred in 399 BCE when Socrates (469–399 BCE) was sentenced to death for corrupting the youth and encouraging belief in false gods. But this was not a widespread or systematic censorship; it was more likely a political put-up job. Athenian citizens (though not slaves or women) enjoyed a generous freedom of speech known as *parrhesia*, which means "frankness" or "outspokenness"; everyone could say what they wanted without fear of legal punishment. Other cultures were not so lucky.

Sparta levied heavy restrictions on its citizens, not least of which included speech. Rome persecuted Christians in particular because they would not integrate their God into the Roman pantheon, making them seem a political threat. Later, when Christians ruled Rome after Constantine's conversion in 312, the state encouraged pagans to convert on pain of, well . . . pain.[1]

Jumping forward, in the early 1500s, authorities in the Western church burned the Bibles William Tyndale translated into English because only certain people (obviously) should be allowed to read the Bible. In 1633, Galileo Galilei was placed under house arrest by Cardinal Belarmine for teaching (after he was told not to) the heresy of Copernican cosmology.

Jumping again, after the Bolshevik revolution of 1917, all non-communist literature was forbidden in Russia, and private presses were crippled by a state ban on print advertising.

---

[1] Pain is, not surprisingly, a very effective motivator. Interestingly, so are kittens; just ask Lord Ventinari.

(Something similar happened in Borogravia on the Disc. The Borogravian army tore town the clacks towers that ended up on their land to prevent signals from interfering with prayers on their way to heaven. See Pratchett, *Monstrous Regiment.*) In the United States, since 1934, the Federal Communications Committee (FCC) has strictly monitored the content of radio and television programming, effectively censoring Elvis Presley's hips, The Rolling Stones' lyrics, conservative Fox Television's big reveal that strippers exist, and PBS's constant use of expletives in a documentary (no joke). And certainly not least, during political protests in 2011, the Egyptian government shut down the nation's internet service (the whole nation's!) in order to prevent news about the protests from spreading inside and outside the nation.

The one thing all these instances of censorship have in common is a fear of the nastiness free speech may cause, whether that nastiness is harm, falsehood, community unrest, heresy, indecency, indignity, or political revolution. The situation is no different in Ankh-Morpork. According to the Bursar of Unseen University, it's not that the *content* of the speech might be dangerous, but that the metal letters might *remember* the words they printed, allowing words to take on physical existence (Pratchett, *The Truth*, 24–25). This fear fades quickly, however, when the Bursar learns just how inexpensive the new printing method is. Similarly, the High Priest of Blind Io is concerned that moveable type might be harmful: "We've got nothing against words being nailed down properly. But words that can be taken apart and used to make other words . . . well, that's downright dangerous" (*The Truth*, 29).

Despite his newly invented occupation of distributing words throughout the city, William de Worde is sympathetic to that fear:

> . . . these dull gray blocks looked threatening. He could understand why they worried people. Put us together in the right way, they seemed to say, and we can be anything you want. We could even be something you don't want. We can spell anything. We can certainly spell trouble. (*The Truth*, 37)

What sort of trouble? Well, that depends on who you are. Words can be harmful to different people for different reasons, usually because people value different things:

> . . . he knew the engravers didn't like it, because they had the world operating just as they wanted it, thank you very much. And Lord Vetinari was said not to like it, because too many words only upset people. And the wizards and priests didn't like it because words were important.
>
> . . . if you took the leaden letters that had previously been used to set the words of a god, and then used them to set a cookery book, what did that do to holy wisdom? For that matter, what would it do to the pie? (*The Truth*, 37–38)

The engravers valued their profession, and their livelihood was threatened by the efficiency of moveable type. Vetinari valued a mollified populace, so it would be easier for him to run the city. The priests need to keep the theological peace, and mixing the miraculous with the mundane may presage spiritual unrest.

Of course, none of the examples given so far (from our world or from Discworld) are *good* reasons to censor. Despite the claims of all these censors, the speech in question really isn't nasty or obviously dangerous at all; some of it just isn't *preferable* to some people for some purposes, and those are usually people on the wrong side of an issue—reading the Bible in your own language; the freedom to pick your own church (or start one!); democratic elections; shaking what your mama gave you (in Elvis's case); etc. But shouldn't we be concerned about some kinds of speech? Isn't racist speech harmful? (Trolls are people, too!) Sexist speech? Janet Jackson's exposed breast?[2] Isn't some censorship *necessary*?

Words Are Weapons

Before considering some good reasons for censorship, there are a couple of important things to note about censorship and free speech. First, freedom of speech is a political idea about the relationship between citizens and their government. If you have the freedom of speech, you have it in the public sphere,

---

[2] Although Discworld doesn't quite have the equivalent of Janet Jackson, it is widely acknowledged that if the same wardrobe malfunction happened to Tawnee from the Pink PussyCat Club, public safety would be decidedly in jeopardy. (See Pratchett, *Thud!*)

but not necessarily in private sphere. If you went into Granny Weatherwax's house, and she asked you to refrain from talking about whether the Great A'Tuin is male or female, she would be within her rights to do so (it's her house), and she would not be censoring you in the sense at issue (you are free to curse whomever you wish in your own home and in others' homes who don't object). So, private instances of "censorship" are not in question.

Second, as a political concept, private employers, like the owner of the Mended Drum (formerly the Broken Drum),[3] and religious organizations, like the Temple of Offler the Crocodile God, reserve the same rights to restrict your behavior and speech in their establishments as Granny Weatherwax does in her home. The latter are private organizations that serve the public in some capacity; but they are not public entities. Only governments can *censor* speech. If your company starts a "no cursing" rule, that's not technically censorship. When Egypt blocked Facebook, that *was* censorship. So, why do some patricians want to censor people? What's so worrisome about free speech?

The Direct Harm Argument

Most people admit that hurting someone without a good reason or consent is a bad thing.[4] Giving your child a vaccine or puncturing the skin of someone who is donating blood is okay. But stabbing an unsuspecting stranger with a needle or helping yourself to someone's blood via smooth application of *eroticus*

---

[3] In fact, if the proprietor of the Mended Drum decided to restrict free speech, the bar might find itself with far fewer "suicides" but what fun would that be? After all, watching "Little Jim" Rupert having his head playfully bounced against the floorboards by Cment the Troll,* who doesn't appreciate having his mother called, well, anything is an important part of the tourist trade in Ankh-Morpork. (*While trolls in Ankh-Morpork have moved with the times and often name their children after the solid foundations of the city,** like Brick, their spelling could still use some work.) (**Yes, I too suspect that any day now there will be a troll named "River." Truly, what can be said to be more solid than the lovely River Ankh upon which citizen can take a leisurely stroll while admiring the sewage?)

[4] The School of Assassins is the exception that proves the rule. In fact, hurting someone without good reason is part of the comprehensive exam at the end of the first term. This exam has become controversial, however. Critics say hurting someone for money *is* a good reason.

pointier denticus[5] is most certainly not okay. But words don't hurt the way needles and punctures do, "sticks and stones" and whatnot. And having freedom of speech helps us to make progress! If we weren't free to say what we want, we wouldn't have cool new ideas like "The earth revolves around the sun" and "Hey, slavery is not nice; you should stop that!" So, according to classical political views, speech gets a free pass: anyone may say whatever he or she (or it) wants without fear of official punishment.[6]

Nevertheless, some folks argue that, in spite of the old adage, words *can* hurt you, and sometimes very intensely. For instance, some minority groups have been so mistreated by majority groups, that simply using derogatory epithets is emotionally and psychologically hurtful. If this is right, they argue, some speech should be prohibited by law for the same reason sucking innocent strangers' blood is. This is the "direct harm" argument for censorship. And there is ample evidence that some speech rises to the level of abuse, for instance, regular, angry screaming at people does bad things to them over time, even if you never lay a hand on them.

The villains of Discworld discovered the *harm* part of the direct harm argument long before the printing press. In *The Truth*, in the dark hallows of a dark ballroom where conspirators sat in dark shadows, one course of action was so obvious it didn't need to be spoken: "Character assassination. What a wonderful idea. Ordinary assassination only works once, but this one works every day" (Pratchett, *The Truth*, 173). Character assassination is assassination precisely because words can hurt regardless of whether sentences formed with them are true.

---

5 Ancient Überwaldian for "sexy pointed teeth." To allay public fears over the increased number of vampires in Ankh-Morpork, a group of enlightened vampires started the Temperance League, recognizable by their black armbands.

6 "Official" punishment is important here because there are many ways of being *un*officially punished. For instance, if everyone can speak freely, some people may call you bad names for saying what you say. They may even give reasons for thinking you're wrong. They may even give reasons you think are good reasons. And having to admit you are wrong may be the worst punishment of all.

The Indirect Harm Argument

If you're not convinced by the direct harm argument that censorship is a good thing, there is also the "indirect harm" argument—which concludes that hateful or derogatory speech can cause indirect harm to a whole culture. For instance, if speciesist[7] or sexist jokes are accepted or considered normal, members of that race or sex might feel alienated and undervalued. The concern here is about power: if powerful people can speak freely, they can disempower others just by overwhelming them with one way of speaking or one way of framing an idea. A whole culture might then make some people feel that they have fewer opportunities than others.

Consider the term *Holocaust* used to describe the extermination of Jews in Nazi Germany. *Holocaust* derives from Greek meaning "burnt offering," which is a type of religious sacrifice to God. Now, it's pretty obvious why a Jewish person would not want to regard Hitler's actions as a religious rite, and the standard Jewish term for the event is *Shoah*, which means "catastrophe." Nevertheless, Western culture has allowed historians and scholars, rather than Jews, to choose what to call the extermination of Jews—and they chose a pretty offensive term. Intentionally or not, words are used to divide and intensify prejudice. On the Disc, some Deep-Downers, dwarfs who reject most modern advancements, perpetuate the myth that trolls and dwarfs went to Koom Valley to fight a war, when in reality they were meeting in order to settle their differences.[8] (See Pratchett, *Thud!* for how the drama plays out.) There are many other examples. (Think of the awkward pressure to call a black man from England "African American" when he is neither African nor American.)

This may seem like a minor quibble over words, but it has radical implications for how we treat people. It allows us to adopt stereotypes that quickly turn into expectations. For instance, "low income" is often used to imply "stupid" or "underprivileged," and phrases like "She is so hot!" can make other

[7] On our world, we might also stick racism in here, but "Racism was not a problem on the Discworld, because—what with trolls and dwarfs and so on—speciesism was more interesting. Black and white lived in perfect harmony and ganged up on green" (Pratchett, *Witches Abroad*, 195).

[8] I FIND THIS CONFUSION OFTEN GOOD FOR BUSINESS.

women feel self-conscious and less valuable. In *Thud!* (11), the vampire Mr. Winkings takes offense when Commander Vimes tells him that vampires are "just not mentally suited to a copper's way of life" (even though Vimes says it is because they are intelligent!).[9] As a result of this sort of unreflective and hurtful language, some opportunities for pursuing the good life may not be open to minorities, or minorities may feel less inclined to pursue them to avoid discomfort or discrimination. This is called the "indirect harm" argument.[10]

Because of all these various possibilities for harming people with words, you might think this shows the absurdity of "political correctness." No one could ever possibly know all the ways they could accidentally offend people, so we should just stop trying. The problem with this response is that it often gives a free pass to people in cases where they should know better. We construct little phrases, like "no offense," to excuse our obtuseness. On the Discworld, Mr. Longshaft, a dwarf lodging at Mrs Eucrasia Arcanum's Lodging House for Respectable Working Men, has a tendency to excuse himself this way. But de Worde thinks this is a questionable tactic: "Mr. Longshaft smiled faintly as he buttered the toast, and William wondered why he always disliked people who said 'no offence meant'. Maybe it was because they found it easier to say 'no offence meant' than actually refrain from giving offence" (Pratchett, *The Truth*, 93). Political correctness may indeed have its place, if for no other reason than to raise awareness about the ways we can hurt each other with words.

If words can really cause harm, directly or indirectly, just think how easy and quick it would be to cause harm with a printing press! Or the internet! Offenses could go flying faster than the speed of light.[11]

---

[9] Plus, they can't pronounce "W," as Vimes prejudicially thinks to himself: "Say 'Watch,' why don't you? I know you can. Let the twenty-third letter of the alphabet enter your life" (*Thud!*, 10).

[10] As they say around the Hublands: *he who has the biggest horn makes the most noise*. Or, as one scholar on our world puts it: "the speech of the dominant is protected, the more dominant they become and the less the subordinated are heard from" (MacKinnon, "Only Words," 152).

[11] Which, admittedly, isn't saying much on Discworld.

The False Beliefs Argument

Other folks are concerned about free speech because there is so much nonsense floating about. If we let people say just anything they want, some of what they say will be false, and we don't want people trading in false beliefs. This is called the "false beliefs" argument for censorship. Now, people believe all sorts of nonsense no matter what you tell them they can or can't say, so what's the worry about a little more?

This worry is primarily about those who have the power to impose false beliefs on others, like school teachers and media outlets. Typically worrisome examples are claims like: *the world is only 10,000 years old*; *the Disc is more like a sphere than a disc*; *African slavery was a good thing*; *there is biological evidence showing that trolls are inferior to humans*, etc. Those who defend the false beliefs argument say that power imbalance is a good reason for prohibiting teachers from teaching things like this. Further, advertisers should not be allowed to imply false beliefs in their ads and philosophers and scientists should not be allowed to publish them in books—these people exert a certain authority over their audiences and, well darn it, audiences are impressionable.[12]

And, of course, more is at stake than merely the truth; *values* are also at stake. According to some ways of understanding humanity, people thrive when they pursue some very specific values (like monogamy, heterosexual marriage, sobriety, and not having vampires in the Watch) and deteriorate when they pursue others (such as promiscuity, homosexual relationships, partying, and having vampires in the Watch). The former values are often called "traditional values," and they are used as reasons to promote certain types of political policies. When some people play fast and loose with what others think is the truth about values, the others feel threatened; they form leagues of "concerned citizens" to advocate censoring those ideas.

---

[12] In *Monstrous Regiment*, Sergeant Jackrum expresses a similar worry about all reading and writing, saying, "You can't trust the people who do that stuff. They mess around with the world, and it turns out everything you know is wrong" (181).

To be sure, it matters who the concerned citizens are. Mr. Pin, one of the assassins hired to kill and replace the Patrician in *The Truth*, recognized that his employers (the conspirators) were concerned citizens. And "He knew about *concerned citizens*. Wherever they were, they all spoke the same private language, where 'traditional values' meant 'hang someone'" (Pratchett, *The Truth*, 68).

The worry comes down to this: on the Discworld, like most places, people have a difficult time distinguishing real authorities from authorities-in-sheep's-clothing (to mix metaphors). When a dispute arose among the lodgers at Mrs. Arcanum's over the number of people hurt in a brawl, Mrs. Arcanum resolved it by appeal to the authority of the printed word: "It must be right . . . otherwise they wouldn't let them put it in" (Pratchett, *The Truth*, 72). When the question was raised as to who *they* are, despite the fact that the author, William de Worde, was sitting in their midst, Mrs. Arcanum assumes it is "special people," and Mr. Mackleduff agrees, "They wouldn't allow just anyone to write what they like. That stands to reason" (Pratchett, *The Truth*, 72). If people believe there are special people behind the printed word, maybe there should be! Someone who can guarantee that everything that's printed is true.

The Horrible Necessity of Free Speech

Traditionally, there is a presumption in favor of free speech and against censorship. And there are two very good reasons for this. The first is the knowledge problem: we don't know everything, and if we don't let people say what they think, come up with new ideas, or challenge currently held beliefs, we will make very little progress and will be stuck with a lot of false or useless beliefs. The second reason is the equality assumption: no one is more valuable than anyone else, and therefore, no one's *ideas* are more valuable than anyone else's. That doesn't mean some ideas are not false or that some ideas are not more useful than others. But we cannot know which are more likely to be true or useful until they are out in the open, until they are spoken. Given these two reasons, censorship is bad.

The three arguments we have considered (direct harm; indirect harm; false beliefs) challenge these two reasons. Those who offer these arguments tend to believe free speech is important, but they claim its importance is sometimes outweighed by the way people act. They say that people speak in horrible ways, intentionally or not. People use words to hurt others instead of to reason with them. They use words to let off steam in insensitive ways. They use words out of frustration and helplessness rather than to make the world better. And they often say false things. They conclude that, despite the importance of free speech, censorship is sometimes good.

So, the question facing us is this: do any of the arguments for censorship override the arguments against it? Evidence from Discworld suggests not. But before we look at that evidence, we should take note of a difference between the *badness* of something and the *legality* of it. Not all bad things should be illegal (for example, lying to your Bursar) and not all things that are illegal are bad (like selling meat pies without a license).[13] This is important because, even if some speech is bad—even really bad—that might not mean we should censor it. We can call it bad, explain why it's bad, and teach our children differently without passing any law banning it. With that difference in place, there are two reasons to believe arguments against censorship prevail against the arguments for it.

First, whether speech is harmful depends on *culture at a time* and *individuals' sensitivity to it*. In some cultures, speech we would now consider harmful was widely regarded as acceptable, even by those it would harm today. This means that instituting a law would make the speech illegal timelessly. On the Disc, it would be silly to have a law today against calling someone a *witch* or a *troll* even if the term was hurtful in the tenth century or before the Battle of Koom Valley. If some speech is harming someone, we can address the harm and ignore the particular content of the speech. Also, different individuals react to speech in different ways. Some members of a minority may not experience racist or sexist epithets as harmful, while

---

[13] Cut-Me-Own-Throat-Dibbler's meat pies have been the subject of concern among Ankh-Morpork's ethically minded citizens for some time. Though Dibbler always observes the proper legal measures,* there is some concern about whether his "meat pies" contain any meat or meat by-products, or, if they do contain meat by-products, whether they are of a sort fit for human consumption. Both criticisms challenge Dibbler's honesty independently of any legal concerns. (*He observes them and finds them . . . quaint.)

others may. In fact, other words, like "fat" and "stupid," can be much more harmful, especially to children. But we cannot reasonably censor every word that might be harmful to some groups at some time under some circumstances because we cannot predict which will and under which circumstances and for how long.

This doesn't mean there aren't obvious cases where we can predict harm, for example, Westboro Baptist Church's protests of military funerals. But in the Westboro case and the horrible cases of racism and sexism, culture does a much better job of regulating speech than law. Think of the massive backlash against Westboro's protests. Consider also, even though there is currently no Federal Equal Employment law in the U.S. protecting homosexuals against discriminatory language, certain industries, like real estate and universities, explicitly protect their employees and customers against such language. And many individual companies, like Starbucks and Disney, proudly advertise that they endorse such protections. In *Monstrous Regiment*, Corporal Polly Perks has a realization that, "The pen might not be mightier than the sword, but maybe the printing press was heavier than the siege weapon" (335). Culture both adds and subtracts language from society based on hurtfulness in a much smoother way than government. For example, the word "slut" is currently being phased out, while the term "Indian" for "Native American" has become acceptable again. If the law cannot predict hurtful words, it is difficult to apply over time, and if culture does a better job of adjudicating harm than the law, censorship is inefficient and unnecessary.

Second, if the government is going to censor, then someone must be appointed to determine whether a claim is true or hurtful. As the dwarfs would say, we would need a *Zadkrdga*.[14] And once a censorship decision is made, it is made for everyone under all circumstances. But electing someone to judge the truth of claims is very difficult. You might say: *Well, we can find the experts*. But as we all know, just because someone is an expert doesn't mean she has *true* beliefs. Even scientific beliefs, rigorously tested and useful, often turn out to be false. The same is true on Discworld, as Lord Vetinari notes:

---

[14] Literally, "one who smelts," but more importantly, "one who finds the pure ore of truth in the dross of confusion" (*Thud!* 71–72).

> "A thousand years ago we thought the world was a bowl," he said. "Five hundred years ago we knew it was a globe. Today we know it is flat and round and carried through space on the back of a turtle." He turned and gave the High Priest another smile. "Don't you wonder what shape it will turn out to be tomorrow?" (*The Truth*, 33)

Note the ironic use of "know" in this passage. Part of what it means to know something is to have a *true* belief. But the point here is that these beliefs can't all be true. So, if not even experts can figure out whether beliefs are true, it is unlikely that any law that depends on experts will be a good one.

And here's a quirk about experts: they don't become experts overnight. In fact, when we do end up with a bit of truth, it often comes from *non*-experts! It's often only after someone has the freedom to discover something interesting that she is considered an expert. Remember, one problem with free speech is the imbalance in power that some people gain when they have the money and influence to speak over others. If we appoint someone as an expert on some subject to determine which beliefs get a free pass and which must be censored, then that person's faults and ideas become the standard for everyone else's. And now we *really* have a power problem.

One of the central themes of *The Truth* is how information changes power structures. Early in the novel, Hughnon Ridcully, High Priest of Blind Io, and Vetinari are discussing the nature of commerce and progress, and Vetinari suggests, in contrast to Ridcully's conservatism, that Ankh-Morpork must prepare for the fact that information will be bought and sold just like prawns:

> what was once considered impossible is now quite easily achieved. Kings and lords come and go and leave nothing but statues in the desert,[15] while a couple of young men tinkering in a workshop change the way the world works.[16] . . . We always thought change came from the outside, usually on the point of a sword. And then we look around and find that it comes from inside the head of someone you wouldn't notice on the street. (*The Truth*, 32)

---

[15] Think Shelley's "Ozymandius" here.

[16] Think Steve Jobs and Steve Wozniak here (or, for that matter, Bill Gates and Paul Allen).

Think of all the things that today we think are false, for instance, that people with dark skin are not people, that women are intellectually inferior to men. At the time many of these false beliefs were promoted, they were widely held by experts and novices alike. The famous educator Maria Montessori (1870–1952) agreed with Paul Broca's (1824–1880) claim that brain size is correlated with intelligence—but she disagreed with his conclusion that men are smarter than women. She concluded the opposite: once we correct for body size, she argued, it will turn out that *women are actually smarter than men*. Now, imagine you lived at that time: which "false belief" should have been censored? Which belief was false? How might we have known?

Third—and this is the really serious problem for censorship—those we put in charge of censoring harmful or false beliefs, no matter how smart they are or how well intentioned we think they are, often have agendas of their own. When powerful people get together, they develop certain "tendencies." Vetinari admits this when he says: "I have certainly noticed that groups of clever and intelligent people are capable of really stupid ideas" (*The Truth*, 337). Some of those ideas just involve bad assumptions or silly agendas like "the common good," as Rincewind the Wizard explains: "I know about people who talk about suffering for the common good. It's never bloody them! When you hear a man shouting 'Forward, brave comrades!' you'll see he's the one behind the bloody big rock and the one wearing the only really arrow-proof helmet!" (Pratchett, *Interesting Times,* 201).

But some tendencies are downright nefarious. One of the chief proponents of censorship in *The Truth* turns out (spoiler!) to be William de Worde's father, Lord de Worde. Lord de Worde is powerful, intelligent, and wealthy. Would he make a suitable *Zadkrdga*?

> The worst part, the *worst* part, was that Lord de Worde was never wrong. It was not a position he understood in relation to his personal geography. People who took an opposing view were insane, or dangerous, or possibly even not really people. You couldn't have an argument with Lord de Worde. Not a proper argument. An argument, from *arguer*, meant to debate and discuss and persuade by reason. What you could have with William's father was a flaming row (315).

Lord de Worde would seem to be a bad choice. But who would be a good choice? We all have shortcomings, biases, and agendas. And if experts and politicians are biased by their own interests and shortcomings like the rest of us, it is hard to imagine anyone who is intelligent, knowledgeable, sensitive, and prophetic enough to make decisions about what is bad for any of us to hear or say.

In our sober moments, we would all prefer to agree and to get along. But without disagreement and a little bit of antagonism, we wouldn't learn anything new—we wouldn't be as likely to discard bad ideas (because no one would tell us they're bad!); and new ideas wouldn't be heard (because people would be too afraid of hurting someone). We would like to be optimistic and conciliatory, like William de Worde when talking with Vetinari ("I'm sure we can all pull together, sir"). But for all its horribleness, the freedom to speak freely is, as Vetinari understands, necessary: "Oh, I do hope not, I really do hope not. Pulling together is the aim of despotism and tyranny. Free men pull in all kinds of directions . . ." (*The Truth*, 340). Free people pull in uncomfortable directions, in good directions and bad. They explore ideas we're afraid to explore; they challenge our unreflective beliefs and attitudes; they provoke us with bad arguments. But it is only in their freedom to pull in these directions—and in ours to pull right back!—that the world (whether shaped like a disc or otherwise) continues to be a place worth living in. As Vetinari says: "It's the only way to make progress" (*The Truth*, 340).[17]

[17] Thanks to Jarrett Heintz for introducing me to the magic and mayhem of Discworld.

II

Truth, Logic, and Law Are Nice, but Someone Still Has to Do the Wash

6
The Absurdity of the Luggage

BRANDON KEMPNER

A tongue red as mahogany, teeth white as sycamore. Hundreds of little feet. A loyalty so deep that it extends beyond the limits of time and space. A roomy interior, with plenty of storage space. An unfortunate tendency to savagely eat anyone who gets in its way.

Behold the Luggage.

Of all the bizarre things that occur in Terry Pratchett's Discworld series, the Luggage is perhaps the strangest. A sentient chest that follows its owner no matter what, the Luggage is at once comical and violent, amusing and disturbing, profound and meaningless. The Luggage obeys its own rules, no matter what the terrified inhabitants of Discworld want, and it is in this very defiance of human logic, reason, and order, that the Luggage comes to play such an essential role in Pratchett's fantasy world. Even its frightened owners don't know how to understand this killer chest. Is it a friend or a foe? A joke or a curse? A loyal companion or a homicidal maniac?

The Luggage is all those things and more.

With the Luggage, Pratchett is forcing us to accept the universe—both Discworld and our own—as fundamentally absurd. The Luggage sums up the brilliance of Pratchett's fictional project. In this murderous walking suitcase, he's made something that's both real and unreal, something that both speaks to the human condition and doesn't speak to the human condition, because, after all, it's a sapient chest that eats people. The Luggage forces us beyond simple categories of "meaning" or "not-meaning" and into the giddy landscape of the absurd.

Absurd! Absurd!

The absurd is a complex idea, but we can boil it down to a simple dilemma: we want the world to make sense. We want it to be ordered, to follow clear rules. We want our lives to "mean" something in a profound way. The world—in this philosophical tradition, anyway—doesn't care. The rocks, the trees, the ocean, and the sky, they don't care if your life means anything. Because the world is indifferent, humans are frustrated in their attempts to insert meaning into the chaos and confusion of existence. This gap, between our desire for meaning and the world's lack of meaning, gives rise to a feeling of the "absurd." We can sum up that feeling as the creeping suspicion that nothing really makes sense, or, to put it more clearly, as the exact feeling we have when we think about the Luggage.

Sounds depressing, huh? Don't worry.[1] Philosophers of the absurd push this idea even farther, arguing that the absurd, rather than making life pointless, actually enhances and defines the human experience. To get to that point, we must understand two things: how philosophers have already embraced the idea of the absurd, and how Pratchett has sent the Luggage (and us) on an absurd journey over the course of his series. This voyage of the Luggage, from an impossibly threatening monster to a snuggly, friendly chest (complete with children!), embodies the philosophical embrace of the absurd. Just as the Luggage grows, we readers grow with the Luggage, and through him we come to accept—not reject—the undeniable non-meaning of existence.

If you're thinking this boils down to Rincewind, you're absolutely right. Rincewind has to grow to accept the Luggage, and once he does—bam!—he finds his place in Discworld, and grows to be the true hero of the series.

The Color of the Absurd

Albert Camus (1913–1960) was a well-known French-Algerian philosopher and novelist, who even won the Nobel Prize for

[1] One time, I was doing a great job of explaining how the absurd wasn't depressing. I was really getting into the flow of the argument and making some great points, but then the bar closed and the bartender made me go home. If anything is depressing, it's a bar closing. That's the real philosophical problem.

Literature in 1957. Often associated with fellow Frenchman and existentialist Jean-Paul Sartre (1905–1980), Camus's most important philosophical work is found in *The Myth of Sisyphus* (1942). In this long essay, Camus argues that human beings want to understand what life means. Unfortunately, the world doesn't care. Since the world exists outside of us, and not for us, it doesn't correspond to human hopes or human desires. Still, people can't accept the indifference of the universe, and instead try to make sense of existence in human terms: "understanding the world for a man is reducing it to the human, stamping it with his seal" (*Myth of Sisyphus*, 17). According to Camus, this enterprise is doomed to fail. You can't find human meaning in the non-human; it just doesn't make sense. And if the quest for meaning doesn't work in our rather sensible universe, just imagine how badly it'll go in a land filled with dragons, giant turtles, and librarian orangutans.

This is exactly where Camus finds the absurd, in the "divorce" between a human desire for order and reality itself. To put this in simpler terms, we feel the absurd when we notice the gap between how we *want to understand* the world and how the world *actually is*. The world we live in is fundamentally unreasonable, because it doesn't respond to the most human of inventions: reason. *Unreasonable*. A tempting word—and a word that perfectly describes the Luggage. If we bring in Camus and Pratchett, we can come up with a simple conclusion: the Luggage operates as the absurd in Pratchett's fictional universe.

The Luggage Fantastic

The Luggage makes its first appearance in the first Discworld novel, *The Color of Magic*. As that book opens, the clueless tourist Twoflower is visiting the city of Ankh-Morpork. Naïve beyond belief, and completely unaware of the vicious dangers of the city, Twoflower has arrived with copious amounts of gold and an unshakeable belief that nothing bad can happen to him. He meets our other main character, the wizard Rincewind, while drinking in a seedy bar. Twoflower, delighted to be in such a scenic spot, flashes his gold about, which in turn attracts dozens of thieves. Shenanigans ensue.

The novel rolls on from there, with Rincewind doing his best to keep Twoflower alive as he cluelessly wanders from crisis to crisis. Rather than focusing on the plot of *The Color of Magic* and its sequel *The Light Fantastic,*[2] we should turn our attention to how the novel introduces us to Discworld. Just like Twoflower, readers are tourists in the city of Ankh-Morpork. We see the barbarians, the thieves, the wizards, the stinking streets, the magic, all of it for the first time. There's a problem, though: it's too easy to accept the fantastic as the normal. After a few pages, a reader could fall into a sort of "been there, done that" attitude. A world travelling on the back of a giant turtle? No big deal. A world where magic has its own eighth color? Cool. A world where Death stalks the streets? Yawn. Just like Camus was talking about, we have the tendency to impose our idea of order on the chaos of "reality" (in this case, Discworld). Then we feel like we "understand" the rules of Discworld, and we just accept those rules like we accept the rules of our everyday lives.

Discworld is in danger of becoming ordinary.

Enter the Luggage. Its absurdity forces us to recognize the entire absurdity of the Discworld fantasy. If we go back to Camus, we experience the absurd when our understanding of the world clashes with the world itself. This is the Luggage in a nutshell, both for us as readers and for the people of Discworld. The Luggage snaps us out of our complacency; it keeps us on our toes. Pratchett achieves this by having everyone in Ankh-Morpork freak out whenever they see the Luggage. Their fear—and lack of understanding—becomes our fear. Consider the Luggage's first appearance. A beggar named Blind Hugh (who sees just fine) has identified Twoflower as an easy target until he notices the Luggage trundling behind him. We quickly get a horrifying description:

> The massive wooden chest, which he had last seen solidly on the quayside, was following on its master's heels with a gentle rocking gait. Slowly, in case a sudden movement on his part might break his fragile control over his own legs, Hugh bent slightly so that he could see under the chest. There were lots and lots of little legs. (*The Color of Magic,* 15)

---

[2] Seriously, don't be lazy. Just read the novels.

Hugh then rushes off to get drunk.[3] By utilizing words like "gibber" and "fragile control," Pratchett clearly communicates Hugh's fear. In a world full of magical objects, the Luggage is the most magical, the most bizarre, the most violent. Everyone in Ankh-Morpork is terrified of it. Throughout *The Color of Magic*, it's described alternatively as absolutely terrible, a Monster, and having "an elemental nature, absolutely no brain, a homicidal attitude toward anything that threatened its master, and he wasn't quite sure that its inside occupied the same space-time framework as its outside" (269).

That last part is particularly important. The Luggage doesn't obey the laws of reality, even Discworld reality. Sometimes, it's full of Twoflower's clothes—which it even launders—and other times it's full of gold. When it's lost—as it almost always is—it pops through space to find Twoflower and Rincewind. It can't be controlled; it can't be bossed around; it's simply the Luggage, above and outside everything else. At one point, it even forces Rincewind to rescue Twoflower. Rincewind tries to resist, but he is helpless in front of the Luggage's might. He tries to speak to the Luggage, but the Luggage just smacks its lips in anticipation of a tasty Rincewind-sized snack. The Luggage always gets its way. So while it's easy to see that the Luggage challenges the characters of Discworld, what exactly do these Discworld inhabitants, Rincewind in particular, want, and how does that fit in with the idea of the absurd?

Going Absurd

Camus argues that the one thing humans can't avoid is their desire for order. Camus tells us that we can give up everything else—our nostalgia, our love, our hopes—but that we still cling to our sense of order, our longing to solve, to understand, *to know*. Within the Discworld novels, it's Rincewind who constantly expresses this desire. As a counterpoint to the Luggage's absurdity, Rincewind dreams of a scientifically ordered universe, one built on logic and good sense. He even goes so far as to dream of a science, a sensible world where the lightning is harnessed, and everything fits together like the

---

[3] Probably the most sensible response. I highly recommend it.

pieces of a puzzle. Poor Rincewind. No science for him. He's constantly missing out on anything that has a "bit of sense to it." As he stumbles from absurd adventure to absurd adventure, he's never able to find any peace or any logic. Cast adrift in a senseless world, he may be in danger of endlessly suffering—unless he finds a way to accept the absurd.

The torture that Rincewind goes through is deliberate, flouting logic at every turn. Pratchett doesn't hide this from his readers; he rubs it in our faces: "It was all very well going on about pure logic and how the universe was ruled by logic and the harmony of numbers, but the plain fact of the matter was that the Disc was manifestly traversing space on the back of a giant turtle and the gods had a habit of going around to atheists' houses and smashing their windows" (*The Color of Magic*, 90). Here, Pratchett almost perfectly coincides with Camus. Both show reality as having a nasty habit of knocking us over and breaking apart our tidy philosophical structures. We don't need to abandon hope, though. Just like Camus, Pratchett doesn't leave us in the lurch. With Rincewind, Pratchett is giving us a perfect example of a character who longs for order but can't find it—but in Rincewind, Pratchett also gives us a character who learns to cope with the absurd. Rincewind becomes what Camus identifies as the "absurd hero," someone who can perceive the absurdity of existence and, instead of fighting against it, learn to embrace it.

Equal Absurds

So far, we've only tackled half of Camus's argument. So the world is absurd, so what? Camus ends his discussion with a section about Sisyphus, a poor bastard who has been doomed to everlasting torment in the Greek version of Hell. A trouble-maker who has angered the Zeus and the other Gods, Sisyphus has been sentenced to roll an enormous rock up a hill for all eternity; every time the rock reaches the top, it rolls back down. Camus uses this story as a metaphor for absurdity. Push the rock up, the rock rolls back down, push the rock up, the rock rolls back down. That seems a lot like life. Things happen for no particular reason, and you end up getting nowhere. Instead of giving into despair, Camus uses this myth to make his most profound argument: the way to deal with the absurd is to embrace it.

Camus flips the seeming despair of the Sisyphus story around. Because Sisyphus is aware of the futility of pushing the rock, he transcends that futility. Instead of seeing Sisyphus as deeply miserable, Camus argues that we must view him as full of "silent joy" because "his fate belongs to him." Instead of clinging to his past life, his memories, his desire to make sense of the world, Sisyphus accepts the absurdity of his condition. The world is absurd; simply take it as it is: "The absurd man says yes . . . he knows himself to be the master of his days" (*Myth of Sisyphus*, 123). It is only when we fight the absurd with the false promise of logic and philosophy that we make ourselves unhappy. When we give in to the absurd, we find true peace.

Pratchett has pretty much the same doubts about traditional philosophy that Camus does. In one sequence from *The Light Fantastic*, Rincewind encounters a group of trolls, monsters made entirely of rock. He quickly learns that trolls "suffer from philosophy." They eventually spend all their time thinking about their lives and their worlds, and this paralyzes them to the point they can no longer move. They slip off into eternity: "Oh yes. Martyrs to it. It comes to all of us in the end. One evening, they say, you start to wake up and then you think 'Why bother?' and you just don't" (*The Light Fantastic,* 148).

To place this in the terms of Camus: we live a world that doesn't make sense. It can't make sense; it exists outside of us, and it doesn't exist to make us happy. We try, as hard as we can, to organize it, to find an order, but that effort is doomed to fail. Eventually, this quest for order paralyzes and destroys us, just like it does the trolls. Camus's answer: you need to stop searching so hard. You need to accept the universe for what it is, or else you're going to wind up a lump of rock, uselessly racking your brain for answers that don't exist.

Think about this as an example: is the Luggage good or evil? Well, what does good mean? What does evil mean? The Luggage is protecting its owner, but it does so at the expense of other lives. Is that ethically acceptable? Or do ethics only apply to the Luggage in certain circumstances? Which circumstances? And do the same kind of ethics apply to a wooden box as to humans?

Those questions will drive you mad.

Our only alternative: to accept the absurd.

Where's My Luggage?

Over the course of the series, Rincewind—and by extension, the reader—comes to love the Luggage. Instead of finding its absurdity horrifying, we begin to find it comforting, like an old friend. Rincewind actually wants the Luggage to stick around, and other characters begin finding the Luggage sweet, loyal, and an all-around cuddly household pet. The Luggage is even instrumental in saving the world at the end of *The Light Fantastic*. Just think of how far Pratchett has taken us. We're actually beginning to *like* a homicidal suitcase.

By the time Twoflower gives the Luggage to Rincewind at the end of that novel, we're ready to make a change in our relationship to the absurd. Rincewind initially tries to run away from the Luggage, snapping out "I don't want you!" and even kicking it. The Luggage reacts almost like a dog: "The Luggage sagged. Rincewind stalked away." Rincewind eventually relents: "When he turned the Luggage was where he had left it. It looked sort of huddled. Rincewind thought for a while. 'All right, then,' he said. 'Come on'" (*The Light Fantastic,* 277). By accepting the Luggage, Rincewind has accepted absurdity into his life. Readers have almost no choice but to do the same. Since we now find the Luggage pathetic ("huddled"), our relationship to the absurd has shifted from terror to acceptance, even affection.

If Rincewind chooses the Luggage, he is no longer victimized by it. If an absurd hero chooses the absurd, he or she is no longer traumatized by it. If a reader chooses to enjoy the absurdity of Discworld . . . you get the point. By abandoning the quest for order, we've transformed the absurd from a source of pain to a source of pleasure.

Moving Luggage

To push the metaphor as far as we can—something that Sir Terry would no doubt want us to do—we can think of Rincewind as Sisyphus and the Luggage as the rock. Just as Sisyphus is damned to push the rock up the hill only to have it forever roll back down, crushing any false dreams he might have of progress or meaning, so too is Rincewind hounded by the Luggage. Rincewind is constantly trying to make sense of his life, to reach his goals, which are mostly to slink off into relative obscurity.

The Luggage won't let that happen.

No matter what, the Luggage is always there, defying all logic, order, and sense. The Luggage pulls Rincewind back into the absurdity of Discworld. Just like the rock rolling down the hill, it returns Rincewind to the reality of his situation. Then the twist: just like Sisyphus comes to love his rock, Rincewind comes to love the Luggage. By being absurd, the Luggage grounds Rincewind and allows him to exist within the madness that is Discworld.

Since the universe we live in is absurd—at its most basic level, the universe is not constructed for human meaning or human happiness—the only way to survive is to accept the craziness. Without the Luggage, Rincewind would be lost in the fantasy of Discworld, and, even more profoundly, so would we readers. Without the Luggage, we would forget the strangeness of Pratchett's fantasy realm. We would become comfortable, complacent. We'd start—shudder!—thinking that Discworld makes sense.

That's where the Luggage saves us. It clumps up behind on hundreds of little feet, chomping its wooden teeth, rolling its red tongue. It's a never-ending reminder that life doesn't make sense, that *life can't make sense*, so we might as well just get on with the business of living.

Interesting Luggages

The Luggage recurs through all the other Rincewind novels, chasing after Rincewind and generally keeping him safe.[4] Before we wrap up our interpretation of the Luggage, let's take a look at one last sequence, when the Luggage falls in love. For the first time, this forces us to consider what the Luggage actually wants. If Rincewind's experience in Discworld is absurd, just imagine what the Luggage thinks and feels. He's trapped in a world of fleshy strangers, forced to ingest dirty clothes, and to trundle after tourists who are constantly getting lost. If anyone's experience in Discworld is absurd, it's the Luggage's. This

---

[4] RINCEWIND'S SURVIVAL IS OCCASIONALLY ANNOYING. YET, FEW PROVIDE ME WITH . . . AMUSEMENT.

all comes to a head in *Interesting Times*. In this novel, Rincewind has been teleported to the Counterweight Continent, Pratchett's version of China, where he gets caught up in court intrigues, reunites with Twoflower, aids some rampaging elderly barbarians, and deals with the general Discworld madness we all know and love.

The Luggage does what it always does: it has to find Rincewind and rescue him from whatever danger he's fallen into this time. Early on, Rincewind makes a startling discovery. The Luggage is not alone! When Rincewind brags to a stranger about his Luggage (showing a newfound pride in the Luggage's absurdity), he's shown an entire group of Luggages. Apparently, sapient pearwood is common in the Counterweight Continent, and hundreds of the sentient chests are just running around, living their Luggage lives.

This might seem to wreck the uniqueness of the Luggage. If it's just one walking box of many, how is it absurd? Pratchett still has some tricks up his sleeve: he utilizes the many Luggages to launch one of the most absurd love plots in all of fiction. When the Luggage finally makes it to the Counterweight Continent, it runs into a female Luggage, complete with dainty feet and a fancy inlaid lid. This female Luggage—she never gets a name—is initially trapped outside in a Luggage corral when she gets attacked by three evil Luggages, who are ominously covered in studded leather. Our heroic Luggage bursts into the corral and saves the female Luggage, chasing the bad Luggages onto the roof and out into the countryside.

Take a second and reread the last paragraph I wrote. There's Pratchett's absurdity for you. You've been forced to accept not only the idea of a sentient Luggage, but also female Luggages and male Luggages, good Luggages and bad Luggages. How did it come to this? It only gets stranger. When the Luggage finally catches up with Rincewind, it (now a he, I guess) has the other Luggage in tow:

> The Luggage shuffled its feet. From out of an alleyway came a slightly larger and far more ornate version of itself. Its lid was inset with decorative wood, and, it seemed to Rincewind, its feet were rather more dainty than the horny-nailed, calloused ones of the Luggage. Besides, the toenails had been painted. (*Interesting Times*, 314–15).

Rincewind is forced—much against his will—to start thinking about the Luggage and sex: "Rincewind's own sexual experiences were not excessive though he had seen diagrams. He hadn't the faintest idea how it applied to travel accessories"[5] (*Interesting Times,* 314–15).

Once again, we have to rethink our relationship to reality, from the Luggage to Luggages. Nothing is fundamentally stable in Discworld; Pratchett can—and does—change the rules as he sees fit. By the end of *Interesting Times*, the Luggage even has children, four little chests toddling behind his new Luggage—wife? Companion? Mate? Pratchett never gets into the details of Luggage marriage. Also, Luggage reproduction only takes a matter of hours. Who knew?

There is no escape from the absurd in Discworld. Not even the Luggage is spared. Instead of having a chance to settle into his new life as a father and husband, Rincewind is whisked off to another continent—this time to XXXX, for *The Last Continent*—and the Luggage duly has to follow him again. Just like Rincewind, and just like us readers, the Luggage is trapped pushing the rock up the hill. His experience is absurd. We can only hope he accepts his fate with as much grace as Sisyphus. The round of Discworld never ends: more adventures, more absurdity, and never any final meaning.

Carpe Luggage

In *The Light Fantastic*, Pratchett sets up a rather labored pun. When discussing the Luggage, Twoflower reveals he purchased it at a magical shop, because "I said I wanted a traveling trunk" (*The Light Fantastic*, 166). Ha, ha! Twoflower got what he wanted: a trunk that travels. I imagine Pratchett enjoys the groans this elicits from his audience. It's in the sheer badness of this pun that the genius of Pratchett lies. You can understand the Luggage in many ways: as a joke gone too far, as a tragic figure doomed to follow Rincewind, as a monstrous nonhuman entity that makes a mockery of all sense. The Luggage

---

[5] I'd advise you not to think about the Luggage having sex, but I imagine it's too late by now. Sorry.

is all these things at the same time: it is the living, breathing, wooden, hundred-legged absurd.

Instead of fearing that absurd, or running away from it, or minimizing it, Pratchett embraces it. The Luggage takes us on the same philosophical journey that Camus outlines. As he argues, only in the absurd lies freedom from the tyranny of logic and philosophy. Rincewind frees himself by embracing the absurdity of the Luggage. The Luggage frees himself by embracing the absurdity of Rincewind. Can we, as readers, do anything else? Let us not be like the trolls, curled in on ourselves, trapped by philosophy. Let us be like the Luggage, forever chasing after Rincewind, free and unbound.[6]

[6] And occasionally terrifying hapless passersby.

7
Pratchett's *Republic*

BRANDON KEMPNER

Humans.

Dwarfs.

Trolls.

Vampires, werewolves, gnomes, golems, and zombies.

Thieves, assassins, witches, wizards, and prostitutes. A stinking city prone to every kind of wickedness, depravity, drunkenness, scandal, perversity, and sausage-selling salesman that you could imagine.

A place where Death himself stalks the streets.[1]

A whole pantheon of crazed gods ready to stick their noses into everything they can.

Steam engines, moving pictures, guns, trains, newspapers, paper money, and a postal service.

That's the toxic stew that makes up the wonder and terror of Terry Pratchett's Ankh-Morpork.

How do you rule all of that?

Quite well, as a matter of fact. Against all odds, the Patrician manages to keep that great city spinning. No problem is too big, no detail too small, for the watchful eye of Havelock Vetinari, long-time ruler of Ankh-Morpork. The Patrician is a man so corrupt he rises above corruption, a man so devious that he is honest, a man so powerful that he appears powerless. In him, we have the ultimate Philosopher King, someone who has faced the grim realities of Nature and found the most effective way to rule. Through his benevolent shepherding of

[1] STALKS? THAT SEEMS A BIT UNKIND.

Ankh-Morpork, Pratchett is presenting his view of the ideal city and how such a place might be run.

Or, in other words, Pratchett is Plato and Discworld is his *Republic*.

Ankh-Morpork: Perfect City or Perfectest City?

Plato (428–348 BCE) is one of the great Greek philosophers. Alongside Socrates and Aristotle, Plato explored questions about knowing, the immortality of the soul, the definition of terms like justice and truth, and what would make a perfect city. Pratchett puts a playful spin on each of these big philosophical concepts. His wizards at the Unseen University are his take on how we learn and acquire knowledge.[2] The character Death is Pratchett's inquiry into the immortality of the soul. The Patrician—and the antics of the City Watch—are Pratchett's take on justice and the perfect city, two ideas closely connected because the perfect city *is* the just city.

Plato is famous for a great many books, but it's his towering *The Republic* (380 BCE) that lays out his vision of the ideal city. In this work, Plato is obsessed with the "true" nature of reality, which he envisions as Forms, abstract ideas that (to him at least) undergird the reality we live in. These unchanging, transcendent "Truths" shape our world, giving form, logic, and order to all things. Plato argues that if we are able to see and understand these abstract ideas, we could use them to construct the perfect city, just as Dibbler uses his perfect knowledge of meats to construct the ideal sausage-in-a-bun.

The Republic is written in Plato's typical "dialogue" style: Plato shows us the philosopher Socrates making fools of everyone who doubts him. Socrates strikes up a conversation with some various patsies about the perfect city, and proceeds to school them on just what such a city should be. Socrates, at least in Plato's depiction of him, is the most vicious debater of all time: he asks seemingly innocent questions that trap his audience into certain conclusions, and then he hammers those home with vicious intensity. Over the course of some 300+ pages of excruciating detail, Plato (through the mouth of

---

[2] Haphazardly and often involving fire and explosions.

Socrates) expounds on the nature of the "just" and "beautiful" city. The picture built up by *The Republic* is one of immaculate order, with perfectly behaved citizens all happily obeying the dictates of our true rulers: the Philosopher Kings. He even gives the city a grand name: Kallipolis, a mash-up of the Greek word for beauty (*kalos*) and city (*polis*).[3]

On the surface, nothing could be more different from Plato's "Beautiful City" than the rotting cesspool that is Ankh-Morpork. Dig deeper, though, and you'll see that they're much the same. In *The Republic*, Plato proposes a class called "the Guardians," a group dedicated to protecting and ruling the city. Plato wants his Guardians to be those "most likely to devote their lives to doing what they judge to be in the interest of the community, and who are never prepared to act against it" (*The Republic*, 113).

That's a near perfect description of the Patrician and the City Watch. Pratchett's Guardians (or, in this case, the Guards) always operate in the best interests of Ankh-Morpork, never their own. Their selfless embrace of justice in its highest form makes Ankh-Morpork the perfect city for Discworld—or as perfect as a city can get in Discworld. Plato has to play by the rules of our world, and the Patrician by the rules of his, but when we compare the two, we can see that Discworld truly offers us Pratchett's guidebook for building the perfect city.

To Serve, To Protect, and To Flee

In *The Republic*, Plato imagines the Guardians, an elite group of citizens trained to protect and shepherd the perfect city.

In *Guards! Guards!*, Pratchett imagines the Watch, an elite group of citizens trained to protect and shepherd the city.[4]

Same goal, but different cities, different methods, and different realities.

Plato states his goal early in *The Republic*: "our purpose in founding our state was not to promote the particular happiness of a single class, but, so far as possible, of the whole community" (*The Republic*, 120). As we'll also see, that's the Patrician's goal for Ankh-Morpork, although he achieves his end quite

---

[3] That name is only slightly less funny than Ankh-Morpork.

[4] And by elite, I mean elite at sleeping, snoozing, and drinking.

differently. In Discworld, the City Watch is directly responsible for keeping the peace of Ankh-Morpork. To start with, they're doing an absolutely terrible job. Their leader, Sam Vimes, is an alcoholic wreck, indifferent to his highest responsibilities, and the other members of the Watch are just as likely to run from a crime as towards it.

Guards! Guards! shows the transformation of this flawed Watch into something that actually serves the greater good of the city. The story begins with the idealistic Carrot. He's your typical human raised by dwarfs, brimming with dreams of moving to the big city and joining the Watch. He's spent his youth studying the *Laws and Ordinances of the Cities of Ankh and Morpork*, mastering every statute and nuance. He knows he can make a real difference. He's utterly disconnected from reality and sees the Law as an end in itself, not something that needs to work for the people.

Aflame with his naïve ideas of abstract justice, Carrot sets out for the city. Once there, he clashes with the Watch's moral and cultural decay. No one has volunteered to join the Watch for years, and to actually want to enforce the Law—it's unthinkable. For the past decade, the Watch has been keeping its head down, ignoring crime and everything else that happens around them. As Nobby exclaims early in the novel, "You're in the City Watch! Don't give me anymore of this law business!" (*Guards! Guards!*, 72). Carrot won't listen. He quickly arrests the leader of the Thieves' Guild. Why? For being a thief. As you can imagine, this gets everyone quite upset. If the Watch is going to enforce the Law, what's next? How are the guilds going to operate? This brings the Watch to the attention of the Patrician. You'd think that big trouble would result. Instead, Vetinari decides to see if he can use them, and, by doing so, transform them into true Guardians of the city.

Carrot's idealism has threatened to overturn the whole apple-cart (or sausage-cart, or whatever you upset in Ankh-Morpork). At this point, he's not working for the good of the City—he's so idealistic he doesn't even understand what is *good* for Ankh-Morpork. Angering the thieves, the assassins, and the prostitutes, is the quickest route to destabilize the city. On the flipside, Vimes and the Watch's indifference to social justice is equally a threat to the city, a point that Pratchett makes abundantly clear in the plot of the novel. Unbeknownst to anyone, the city is on the verge of crisis. A secret society has been plotting to bring Kings back to Ankh-Morpork, and they're planning to do so by summoning dragons into the city.

Good plan, huh?

It's a little more involved than that. They've dug up a dupe to act as King, and they figure if he defeats a dragon, he'll be so beloved that the citizens will crown him King, kicking the Patrician out in the process. The fragile peace of Ankh-Morpork would end, and the city would be transformed into a monarchy, ruled for specific interests, not the good of all. This is what brings us back to Plato: is Ankh-Morpork going to be ruled for the good of the whole community, or for the good of the few? Will it be a just or an unjust city?

Neither Carrot nor the Watch alone is going to be adequate. They have to pull together, become more philosophical, and act like true Guardians. Over the course of *Guards! Guards!* that's exactly what they do. Carrot learns to control his idealism, Vimes learns to control his indifference, and the mixture of the two saves the city from dragons, Kings, and general skullduggery.[5] Carrot accepts the guilds as being part of the machinery of the system, and Vimes accepts that he does have to enforce the Law at times. That's a powerful one-two punch of idealism and pragmatism.

We're still missing one last part of Plato's picture, though: the ruler of the city, or what Plato calls the "Philosopher King." That's the Patrician, the mysterious and shadowy figure who operates as Ankh-Morpork's ruler. It's only when Carrot's idealism, Vimes's practicality, and the Patrician's cleverness come together, that the city of Ankh-Morpork can survive and thrive.

The Perfect Pratchett Philosopher King

Thus we come to the Patrician, absolute ruler of Ankh-Morpork. On the surface, he may seem like a self-interested, Machiavellian dictator, but, scratch beneath that crusty exterior and you'll find a dedicated public servant. Plato begins Book V of *The Republic* with a seemingly impossible claim: that

---

[5] Well Dibbler is still around, but he's really like the little burnt greasy bits you get in a sausage-inna-bun—he gives the city *flavor.** (*and heartburn.)

a perfect city can't arise until the philosophers become kings. These Philosopher Kings, blessed with unerring wisdom, will guide their city with perfect logic, insight, and efficiency.

Fat chance.

That is, until you think about the Patrician. He's a perfect example of the Platonic Philosopher King. By closely observing his behavior, we can get a glimpse of the selfless ruler in action. While the Patrician was a bit player in earlier Discworld novels, *Guards! Guards!* gives him his first real chance to shine. As we saw above, he teams up with the Watch to turn aside the threat of monarchy and to preserve the Ankh-Morpork we all love and cherish. But is he doing this for his own personal gain (the pleasure he takes in being ruler), or is he doing it for the city?

Pratchett explains Vetinari's own political philosophy in some detail:

> Under his hands, for the first time in a thousand years, Ankh-Morpork *operated.* It might not be fair or just or particularly democratic, but it worked. He tended it as one tends a topiary bush, encouraging a growth here, pruning an errant twig there. It was said that he would tolerate absolutely anything apart from anything that threatened the city.[6] (*Guards! Guards!*, 94)

Vetinari keeps the city organized by keeping everything in its right place. Instead of outlawing thieves and assassins (an impossibility), he licenses them, forming guilds so that their behavior can be regulated and controlled. His goal is not his own enrichment, but rather the smooth functioning of Ankh-Morpork. In *The Republic*, Plato even argues that justice is keeping everything in its right place, of minding your own business and not messing with other people.

That's the Patrician in a nutshell.

A great example of this can be found once the monarchists take over in *Guards! Guards!* Buoyed by their crazy dragon plot, they arrest and imprison Vetinari in his own dungeon. Vimes visits him down there, only to realize that Vetinari has plotted all of this out in advance. The cell is sealed with an enormous door, bristling with locks, *but all the locks are on the inside*. Vetinari is always thinking ten steps ahead. He doesn't

---

[6] And mimes.

do this for his own benefit, though. He knows that if he's imprisoned, his city must be in trouble. By allowing himself the means to escape, he can once again act in the public good. That's exactly how *Guards! Guards!* plays out. The dragons have gotten out of control, and Vetinari and the Watch have to step in and straighten the whole thing out. If Vetinari had followed the "rules," he'd still be stuck in prison. By following a higher mandate—of keeping the city safe—he's able to save the day.

Vetinari's commitment to Ankh-Morpork, his perfect understanding of reality, and his ability to think ahead, are what make him a Philosopher King. Instead of ruling from a place of power, he rules from a place of knowledge, and it's that supreme understanding that helps Vetinari work with the Watch and dump the dragons. What's key here is that he does all of this for the city's benefit, not his own. Just like Carrot has to learn that the Law can't be equally applied in all instances but rather has to be tailored to the needs of Ankh-Morpork, that's exactly how Vetinari rules. He doesn't rule the city. He rules for the city.

Every city receives the Guardian it deserves.

The Truth and Nothing but the Truth

To truly nail our point home, let's take one last look at the Philosopher King in action. Much of Plato is spent exploring the idea of the "Truth" (you should imagine that in glowing capital letters), which Plato defines as an impersonal, transcendent "rightness" that manifests itself in our reality. If the need for an overly idealistic Truth to balance out with a grim and pragmatic Reality is the core theme of *Guards! Guards!*, that's kicked up a notch in Pratchett's novel *The Truth*. As usual, Pratchett approaches this idea playfully, but hidden within the chaos and frenzy of *The Truth* are some Platonic messages: the Truth is more powerful than deception, and that seeking the Truth will make for a better Ankh-Morpork.

The Truth is Pratchett's Discworld volume about starting and running a newspaper. Sudden advances in dwarf technology have resulted in the first moveable type printing press, and William de Worde has launched Ankh-Morpork's first daily newspaper: *The Ankh-Morpork Times*. Complete with a catchy slogan of "The Truth shall make ye free," it begins life as a trashy human-interest rag, featuring stories about odd-looking vegetables, riots, and what not. Worde and *The Times* are quickly drawn into a political scandal: the Patrician seems to have been caught trying to flee town after apparently stabbing someone, his donkey loaded down with 70,000 Ankh-Morpork dollars' worth of public silver. Ankh-Morpork is thrown into chaos, the Patrician imprisoned, and Worde finds himself on the trail of the story, seeking the Truth his newspaper has so naïvely promised to deliver.

The governance question investigated by Pratchett in *The Truth* is the proper relationship between words, truth, and the ideal city. Although *The Republic* was written long before the emergence of the press, Plato had some strong words for people using art and other written works to spread what he saw as "lies." For Plato, stories—particularly stories about the gods—were incredibly dangerous. Plato's basic argument is that words don't represent "the Truth." Since words are a representation of reality, and not reality itself, they move us away from true knowledge, not towards it. Throw in the fact that words can also lie, and Plato comes to a pretty strong conclusion: writers, poets, and newspaper men (if they existed back then), need to be banned from the perfect city.

Pratchett doesn't quite agree—but, if you dig deeper, you'll find that Pratchett isn't disagreeing in principle with Plato, but only in practice. Instead, Pratchett is going to show us how words and newspapers might operate in service of the just city, rather than in opposition to it. Pratchett frames *The Truth* with some early passages that discuss the importance of words and governance. At the start of the novel, the Patrician makes two revealing comments, namely that "flexibility and understanding have always been my watchword" and that "a civilization runs on words, Your Reverence. Civilization *is* words. Which, on the whole, should not be too expensive. The world turns, Your Reverence, and we must spin with it" (*The Truth,* 37 and 39). Expert manipulator that he is, Pratchett gets our minds buzzing with the core ideas of *The Truth*: namely, how words, truth, and good governance all need to work together.

Pratchett puts this plan into action when Worde teams up with the Watch and Sam Vimes to investigate what exactly happened to the Patrician. Remember, the Patrician has been accused of murder, and the whole city is sliding into chaos as new powers jostle to take over. Worde commits himself to finding "the Truth" of what happened, and he goes farther than even the Guard in investigating the alleged crime. At first, he's doing this just to get the scoop, hoping to sell more newspapers. As the book goes on, though, his quest for the Truth begins to converge with the Good of the City, and we, as readers, find out that those two things are one and the same.

Worde discovers that Vetinari has been framed for the crime, and that it's his own aristocratic father that doing the framing. Worde's father thinks that the Patrician has become too populist: he isn't helping the rich get richer, but rather ensuring the city works for all. How dare he! Worde has to set aside his own family loyalties: "*Someone* has to care about the . . . the big truth. What Vetinari mostly does not do is *a lot of harm*. We've had rulers who were completely crazy and very, very nasty" (*The Truth*, 291). Not only does Vetinari have to think about "the big truth," so too does Worde, and by aligning his newspaper with the Truth (and Vetinari), he becomes a selfless servant of the city.[7] Worde exposes the plot and saves the day. Vetinari returns the favor by allowing the Press to operate, thus extending the circle of Guardians from just Vetinari and the Watch to now include Worde and the free press. Together, all three can work towards protecting and serving Ankh-Morpork.

Total Discworld

Near the end of *The Republic*, Plato has a truly Pratchett moment. When discussing how much happier Philosopher Kings are than tyrants, Socrates gives us a precise answer: Philosopher Kings are 729 times happier. Socrates tries to back that up with some fancy math, but it's truly a great moment of absurdist comedy. Plato so wants the world to make precise sense, he'll assign a mathematical value to happiness.

Pratchett isn't as precise in Discworld. He just wants things to work. We can't know whether Plato would have been fascinated or appalled by Pratchett's fantasy world. Plato has no patience for fools. He believed that he understood Truth absolutely, and anyone who failed to conform to his vision of the

---

[7] Well, as selfless as any Ankh-Morporkian can be, which really isn't all that selfless, but it's the thought that counts.

Truth was dangerous, subversive, and a downright problem. In *The Republic*, Plato talks about banning poets from his perfect city because they are liars, and anyone who doesn't get with the Platonic program was on the short path to exile.

Pratchett might seem like one of those subversive artists, drawing us away from pure reality with his fantasy. Still, the core of Pratchett reflects the core of Platonic idealism. The Guardians of Ankh-Morpork don't serve themselves, but a higher concept of justice. They believe that the city can be run for the good of the people. The Patrician is still ruling through the Truth, but it's just a different truth than Plato imagined. In Plato's world, the Truth is rigid, dominating; in Discworld, it oozes like slow light.

Plato has often been accused of being a totalitarian. In *The Republic*, he sets up a system of government that excludes democracy, individual choice, and free will. Plato insists that the world we live in conform to the vision of his ideal world. I'd argue that Pratchett and the Patrician do something slightly different. The Patrician accepts the flaws of reality as reality itself, and instead of making people change, he changes that false idealism to match observable reality.

Whether you consider Ankh-Morpork "perfect," with all its squirming ugliness, may be a matter of debate. Maybe you don't like bustling cities full of human anguish and pleasure, of opportunity and promise, of freedom and equality. There's no accounting for taste. Some people like eating snails. Other people don't.[8] I leave you with just one question: would you rather live under the iron fist of Plato, or under the kindly efficiency of the Patrician?[9]

---

[8] Sane people, for the record.

[9] Special thanks to Havelock Vetinari for his feedback on this chapter.

8
Honesty Trumps Cleverness: Sam Vimes and Commonsense Philosophy

MATTHEW SKENE

Fallor, ergo sum; "I err, therefore I am."

"If you spend your whole time thinking about the universe, you tend to forget the less important bits of it. Like your pants" (Pratchett, *Small Gods*, 142). Intelligent characters throughout Pratchett's works usually come across as impractical and ungrounded, often to their own and to others' dismay. Even those with good intentions cause problems. For example, we are introduced to Leonard of Quirm in a conversation with Vetinari over his creation of the gonne.

> "This city is full of clever men," said the Patrician. "And dwarfs. Clever men and dwarfs who tinker with things."
> "I am so very sorry."
> "They never think."
> "Indeed."
> ". . . And then there's the wizards. Tinker, tinker, tinker. Never think twice before grabbing a thread of the fabric of reality and giving a pull."
> "Shocking."
> "The alchemists? Their view of civic duty is mixing up things to see what happens."
> "I hear the bangs, even here."
> "And then, of course, along comes someone like you—"
> "I really am very sorry." (Pratchett, *Men at Arms*, 192)

Most of the time, clever characters fail to see the obvious and develop ideas that are blind to the difficulties this causes.

Meanwhile, slow, straightforward types are hard to mislead and tend to lack the creativity necessary to see things any way other than how they really are. Detritus, for example, is described as having "that special sort of stupidity that is hard to fool" (Pratchett, *Feet of Clay*, 53). Of course, it's not lack of intelligence itself that allows these figures to see things more clearly. Speculation by the masses in his works is a source of mirth as often as speculation by philosophers. Making these mistakes is part of what it is to be human. We exist "TO BE THE PLACE WHERE THE FALLING ANGEL MEETS THE RISING APE" (Pratchett, *Hogfather*, 336). Humans can convince ourselves we shouldn't believe our own eyes, but as for the Librarian, "as an ape he had no doubt whatsoever about his eyes, and believed them all the time" (Pratchett, *Guards! Guards!*, 88). Yet we tend to not trust our eyes, sometimes for good reason.[1] Between the infallibility of divinity and the certainty of animality lies the inevitable error of human existence.

Philosophy is all about answering questions. When it comes to supplying answers to questions, becoming an authority is depressingly easy. Speak confidently, maybe use whatever passes for an argument given your skills, and those listening will assume you have authority over these matters.[2] Silence in others will simply confirm this. Sergeant Colon has been well educated. "He'd been to the School of My Dad Always Said, the College of It Stands to Reason, and was now a postgraduate student at the University of What Some Bloke in the Pub Told Me" (Pratchett, *Jingo*, 34). Whenever characters are standing around trying to figure something out, they can always pull an answer out of their Colon, who is an expert in all matters no one else is informed enough to contradict him on. The reason speaking up with an air of authority often works no matter how clueless you are is because everyone listening is just as clueless; that's why they were looking for an authority in the first place. When addressing the big questions, traditionally those who are challenged on their answers fall back on divine

---

[1] AND SOMETIMES BECAUSE THE TRUTH IS TOO TERRIFYING FOR YOUR BRAIN TO BELIEVE YOUR EYES ARE SEEING IT.

[2] Trolls, for example, are authorities on many topics because it is hard to challenge the logic of the common trollish argument . . . "Because dis fist will make another hole in yer face ta breath tru."

revelation or tradition to justify themselves. Philosophers challenge these sources, trusting their own reason to do a better job with them.

Despite being full of philosophical influences, philosophers don't come across well in the Discworld books. With quotes such as "I used to think that *I* was stupid, then I met philosophers" (*Small Gods*, 368), and "These men are philosophers, he thought. They had told him so. So their brains must be so big that they have room for ideas that no-one else would consider for five seconds" (Pratchett, *Pyramids,* 213), philosophers often come off less well than wizards. Of course, this complaint is often echoed by philosophers, who love the claim that "there is no idea so absurd some philosopher has not held it." Philosophers tend to love clever ideas and developing grand theories, but they often miss out on the obvious in their efforts to develop them.

Commonsense philosophy stands as a bastion of sanity amidst the storm, seeking to get philosophers to follow the lead of those like Sam Vimes who will take honesty over cleverness any day. In commonsense philosophy, the mundane facts of life are given a central role. Theories are developed from them and required to maintain them. An insistence on holding fast to what we know may make us occasionally miss out on things we might have otherwise discovered, as some have said of this approach. Vimes, for example, refuses to believe in the existence of the Summoning Dark because it goes against common sense. It's possible following commonsense philosophy may lead us to fail to believe in floating eyeballs that are really there. On the other hand, since it will also stop us from believing in lots of ones that aren't there, I'd say it's a tradeoff worth the cost. As Vimes proclaims "Common sense and facts! That's what works" (Pratchett, *Thud!*, 366).

There are three aspects of commonsense philosophy that Vimes embodies: opposition to speculation, irreverence for thinkers of the past, and an understanding of the need to check theories against reality. Vimes always gets his criminal member of a multi-vital society, but it's not through cleverness, it's through thoroughness. Vimes hates clues because they invite people to speculate in order to solve things rather than to sit down and think it through carefully. Vimes is also irreverent and anti-authoritarian.[3] He doesn't take on attitudes towards authority that cloud his ability to see things as they are. Vimes is the sort of man who, when asked if he wants truth, freedom, and justice replies that he wants a hard-boiled egg, because he has a chance of getting that. Finally, there is his realism. Vimes has been described as "not the sharpest knife in the drawer, but honest as anything" (*Thud!*, 110). He won't assume that his ideas hold up just because his intellect let him come up with them, instead he insists on ensuring that his opinions are borne out by the facts. Vimes's insistence on checking theories against reality comes through most clearly in his political views, especially as described in *Night Watch*. Here, he clearly sees that so much misery arises out of efforts to force society into patterns that don't work for human beings. In all these respects, Vimes embodies the commonsense approach to philosophy.

Against Speculation

The most famous commonsense philosopher was Thomas Reid (1710–1796).[4] Reid was a family friend of Isaac Newton, and grew up learning from his example. Newton's successes in physics were shaped in large part by his refusal to believe in things on speculative grounds. While everyone else was searching around for non-existent gravitons, Newton didn't bother believing in such things, and instead just figured out the laws of gravitational attraction without the needless addition of hidden gravitons.[5] Reid carried this opposition to speculation into philosophy. According to Reid, "It is genius, and not the want of it, that adulterates philosophy, and fills it with error and false theory," and "when men attempt, by the force of genius, to discover the causes of the phenomena of Nature, they have only the chance of going wrong more ingeniously" (Reid, *Essays*, 534). According to Reid, we can only make progress in philoso-

---

[3] This is despite the fact that he is an authority himself, a point that Vetinari points out is "practically zen."

[4] Of course the word "famous" when referring to philosophers is somewhat relative. It is a bit like saying, "The most famous ditch-digger in history." Who amongst ditch-diggers is a celebrity they all wish they could have met? To those who can't tell the difference between a good shovel and a *really* good shovel, it isn't that big of a deal.

[5] Newton of course turned out to be wrong. Funny how that works.

phy or in any discipline by starting with things we know and resisting the urge to build elaborate theories from inadequate data. Commonsense philosophy insists on a cautious approach to forming philosophical opinions. In particular, it opposes speculation as a grounds for belief. Of necessity, when trying to piece together a picture of reality as a whole, we are working with a limited range of information. Focusing on a few interesting pieces to put together a picture can be one of the quickest ways to get a fascinating, inaccurate theory. Reid thinks we should trust our judgment in areas where we don't have to speculate, but that we shouldn't assume that in those areas where we have to go beyond what lies at the surface, seeing what is beneath will be easy. Instead, we should work slowly from what our common sense can tell us, and only come up with a theory if it is grounded in things we are reasonably sure of to begin with.

In addition to refusing to lie to himself about the world around him, Vimes approaches problems in a way that fits well with common sense philosophy. This can be seen in his mistrust of the Sherlock Holmes approach to policing. Vimes complains about people who claim to be able to know everything about someone from a few little details even though they are fully compatible with lots of other explanations. He says of such figures "What arrogance! What an insult to the rich and chaotic variety of the human experience!" (*Feet of Clay*, 174). The reason the Holmesish characters are beloved is that we all like to think that if we were just a little smarter we could simply see it all and discover the hidden truths from the smallest details.

The dream of easy answers is like a ring for sale on the cheap from Moist von Lipwig; we should know it must be glass, but our hope of getting the prize blinds us to common sense. The reason Vimes hates clues is because he knows this hope is a lie. In philosophy as in policing, "the world was far too *real* to leave neat little hints" (*Feet of Clay*, 174). Intelligence, and the ability to spin a yarn to explain a few minor details doesn't lead to the truth very often. No matter how smart you are, making stuff up to figure stuff out is a bad way to go about things. You need to find all the pieces of the puzzle and fit them together until the picture emerges, not guess it must be a picture of Koom Valley just because you see a piece with a rock in it and another with a battle axe. Following clues leads you to embrace wild theories. Instead, you should just gather the pieces you have and hope that by looking at them you'll start to find the corners and some features that might make the picture become clearer. This process is difficult and slow, but it ultimately gets results.

The Virtue of Irreverence

"It seemed to be a chronic disease. It was as if even the most intelligent person had this little blank spot in their heads where someone had written: 'Kings. What a good idea.' Whoever had created humanity had left in a major design flaw. It was its tendency to bend at the knees" (Pratchett, *Feet of Clay*, 77). The word "kings" can be seen as a simple placeholder here. Really, people want someone to take away the discomfort of freedom, and the uncertainty that comes with it. People don't just want to be told what to do so they don't have to worry that they're doing it wrong, they also want to be told what to believe so they don't have to feel that terrifying freedom Dorfl describes as "Like Having The Top Of Your Head Screwed Off" (*Feet of Clay*, 349). We want answers to the questions that don't seem to go away; the questions that lie at the heart of philosophy. Even the most intelligent are often willing to find an authority they can respect and hold fast to the answers they give. Philosophers have standards, and won't be taken in by just anyone, but they, too, often find authorities in one another or in society to take to heart.

While the idea of Colon as an expert in anything other than sergeanting is an obvious illusion I would hope even the most moderately thoughtful could avoid, others who seek to take up authority will build traditions, or better yet, religions, as a substitute for answers. This is why Grag Hamcrusher speaks about "history and destiny and all the other words that always got trotted out to put a gloss on slaughter" (*Thud!*, 23) and can convince otherwise sensible dwarfs that because it was written in a holy book, exterminating the trolls is their moral duty. When you're trying to sell people on the value of an idea, placing it behind a veil of solemnity and import is a great way to mask its faults.

All philosophy begins with a commandment to love autonomy and think for yourself. Commonsense philosophy goes farther by starting with a healthy dose of irreverence. It recognizes that those who take positions of authority in an area are often simply the brashest, and not the most competent. "One of the hardest lessons of young Sam's life . . . had been finding out that governments were not, on the whole, staffed by people who had a grip, and that plans were what people made instead of thinking" (Pratchett, *Night Watch*, 247). One of the hardest lessons one learns in reading the works of brilliant thinkers is that their brilliance doesn't always mean they have a grasp of things, and that theories are often things people make instead of paying attention to the facts.

Reverence is only needed where respect isn't deserved. If your views are correct, then you should be able to demonstrate this plainly and clearly to others. "Vimes found it better to look to Authority for orders and then filter those orders through a fine mesh of common sense, adding a generous scoop of creative misunderstanding and maybe even incipient deafness if circumstances demanded, because Authority rarely descended to street level" (*Night Watch*, 65). This is good advice in philosophy as well. Philosophers have had a number of brilliant and interesting things to say. By filtering their ideas through common sense, adding in some misunderstandings where necessary to make the idea better than it was at first, and ignoring some of the more outlandish aspects of their views, one can piece together a philosophy that works for the real world.[6] Reverence for authority will only get in the way of the process.

Good philosophy begins in anarchy. It starts with an unwillingness to respect authority and tradition as sources of answers to the big questions. Philosophers seek to use reason to pry apart the joints of the universe and see what lies beneath, and shouldn't take anyone's word for it that they've figured it out and it's all quite simple, really. Socrates is usually credited as the most influential figure in early philosophy. Although he's often presented as humble and solemn, Socrates really spent his life humiliating the Lord Rusts of his time.[7] He

---

[6] This process is known in the discipline as doing "history of philosophy." Those who work on historical figures, however, are contractually obligated to pretend that their own improvements were really there in the text the whole time.

[7] The technical word for such people in ancient Athens was "sophist" from which the word "sophistry" derives.

would find people who put themselves out as authorities on an issue, get them to explain their answer, and then ask them questions until it became clear they didn't know what they were talking about. He took false authorities and stripped them bare for the world to see. He was rewarded for his efforts with a nice stay behind bars followed by a refreshing glass of hemlock. Socrates often claimed to know nothing himself. Other philosophers have not been so reticent. Philosophers have put forth any number of theories and arguments in their attempts to answer questions. But while these efforts are often improvements over the past doctrines, providing accurate answers is really hard, and few have stood up to a thorough examination. However, it's also hard to get people to listen to you if you say "give me a few months or years to think about this and I'll come back with a good answer" while a bunch of others are offering answers free of charge and ready in five minutes or less. The people are usually happy with a panacea. Give them a dose of whatever helps them stop the uncomfortable feeling of uncertainty, and they'll swallow it down without batting an eye. But philosophers should be better than that, even if the person offering the solution is one of our own.

The idea that we shouldn't revere philosophical answers comes across in one of the general arguments for common sense offered by probably the best-known commonsense philosopher, G. E. Moore (Moore, 606–11). Moore considers an argument from famous skeptic David Hume in support of the position that no one really knows if there are things that exist outside our own minds. Moore responds to Hume by grabbing a pencil and essentially saying "it's more likely that I know this exists than it is that you know the premises of your argument, so if I've got to choose, I'll trust my own eyes rather than your philosophical arguments, thanks all the same."

Xeno from *Pyramids* is based on an actual person of the same name who really did think it was logically impossible to shoot turtles with arrows, to beat them in races where they had a head start, or even to fall out of a tree. A healthy dose of common sense suggests that maybe rethinking things is better than trusting in your abilities no matter where they take you. Progress in science is aided by the need to continually test theories against reality. Commonsense philosophy is like science in this regard, with commonsense beliefs playing the role of data to check the theory against. If you devise a clever argument for the view that there are no rocks it shouldn't take Detritus punching you in the head to realize your mistake. Commonsense philosophy recognizes that philosophy is really, really hard, and that humans are not ideally equipped to figure out the questions it poses. Detritus in Antarctica would struggle to figure out plausible answers to these questions. Trusting in your own abilities to answer these questions even when your answers go against your superior ability to figure things out well enough to get around in the world requires misevaluating where you are most competent. Getting others to trust you over their own eyes is a magic trick that can only be pulled off by getting them to think they should take whatever you put forth seriously simply because you're the one who said it. Philosophers are more respectable in that they dazzle you with their intellect in order to create this illusion rather than simply declaring that the gods have handed them the truth, but in both cases, the illusion is all that keeps us from seeing the vanity at the heart of those asking you to take their answers seriously.

In general, commonsense philosophers don't treat thinkers of the past or the present with the level of reverence others do. Reid was a contemporary of Hume's, and he wrote of him with a charmingly insulting respect. He would say, for example, of Hume's view that there is no self, only a set of experiences, "It seemed very natural to think, that the *Treatise of Human Nature* required an author, and a very ingenious one, too; but now we learn, that it is only a set of ideas . . ." (Reid, *Inquiry*, 35). Hume complained about Reid in a letter to a mutual friend that he wished he would leave philosophers to argue among themselves with good manners. But Reid sees value in ridicule precisely because it cuts through reverence. According to Reid ridicule is a sentiment nature has provided us "for this very purpose of putting out of countenance what is absurd, either in opinion or practice" (Reid, *Essays*, 462). Although it is not always a polite means of resolving debates, it may be the most effective. In many respects, commonsense philosophers are the gadflies of philosophy. They depend on an ability to point out absurdity in the hopes that the mask of dignity is removed from these ideas and, if need be, their advocates in order for the craziness to become clear.

When the likes of Sgt. Colon is faced with providing answers and sounding an authority on issues that are beyond him, the results are often humorous, and rarely on target. Philosophers try to grapple with the deepest and most fundamental questions about the nature of existence. It's hardly a wonder that in an area such as this even the most brilliant minds occasionally sound Colon-esque. Common sense can serve as a bulwark to tie our imaginations down from the more far-flung flights of fancy; it can prevent us from feeling that we must have an answer, any answer, and therefore start to accept the first one that sounds kind of plausible to us at the moment. Additions to our knowledge are tricky to get and require labor and patience. We need to get the corner with the sky and the bit of leaves and kind of see how things are shaping up before we guess at the overall picture. And if we speculate that it will be a nude of Nobby Nobbs, we should be able to know in advance that that's wrong, because no one could ever be so cruel to the world, even in Ankh-Morpork.

Vimes's Political Realism

To help see how commonsense philosophy can help in practice, we can look at how it works in political philosophy. The place where Vimes's ability to see clearly helps him most is in political philosophy. Here, his grasp of human nature gives him insight into the flaws of political ideas that the proponents are blissfully unaware of. A large portion of political philosophy has consisted of describing the ideal society and trying to encourage people to create it. There is a whole cottage industry to trying to figure out what everyone could agree to if we were all just perfectly rational and free of prejudice. The answer is probably not much. Philosophers are among the most rational and occasionally least biased people you're likely to encounter, and we've yet to agree on a set of rules for society. But we could at least learn this much from Vimes: people can't be fixed by wishing they were different than they really are. We need to figure out how to make a world work with actual people in it, and they won't simply become the people we want because we make the world where better people could live.

Pratchett's understanding of human nature is unrivaled in literature, and it shapes his political philosophy. As current philosopher Michael Huemer points out, what makes someone's political philosophy utopian is that it "calls for an alteration in a robust aspect of human nature, without proposing a plausible mechanism for bringing this about." (Huemer, *Problem of Political Authority*, 194). This sounds roughly like Vimes's complaint against revolutionaries that "The People tended to be small-minded and conservative and not very clever, and even distrustful of cleverness. And so the children of the revolution were faced with the age-old problem: it wasn't that you had the wrong kind of government, it was that you had the wrong kind of people" (*Night Watch*, 250). Huemer's approach to political philosophy has a commonsense origin. He begins by asking questions about what we know about morality in general.

For instance, if we were to demand others give us money for services they hadn't actually asked for, and then threaten those who didn't pay up, would this be okay? Pretty much everyone says no. Since "taxation is just a sophisticated way of demanding money with menaces" (*Night Watch*, 113), this is pretty much what government does. We therefore must ask in political philosophy what could justify this sort of behavior for members of government. Like other commonsense philosophers, Huemer's anti-authoritarian nature makes him skeptical of answers those inclined to bend at the knees may go for, and the challenge, in his mind, remains unanswered. By starting with the facts of morality as we all tend to accept them and demanding that theories attempting to justify coercion and harm to others by agents of the state explain why we shouldn't extend them to guys in blue uniforms or in nice, white houses, Huemer illustrates how the commonsense approach to questioning theories, including theories about how states should function, can help us in one of the more practical areas of philosophy.

In addition to having commonsense morality test the legitimacy of political views, Huemer insists that they be tested against an accurate view of human nature. Vimes's realism about human nature comes out in page after page of *Night Watch*. His relatively compassionate criticism of Reg Shoe's communist idealism is one example of this. Reg is in way over his head trying to put together a "People's Republic of Treacle Mine Road" in the midst of what some call a revolution and others call hiding behind a barricade to keep yourself from getting run down by cavalry while other people try to replace one evil tyrant with another. Reg can't get people on board with his ideas of communal property and regimented economies, and flails about trying to convince others to share his ideals. After talking Reg down, Vimes suggests that "maybe the best way to build a bright new world is to peel some spuds in this one" (*Night Watch*, 333) and sends him off to actually help those his genuine, if misguided, compassion was intending to help.

While he pities the naivety of Reg, Vimes isn't nearly so understanding of Findthee Swing. Swing is convinced that he can use phrenology to discover people's character, and that his torture chambers are justified by the need to fix the character of criminal types. He has some ideas, like banning weapons and creating a free for all for real criminals, that actually turn people into criminals. But the real problem with Swing is the underlying assumption of his views. As Vimes explains it, "Swing, though, started in the wrong place. He didn't look around, and watch, and learn, and then say 'This is how people are, how do we deal with it?' No, he sat and thought, 'This is how people ought to be, how do we change them?'" (*Night Watch*, 135). Here Vimes is echoed again by Huemer, who says that "any social system must be judged by how it would perform when inhabited by real people, such as we find in the actual world " (197).

Finally, the irreverence in commonsense philosophy is also crucial to an honest examination of one's society. Huemer spends a chapter detailing the psychology behind accepting authority that puzzles and enrages Vimes, and agrees with him that people have a built-in design flaw of bending to authority. He also sees that accepting the status quo and the legitimacy of authority in politics doesn't just get in the way of getting things right, it allows us to stand by while leaders do harm. Nowhere do these dangers come through more clearly than in warfare. In *Jingo*, Lord Rust takes command of Ankh-Morpork when war seems inevitable. His desire for him and his counterpart and soon-to-be war opponent to be friends shocks Vimes, as does his declaration that "War is a continuation of diplomacy by other means" (*Jingo*, 176). In war, those in charge are so distant from the pain it causes that there can even be a sense of camaraderie between those orchestrating the war.

This attitude of mutual respect reached its peak in the British Empire Pratchett is mocking in the person of Rust, but the detachment must be present to explain how leaders have been so ready to subject so many of their citizens to war. Rust is an incompetent at warfare, but is in a great tradition in that regard. He sees battle as glorious, even in defeat, and is ready to march his soldiers into the strength of the Klatchian army prepared with only bravado and mindless, obedient courage. And the people are so obedient that despite knowing that his motto for war is "It matters not that you won or lost, but that you took part" (*Jingo*, 377), people still follow him. Vimes, however, sees war as a crime. After Carrot reminds him that "we could charge them with behavior likely to cause a breach of the peace, sir. I mean, afterall, that's what warfare *is*" (*Jingo*, 387), Vimes decides it's a good idea to arrest both armies then and there. Eventually it hits him that arresting an entire battlefield isn't the sort of thing you can do, but not until he's actually already done it.

The failure to see war as a crime as a result of the blinding force of the illusion of authority is also the point that Huemer ends his book on. In both Vimes and Huemer, we see clarity in the ideas that common sense should provide to us. When we know that something is a crime, making it bigger shouldn't make it better. The failure to apply common sense to warfare grows out of reverence for the decisions of those in charge, and a willingness to let them decide matters, even to the point of one's own death. Irreverence is needed to cut through this, and those in line with the commonsense approach should be well positioned to learn these lessons of political philosophy.

Of course, for all its realism about politics, Ankh-Morpork is itself a bastion of idealized political figures. Vimes is the anti-authoritarian legal authority we all dream of, Carrot is the reluctant good king waiting to take over if things go bad, and Vetinari is the perfect Hobbesian Leviathan, a tyrant who maintains power and stability by always ensuring that it is more in everyone's interests to keep him around than it would be to get rid of him. And yet what makes these characters each so ideal is their grasp of the reality of things. Even Carrot's simple good nature doesn't prevent him from seeing that Vetinari's schemes are working, or that Vimes's cynicism can be helpful. By and large, Ankh-Morpork is in a golden age[8] of growth, peace, and prosperity because of the realism of its leaders.

Om-mission

People respect Sam Vimes. His name is synonymous with honesty and diligence. Vimes is described by 71-Hour Ahmed as "an unbendingly honest and thorough man, if somewhat lacking in intelligence" (*Jingo*, 358). He's cynical and angry, but never mean or cruel. He builds the law around him like a prison for the rage within. He refuses to make himself content with any façade, and starts out two drinks below sober. All of this makes him able to see people clearly. He has neither tact nor decorum to stop himself from forcing others to see it as well. Dishonesty isn't in him. And yet even when the world is bleak, true hatred for humanity, empty nihilism about existence, these are not found, because those, too, are dishonest.

Vimes shows a clear preference for honest realism over clever (or not so clever) speculation. But of course the ideal would be intelligence combined with realism about human nature and the world around us. The great God Om, whose quote begins this chapter, explains that the reason you keep philosophers around is because although ninety-nine out of a hundred ideas they come up with are generally useless, "the hundredth idea is usually a humdinger"[9] (*Small Gods*, 142). Cultivating a Vimesian resistance to chasing ideas rather than sitting down and piecing things together should help philosophers up that rate of humdingers. Imagine a philosopher who doesn't forget his pants, and you'd have a force to be reckoned with.

---

[8] I of course considered including a urine joke here, but decided it would be an insult to the hard work of that other great civic leader and simple, honest thinker, Harry King.

[9] Funny that the ideas we seem to value the most from philosophers as humdingers are the giant mirrors atop of tall buildings that are very good at turning other people's ships into bright spots of kindling.

9
Why Would You Put a Con Artist in Charge of the Money?

DON FALLIS

> *Some tasks need a good, honest hammer. Others need a twisty corkscrew.*
>
> —TERRY PRATCHETT

Moist von Lipwig is a thief, swindler, forger, scallywag, and confidence trickster. As Topsy (née Turvy) Lavish puts it, he is "an all-round bunco artist" (Pratchett, *Making Money*, 47). In his career, Moist (aka the Fibbermeister) has conned the inhabitants of Discworld out of at least one hundred and fifty thousand dollars. And once he has a legitimate job, he still keeps pilfering trivial things like paper samples from Mr. Spools and Drumknott's pencil (three times). Why would Lord Havelock Vetinari, supreme ruler of Ankh-Morpork, put such an untrustworthy individual in charge of the Royal Bank and the Royal Mint (as he does in *Making Money*)?

A Fox Guarding the Chicken Coop

When we first meet Moist in *Going Postal*, he is about to be hanged for his many crimes. Fortunately for Moist, though, Vetinari spares his life and makes him an offer that he can't refuse.[1] Moist gets to choose between becoming Postmaster General of Ankh-Morpork and certain death.

---

[1] Vetinari is a bit of a con artist himself when it comes to hangings. Although he saves Moist as well as Owlswick Jenkins from the gallows, everyone in Ankh-Morpork is left with the impression that these executions were actually carried out.

Vetinari's decision to put "a natural-born criminal, a fraudster by vocation, a habitual liar" in charge of the Post Office seems just as crazy as his later decision to put Moist in charge of the Bank and the Mint (Pratchett, *Going Postal*, 15). After all, the Post Office as well as the Mint can essentially print money. As Vetinari himself points out, "stamps have become a second currency in this city" (*Going Postal*, 393). That is, the citizens of Ankh-Morpork will accept stamps in exchange for goods and services.

Like most con artists, Moist does not use violence, or even the threat of violence, to get people to give him their money. Moist is telling the truth when he says to Mr. Pump, "I have never laid a finger on anyone in my life" (*Going Postal*, 100). Con artists fool people simply by making the world appear to be a way that it isn't. As Moist explains, "before you could sell glass as diamonds, you really had to make people *want* to see diamonds. That was THE trick, the trick of all tricks. You changed the way people saw the world. You let them see it the way THEY wanted it to be." (*Going Postal*, 36). In this way, Moist is able to pass off "a shiny brass ring with a glass stone that was worth fifty pence of anybody's money" as a "genuine diamond ring" (*Going Postal*, 18).

This sort of thing works best if you are careful about *who* you try to con. In particular, someone who is a little deceitful himself might very well like to get a deal on some cheap diamonds. As Moist explains, "fooling dishonest men was a lot safer and, somehow, more sporting. And, of course, there were so many more of them. You hardly had to aim" (*Going Postal*, 18).

But despite their commitment to nonviolence, con artists are still able to separate people from significant amounts of money. As Vetinari says of Owlswick Jenkins, "he never cut a throat but he bled the city, drop by drop" (Pratchett, *Making Money*, 191). So, all other things being equal, we probably don't want con artists like Moist running around free, much less running powerful public institutions.

Moist himself even admits that he is "a liar for the purposes of amusement, publicity, trivial one-upmanship, personal profit, and the gaiety of nations" (Pratchett, *Raising Steam*, 142). He is not at all like the troll lawyer Mr. Thunderbolt who is "diamond through and through and therefore [. . .] cannot tell lies for fear of shattering" (*Raising Steam*, 142). Given his penchant for lying and deception, it seems like a very bad idea to put Moist in a position of power.[2]

Interestingly enough, though, Moist is not the first con artist who has been put in charge of the money supply. And the previous cases didn't work out well. F'rinstance, the Scottish swindler John Law (1671–1729) has a very similar résumé to Moist. As a young man, he too narrowly escaped a death sentence. Despite his checkered past, Law was ultimately put in charge of France's Banque Générale and appointed Controller-Générale of Finances, where (much like Moist) he introduced paper currency to the country. But then, not so surprisingly, things went bad. Law hatched a fraudulent investment scheme (involving a French trading company in North America) that led to the collapse of the currency and the national bank. It was basically a pre-Ponzi, Ponzi scheme.

There is one important difference between Moist and John Law. Thanks to Immanuel Kant (1724–1804), Law is actually famous in the philosophical world for *not* being a liar. In order to give himself time to get out of France after the "Mississippi Bubble" burst, Law had to convince everyone that he was not going to run away. But as Kant pointed out, Law did this without lying: "he kept on building his house, and when everyone was thinking: He'll never leave, off he went" (*Lectures on Ethics*, 203).

For the Good of Ankh-Morpork

Although it seems like a crazy idea, it actually makes sense for the Patrician to put a con artist in charge of the money supply. On several occasions, Moist is able to use his skills at lying and deception for the good of Ankh-Morpork. F'rinstance, he tells everyone that the gods have told him where to find a buried treasure. With this cover story, he is able to dig up his own ill-gotten gains so that he can rebuild the Post Office. Also, in order to expose the crimes of Reacher Gilt and the Grand Trunk Semaphore Company, Moist performs what computer hackers would call a "man-in-the-middle attack." He makes an old wizarding tower that is a short distance away look like it's

---

[2] In an odd moment of paradox it seems that politics, however, would be perfect for him . . .

really a huge clacks tower much further away. As a result, he is able to insert a message into the system which appears to have been sent by "dead clacksmen" (*Going Postal*, 378).

(Pratchett himself is actually all about using deception to do good. In *The Science of Discworld*, he coined the term *lie-to-children*. This is "a statement which is false, but which nevertheless leads the child's mind towards a more accurate explanation, one that the child will only be able to appreciate if it has been primed with the lie"[3] (Pratchett, Stewart, and Cohen, *The Science of Discworld*, 38). An example is when a teacher tells a student that electrons orbit the nucleus of an atom like a little solar system, even though the reality is nothing like that.)

But despite his rehabilitation, Moist is always tempted by the exciting, and self-serving, life of the con artist. When he learns about the unscrupulous characters from the "up-and-coming Big Cabbage Railway Company" who just want to fleece investors, "part of him longed to be one of them" (Pratchett, *Raising Steam*, 100). Now, Vetinari is undoubtedly much better at keeping Moist under control than Louis XV was at staying on top of John Law. The Patrician puts the indefatigable golem Mr. Pump in charge of watching over Moist twenty-four hours a day. But why take the risk in the first place? Well, it turns out that Moist (or someone very much like him) is really the *only* person who can do the job that Vetinari needs done.

It Takes a Thief

Government institutions, such as the Mint and the Post Office, are potential targets of criminals, and not just violent criminals like armed robbers. Counterfeiting, in particular, can have an extremely deleterious effect on the economy. If people are worried about counterfeit currency being in circulation, they will be less likely to accept money in exchange for goods and ser-

[3] Before you read any Ludwig Wittgenstein (1889–1951), you should know that he admitted that a lot of his philosophical work consists of such lies. His reader "must, so to speak, throw away the ladder after he has climbed up it. He must transcend these propositions, and then he will see the world aright" (Wittgenstein, *Tractatus Logico-Philosophicus*, 74). So, "lies-to-children" are also known as "Wittgenstein's ladder."

vices. Also, if a lot of counterfeit currency is out there, it can lead to inflation since each "dollar" is worth just a little bit less. Thus, people like the forger Owlswick Jenkins who create counterfeits that appear to be genuine can be a serious problem for society.

An important reason to have someone like Moist in charge of the money supply is captured by the venerable old proverb, "It takes a thief to catch a thief." Or as Moist tells Mr. Bent, "I'm a scoundrel, and I can spot them a mile off" (*Making Money*, 162). Since Moist knows counterfeiters and how they operate, he is in a good position to thwart them.

But before looking at how to make things difficult for counterfeiters, it is important to be clear about what *counterfeits* are in the first place. This is where philosophers, with their expertise in conceptual analysis, can help. Ever since Socrates, philosophers have been trying to give concise definitions of important concepts, such as knowledge and justice. A few have recently studied the concept of counterfeits.

The term *counterfeit* is typically reserved for currency (that is, coins and banknotes), stamps, and sometimes articles of clothing and handbags. But all sorts of things, including documents and jewelry, can be counterfeits or *forgeries*.[4] F'rinstance, Moist forges Form 37 in order to get Owlswick released from "the condemned cells down in the Tanty" (*Making Money*, 10). Also, Heretofore counterfeits Ventinari's stygium signet ring as well as his sword stick. *Forged works of art* have been the primary focus of philosophers. But what they have to say on this topic applies equally well to counterfeit currency and stamps.

A Counterfeit Definition

As you might expect, counterfeit Xs are defined by contrasting them with *genuine* Xs. So, we should start there. Being a genuine X requires having a certain history of production. For instance, in order to count as a genuine Vermeer, a work of art

---

[4] Most philosophers think that only *artifacts* can be forged. But in *Making Money*, it certainly seems like Cosmo Lavish is trying to turn himself into a counterfeit Lord Vetinari. So, who knows? Maybe people as well as things can be forged.

must actually have been painted by the Dutch artist Johannes Vermeer.[5] Similarly, a genuine Bank of Ankh-Morpork banknote must have been produced by the Royal Mint of Ankh-Morpork.

But after that, things get a little tricky. An obvious suggestion that several philosophers have made is that a counterfeit X is simply a *copy* of a genuine X that doesn't have the requisite history of production. For instance, a counterfeit Vermeer is a copy of a genuine Vermeer painted by someone else. Also, a counterfeit five-dollar Bank of Ankh-Morpork banknote is a copy of a genuine five-dollar Bank of Ankh-Morpork banknote that was not produced by the Mint.

There are at least two problems with this definition, however. First, despite being copies of genuine Vermeers, the reproductions that you buy in the museum gift shop are not counterfeit Vermeers. In a similar vein, "in Ankh-Morpork sensible goblins were making quasi unggue pots for sale, looking like the real thing, Adora Belle said, but with the magic taken out and the wonderful sparkle left in" (*Raising Steam*, fn. 44). Also, the sample "banknotes" that came with the first edition of *Making Money* from Waterstones are not counterfeit currency. In none of these instances is there any suggestion that the copies are the genuine item.

Second, something can be a counterfeit X even if there is no genuine X that it is a copy of. In fact, forged works of art often purport to be the "lost works" of some famous artist. For instance, two hundred and fifty years after Vermeer's death, another Dutch artist, Han van Meegeren, created several paintings in the *style* of Vermeer and successfully passed them off as genuine Vermeers. Similarly, Heretofore could forge Vetinari's sword stick "made with iron taken from the blood of a thousand men" even though the Patrician never owned a blade with such provenance. (The stick that Vetinari carries around is itself a counterfeit without an original!)

Now, counterfeit stamps and currency usually are copies. But they don't have to be. Remember that Moist introduced the very idea of stamps to Discworld. What if another con artist

---

[5] If Vermeer were to make a copy of his *Girl with a Pearl Earring* and try to pass it off as the original, however, it would be a genuine Vermeer, but it would be a counterfeit *Girl with a Pearl Earring*.

(and there are many in Discworld) had found out about Moist's plan before he was able to create the first batch of stamps? If he were quick enough (and con artists are very quick), this other con artist could have put a bunch of counterfeit stamps into circulation before there were any genuine stamps for them to be copies of.

Of course, Owlswick is unlikely to be the culprit in this scenario. When Moist recruits him to design the first one-dollar Ankh-Morpork banknote, Owlswick has to admit that "I can't make things up . . . I don't know how to get started . . . I mean, I need something to work from" (*Making Money*, 186–87).

A Genuine Definition of Counterfeits

Harvard University's Nelson Goodman (1906–1998) has a better idea. He claims that a counterfeit X is "an object falsely purporting to have the history of production requisite for" a genuine X[6] (Goodman, *Language of Art*, 122). This fixes the two problems with the previous definition. Reproductions are not counterfeits according to Goodman's definition. F'rinstance, quasi unggue pots may look exactly like genuine unggue pots. But they do not purport to have held any goblin secretions. In addition, while Goodman still defines counterfeit Xs in terms of genuine Xs, he does not require that any genuine Xs actually exist.

There are at least two problems with Goodman's definition, however. First, it is not clear that inanimate objects can *purport* (falsely or otherwise) to have a certain history of production. Admittedly, the mail in *Going Postal* has a life of its own. But in general, stamps and coins cannot perform intentional actions like purporting. If there is purporting going on, there has to be some *person* (or dwarf or troll) who is doing it.

Second, Goodman's definition does not distinguish between something that is a counterfeit X and something that is simply mistakenly believed to be a genuine X. For instance, suppose that an art expert incorrectly identifies a painting by a lesser

---

[6] Goodman is also famous for inventing the color *grue*. It is not the "lovely bluey green color" of the troll known as Mr. Teasy-Weasy Fornacite though (*Raising Steam*, fn. 25). An object is grue just in case it is observed before time *t* and is green, or it is not observed before time *t* and is blue.

known contemporary of Vermeer, such as Pieter de Hooch, as being a genuine Vermeer. This painting is not a counterfeit Vermeer even though it (or more precisely, the art expert) purports that it was painted by Vermeer.

But we can fix these problems by revising Goodman's definition just slightly. Basically, a counterfeit X is something that someone purports to be a genuine X when she knows that it is not. Of course, this does not necessarily mean that this person overtly lies about the counterfeit X being a genuine X. The counterfeiter just has to intentionally make it appear to be a genuine X. Once Owlswick puts one of his forged halfpenny stamps on an envelope and sticks it in the mail, he is purporting that it is genuine.

Bald-Faced Forgery

The contemporary philosopher Michael Wreen gives a definition along the lines suggested above, but he adds an additional requirement. Wreen claims that the person who represents the counterfeit X as being a genuine X must *intend to deceive* people. Wreen says that counterfeiting is like lying in this regard.

Now, counterfeits usually are intended to deceive. Moist certainly intends the "sympathetic citizen" of Hapley to believe that he is buying a *real* diamond ring for twenty dollars. Also, lies are usually intended to deceive. Moist intends the citizens of Ankh-Morpork to believe that gods have told him where to find a buried treasure. But it is not clear to me that counterfeiting and lying are *always* intended to be deceptive.

Several contemporary philosophers, such as Tom Carson and Roy Sorensen, have recently argued that you can tell a lie even when you know that everyone knows that what you are saying is false. Such "bald-faced lies" aren't intended to deceive anyone. Terry Pratchett already knew that this was possible. Remember when Moist asks why Mrs. Lavish (who used to be in charge of the bank) has crossbows on her desk: "'Family heirlooms, sir,' lied Bent. It was a deliberate, flagrant lie, and he must have meant it to be seen as such" (*Making Money*, 65). This is a lie even though Mr. Bent did not expect to conceal from Moist the obvious fact that she uses the crossbows to protect herself from intruders. (Unfortunately for Topsy, the crossbows turn out to be ineffective against Death.[7]) Also, when Moist tells a story in an attempt to recover some Post Office property, it is a lie, but it is not really intended to deceive Slugger and Leadpipe: "The brothers Upwright probably didn't believe in angels. But they believed in bullshit, and were the type to admire it when it was delivered with panache. There's a kind of big outdoor sort of man who's got no patience at all with prevaricators and fibbers, but will applaud any man who can tell an outrageous whopper with a gleam in his eye" (*Going Postal*, 230).

It seems like counterfeits as well as lies can be "bald-faced" in this way. J. S. G. Boggs is an artist who hand draws United States banknotes. Even though his drawings are valuable artworks, Boggs does not sell them. He only "spends" them at face value. (He sells the change and the receipt to collectors, who usually then try to acquire the banknote itself.) Boggs does not expect the cashier to think that his banknotes really are genuine. But in these transactions, he represents his banknotes as being genuine US currency when he knows that they are not, which seems to be enough to make them counterfeits.

But fortunately, we don't have to conclusively resolve this particular issue in order to deter counterfeiting. Whether or not counterfeits must be intended to deceive, it is clear that a genuine Ankh-Morpork banknote must have a certain history of production. Namely, it must have been produced by the Royal Mint of Ankh-Morpork. So, in order to foil counterfeiters, Moist has to design the genuine currency so that it is very difficult for anybody other than the Mint to produce anything that looks like it. The same sort of thing holds for the Post Office and genuine Ankh-Morpork postage. As Moist explains to Mr. Spools, "the important thing is to make stamps hard to forge" (*Going Postal*, 172).

The *Ankh-Morpork Times* inadvertently makes the job of the counterfeiters easier by printing the front and back of the one-dollar note in color on the front page. As Ventinari laments, "even now, Drumknott, even now, honest citizens are carefully cutting out both sides of this note and gluing them together" (*Making Money*, 381). But Moist is able to thwart even much

---

[7] VERY INEFFECTIVE.

more sophisticated counterfeiters by using special paper supplied by Teemer and Spools. As Mr. Spools explains, they use "watermarks, special weaves in the paper, all kinds of tricks" as well as "chemical voids, thaumic shadows, timed inks, everything" (*Going Postal*, 158 and 173). Moreover, they "change the plates often to keep it sharp, little tricks with the design . . . and make it complex, too" (Pratchett, *Making Money*, 164). In fact, the reason that Moist breaks Owlswick out of jail is that he can design "a note so good that no one else could do it" (*Making Money*, 186).

Selling the Fantasy

While Moist's ability to thwart counterfeiters is important, the best reason to put a con artist in charge of the money supply is that money itself is a kind of con. As Pratchett himself noted in a 2007 interview, "money itself is a major fantasy in the 'real' world. We've agreed that these numbers of conceptual things like dollars have a value" (Pratchett, "Meeting Mr. Pratchett"). Like the entrepreneur Harry King, most people are pretty happy with "money that clinks" (*Making Money*, 161). After all, a twenty-dollar gold piece can always be melted down for the gold.[8] But unless you need some kindling to start a fire, small slips of paper with some printing on them don't have much intrinsic value.

Don't get me wrong. Money *really is* valuable. However, it is not valuable because of the physical properties of these slips of paper. Money is valuable because of how humans (and dwarfs and trolls) have learned to treat these slips of paper.

Money is like many other aspects of "social reality" in this regard. Borders only exist because we treat these imaginary lines between city-states as being real barriers.[9] Also, it is

---

[8] Unless you are building electronic equipment of the sort that Discworld does not yet have, gold is not as directly useful as food and clothes. But since people do like to decorate themselves with bits of rare, shiny metals, gold tends to be valuable to people in a way that small slips of paper are not. Of course, there are crazy collectors like Apprentice Postman Stanley Howler who seem to find small slips of paper with just the right printing on them intrinsically valuable.

[9] Governments often turn them into physical barriers. But there aren't many social or physical restrictions at the border between Ankh-Morpork and

physically possible to put the pieces of "basalt, which is the very devil to carve," from Vetinari's Thud set anywhere on the board (*Going Postal*, 78). But because the players agree to abide by the rules of the game, the troll pieces and the dwarf pieces are only able to move in certain specified ways. As Berkeley's John Searle explains, we collectively construct these sorts of "institutional facts" by just agreeing that "X counts as Y in context C" (*The Construction of Social Reality*, 55). For instance, the citizens of Ankh-Morpork might agree that slips of paper with a particular pattern printed on them count as being worth five dollars in the context of the Ankh-Morpork economy.

But since Moist is trying to introduce paper currency for the first time, the necessary norms of behavior don't yet exist in Ankh-Morpork. These small slips of paper with some printing on them are just slips of paper (even when they do come from the Royal Mint). It takes a confidence trickster to convince the levelheaded, no-nonsense merchants of Tenth Egg Street to "loosen their grip on the idea that money should be shiny" and to *start* accepting these slips of paper in exchange for goods and services (*Going Postal*, 393). Fortunately, "Moist was good at selling dreams. And if you could sell the dream to enough people, no one dared to wake up" (*Making Money*, 115).

Moist von Lipwig "may be a Slippery Jim but he gets things done, no doubt about it" (*Making Money*, 137). Even so, as the case of John Law illustrates, it's a good thing that Vetinari keeps a very close eye on him![10, 11]

Quirm: "the only obstacle was a gate, theoretically locked and manned by a couple of officers, one on each side. However, such was the nature of international relations that they were quite often asleep or, if not sleeping, were happily cultivating their little gardens on either side of the border" (*Raising Steam*, 145).

[10] Otherwise Vetinari is likely to find himself without any pencils.

[11] I would like to thank Tony Doyle, James Mahon, Kay Mathiesen, and Ken McAllister for helpful feedback on earlier drafts.

10
Lord Vetinari's Friendly Guide to Tyranny

DANIEL MALLOY

> *Ankh-Morpork had dallied with many forms of government and had ended up with that form of democracy known as One Man, One Vote. The Patrician was the Man; he had the Vote.*
>
> —TERRY PRATCHETT, *Mort*[1]

Lord Havelock Vetinari, Patrician of Ankh-Morpork, was enjoying his morning. It was early yet—so early that some might say it was still night. He generally enjoyed this time of day. The Palace was quiet and seemingly occupied by just himself and his faithful clerk, Drumknott, who was silently busying himself with his morning office supply rituals. Vetinari was similarly engaged in his ritual, seated at his desk in the Oblong Office, perusing a file that Drumknott had prepared for him. The file consisted of several clippings from the "Letters to the Editor" page of the *Ankh-Morpork Times*, along with notes about their respective authors and a memo requesting further instructions.

Vetinari, a loyal reader of the *Times*, was already familiar with the letters in question, but had the file prepared on the grounds that it might prove useful to have the entire exchange in one place—it had taken place over the course of a couple of weeks. Now he selected the earliest of the letters and began to read.

---

[1] ONE MAY WONDER IF I MISS MORT . . . CAN ONE MISS ONESELF?

Although his name was in the headline, the letter concerned not Vetinari, but Vimes. Of course it would start with Vimes. The Patrician almost smiled.[2]

Vetinari's Terrier Out of Control

Dear Mr. De Worde,

Commander Vimes and his motley crew have gone too far this time. They have trampled on all standards of decency and decorum. Last night they came right through my rose bushes! "Hot pursuit," they said, chasing down some miscreant who was only even in the area because he was being chased by the Watch. Oh, they won't tell you that. No, they'll insist he was trying to burgle the place, but I'm paid up with the Thieves' Guild, so I know I was in no danger.

Tell me, why should I put up with having my rose bushes trampled—and worse (I won't mention what that repulsive Corporal Nobbs did)—just because someone else in the neighborhood didn't pay their annual fee? I say, if you can't pay, you probably don't have anything worth the thief's effort. And if you can pay and don't, the burglary is on your head.

And even if Commander Vimes was right, and the thief was unlicensed and just as likely to burgle my house as someone else's, let him! And let the Thieves' Guild handle it. That's why I pay my fee! Not so a bunch of coppers can come traipsing through my garden willy-nilly.

Vimes and his gang are just interfering with the due process of the law. The thief should have been dealt with by the Guild, not thrown in the Tanty where he's costing the taxpayers money. The Guild would deal with him swiftly and ensure that he never again bothered the upright citizens of Ankh-Morpork. Instead, he gets three meals a day, a bed to sleep on, and a trial, all at the taxpayers' expense. And in the

[2] For him to actually smile would take an act of Blind Io, and even then it would probably require that the god beat himself about the head with a herring, but hey, anything can happen.

end, he'll be right back on the street, causing trouble for honest, decent people again.

I say why not run the Watch like the Guilds? You call on them when and if they're needed, and perhaps pay them to stay away when they're not. I, for one, should be delighted to pay a small annual fee to keep them away from me and my family. Simply being free of the horrible presence of that Nobbs character would be worth almost any price.[3]

Mr. Vimes is a common street thug who employs others like himself—and that's just the humans! Not to mention all the trolls, dwarfs, zombies, and golems! I have no doubt the rumors of a werewolf on the Watch are true—there's probably more than one. The only one of them worth a farthing is that dashing Captain Carrot. The Patrician should fire Vimes and put Carrot in charge—I have no doubt he would clean out the scum Vimes has patrolling our streets. At the very least, the Patrician needs to bring his terrier to heel.

Sincerely,
Maxima Webern
Isle of the Gods

Anarchy in Ankh-Morpork

To the Editor:

I read what Mrs. Webern wrote in the paper today, and I couldn't disagree more. The problem isn't Vimes or the Guilds. It's Vetinari who's running the show.[4] Firing Vimes and putting Carrot in charge is just trading one puppet for another.

---

[3] Oh let's be honest . . . *any* price.

[4] Roberts, the author of this particular letter, is a very brave or a very stupid man.

And as for bringing the Commander to heel, don't lets kid ourselves: Vimes doesn't do anything the Patrician doesn't okay first.

Vimes and the Guilds interfere with a man going about his business, but at least they do it with a bit of honesty—with a truncheon to your head or a knife to your throat. They've got no right to do it, but at least they don't pretend that they do. But Vetinari just sits in his palace and makes us think we ought to obey him, like he's got the right to rule us. He's got no such right, because there is no such right.

No man has the right to tell another "Do this" or "Don't do that." A man's got to decide for himself. It is the right and duty of each man to choose his own actions. What's more, it's his duty. Until a man can stand up and claim his actions as his own, freely chosen without any interference from any so-called government, he isn't really a man.

Now, I'm not saying we should all go out and act like Vimes and his gang. Just the opposite. We should act like the free golems. They're not out kicking up a fuss. But they're also not slavishly obeying the word of the man in the palace. They can't be forced to do anything, but they act right. Just look at how they act when there's a fire—people and property are in danger, and the golems take the initiative, drop whatever they're doing, and put out the fire. No one makes them, and nothing stops them. They choose to do the right thing because it is the right thing. The clay men are more men than anyone else in Ankh-Morpork.

"Stoneface" Vimes is just a symptom of the problem. The real problem is Vetinari and his whole blasted government. Until we rise up and get rid of the man in the palace, and everything he stands for, the people of Ankh-Morpork will remain children and slaves.[5]

Noli Timere Messorem,
Wolff Paul Roberts
The Shades

[5] Or, in the case of Roberts, in a dungeon.

Our Sovereign Ruler

Dear Sir,

Regarding Mr. Roberts's letter of this morning, I must take exception. It is one thing to say that the Patrician has no lawful authority, which is perfectly right, but quite another to say that there is no such thing as lawful authority, which is utterly false. Mr. Roberts, it seems, is no better than an anarchist, who would gladly see our fair city plunged into a chaotic war of all against all.

Mr. Roberts mentions the golems as a model for men, but fails to acknowledge that the golems only began to gain their freedom after constructing a king for themselves—the clay of their clay, as they said. The golems instinctively—if I may use the word for creatures such as them—understood that freedom is not the same as license. Freedom requires limits, agreed upon by everyone in the community, and enforced by a sovereign ruler.

Every member of every civilized race understands this. As much internal strife as there now is among our dwarfish brothers, not one dwarf anywhere is advocating anything like the extremes that Mr. Roberts calls for. They may disagree about who has the right to sit upon the Stone of Scone, but no dwarf anywhere would even imagine that they could do without a Low King. The mere existence of the Low King is part of what makes dwarfs, dwarfs.

The same is true for the rest of us. Our freedom is not threatened by a true government, but guaranteed by it. Freedom without security is not freedom—unless Mr. Roberts thinks that freedom means the freedom to starve or die a violent death. It is in order to secure true freedom that men have set up governments among themselves by means of contract. And it is secure the terms of the contract that we establish sovereign rulers. The sovereign ruler of Ankh-Morpork, established by the same contract that established the city itself, is her king.

Lord Vetinari, like all the Patricians before him, is a mere usurper. He has no right to rule because he is not our duly established sovereign.[6] Ankh-Morpork has been without a true sovereign since Lorenzo the Kind was so brutally slain by the first "Stoneface" Vimes. For centuries our city has been a shadow of itself, a pale ghost haunting the world awaiting the day when she might once again live. That day will only come with the restoration of the monarchy.

There are some who say that Lorenzo was a monster, that he committed crimes. Such a thing is impossible. A sovereign cannot commit a crime, because it is the sovereign who decides what is or is not a crime. This power is granted by the contract. In assenting to it, men consign their wills to that of the sovereign. When he speaks, he speaks for all. Should the sovereign commit a crime, it would be the city committing the crime. And how, I ask you, can the city as a whole commit a crime?

The death of Lorenzo was a crime. Indeed, it was the highest crime. "Stoneface" Vimes did more than kill a man. He betrayed, and indeed, to the extent that was in his power, even destroyed the city. And the fact that Vetinari has entrusted his descendant with the safety of fair Ankh-Morpork is further proof of his unfitness to rule. Like his predecessors, Vetinari is no sovereign ruler; he is nothing more than a usurper and pretender. The Commander of the City Watch may be the familial descendant of the regicide Vimes, but Vetinari, by continuing the pretense that he has the right to rule, is his spiritual descendant.

The true ruler of Ankh-Morpork is our king, that mortal god descended from a long line that can be traced back to Lorenzo. Whether he is here now or will reveal himself within our life time, I do not know. He may well now walk among us even now. Should he reveal himself, I will be the first to forsake the Patrician and swear my loyalty, but even that is not

[6] One can only assume that Hobbes, like Roberts, will be a guest of Vetinari tonight.

necessary.[7] So long as we live in Ankh-Morpork we have all sworn to abide by the laws of our true sovereign lord, our king.

Gods Save the King!
Thomas Hobbes, Armorers' Guild
Five-and-Seven Yard

The Freedom to Take the Consequences

To the Editor:

"Mortal god," indeed! Mr. Hobbes had best pray that none of the immortal gods are *Times* readers, or he may shortly find himself on the business end of a lightning bolt.

As to Mr. Hobbes's contention that there's a king around, well, that's the rumor, but I'm skeptical. We've seen our fair share of pretenders to the throne over the years, and there's always enough gullible people around to believe them. I'm sure we all remember that unfortunate business with the dragon not so long ago.

But let's grant Mr. Hobbes his premise: suppose there is a descendant of Lorenzo the Kind walking the streets of Ankh-Morpork today. So what? The truth is that it doesn't matter if some bloke's got the blood of a king coursing through his veins. The kings had no more right to rule than Vetinari does. Bunch of inbred loons, the lot of them. Nothing special about them at all, and certainly nothing that demands obedience.

"But," says Mr. Hobbes, "we established the monarchy and the royal line. We all agreed to be ruled by our sovereign lord to secure the blessings of freedom."

[7] The first and likely the last . . . It is hard to follow a man down a hole with lots of spiky things at the bottom.

Who's this we? And when did "we" come to this agreement? I, for one, was not there. But then I couldn't have been, if Mr. Hobbes's reasoning is right because this agreement must have been reached long before I was born. The agreement Mr. Hobbes speaks of would have granted the first king the right to rule over those who agreed to it, if it ever happened. It is in no way binding on anyone today.

So far as this idea that we somehow agree to be ruled by a king by living in his city, well, I don't know how well off Mr. Hobbes is, but I live in the Shades, and me and most of my neighbors would be hard-pressed to set up house anywhere else even within the City, never mind moving away from it. How can I be said to agree to anything when I have no choice in the matter? Until we all get the option to leave Ankh-Morpork, we can't be said to have agreed to live here under anyone's rule.

What's more, I was born here. I've lived here my whole life, just like my parents and their parents before them. Ankh-Morpork is my home. Why should I have to leave my home just because some nob in the palace, whose only claim to authority is who his parents were, decides something I want to do is "illegal"?

A king would have no better claim to rule us than Vetinari does.[8] Mr. Hobbes just wants to trade one bully for another, instead of living like a free man and taking responsibility for himself and his own life.

Noli Timere Messorem,
Wolff Paul Roberts
The Shades

[8] Funny, who would have thought Roberts would have enough hands left to write a second letter?

The Differently-Alive Majority

Dear Sirs:

Regarding the recent doubts entertained about the Patrician's right to rule, I must say I agree with the sentiment, but the reasoning of both Mr. Hobbes and Mr. Roberts is rather slipshod. Mr. Hobbes suffers from a misconception about the purpose of government, while Mr. Roberts fails to understand its necessity. The purpose of government is to make lives (and afterlives) better. That purpose entails providing security, as Mr. Hobbes correctly notes, but it is not limited to that. The Patrician's job is to create the greatest good for the greatest number. His authority is justified to the extent that he succeeds in that goal. Unfortunately, in many ways he fails astoundingly.

All these non-humans that have flocked to our fair city in recent years, most prominently the dwarfs and trolls, have done so in hopes of achieving better lives for themselves. Ankh-Morpork represents the promise of greater freedom and prosperity to all who pass through her gates. That we have extended that promise so much under his rule is to the Patrician's credit. There can be no denying that our city is richer than ever and is more stable than it has been in living memory. In our freedoms, as well, we are better secured now than at any time in our recorded history. The very existence of the *Times* is proof of that—it was not so long ago, after all, that printing was banned and we were all dependent on the engravers.

For all the good he has done, though, I fear the Patrician still falls far short of producing the greatest good for the inhabitants of Ankh-Morpork. As my associate Mr. Reginald Shoe of the City Watch has pointed out, the city's dead far outnumber the living, and yet the Patrician regularly ignores the effects his decisions have upon us. We are still woefully underrepresented in the city's service departments, including the Watch. There is only one vampire and a handful of zombies (and perhaps a werewolf) on the Watch.

Some will no doubt say that the dead don't count. Most of my fellow differently-alive Ankh-Morporkians may indeed be entombed, but it is a mistake to discount us. Merely because many of us are silent does not mean that we are not suffering, or that a responsible ruler has the right to overlook us.

Meanwhile, abominations like our seemingly infinite golem population are allowed to wander around loose, scaring the life (if you'll forgive the expression) out of decent people. I ask you, what good can come of this? Golems feel neither pleasure nor pain, so their only contribution to the good of the city is the detriment caused by their presence. They take away jobs from real people, charge far more than their work is worth, and generally give people the willies. Were the Patrician the true and rightful ruler of this great city, he would declare them all the property of the city and bury them with their Umnian kin, where at least they could do some good for the rest of us.

The Patrician needs to deal with the golem problem. At the very least, he needs to put a stop to their insidious and subversive revolution. Instead he is actively endorsing it! Golems are employed—employed—by the Watch and the Post Office. The city's government is paying these *things* and helping them to buy other golems and set them "free." I ask you, can you free a chair? Or a hammer? No, you can't. Would you pay wages to a truncheon? Or a helmet? Of course not. These things, like golems, are just objects. And yet the Patrician is aiding them in their attempt to undermine the order of nature!

Instead of cracking down on the golems, the Patrician chooses to waste his time and that of the Watch by cruelly persecuting innocent mime-artists, whose only crime is the desire to entertain quietly.[9] Rather than confront the golems, he has these poor, harmless performers thrown into the scorpion pits! What sort of use of resources is that?

I suggest that it is high time Ankh-Morpork had a differently-alive ruler—perhaps even one of the old kings. I'm sure there are still some around who, with a bit of coaxing, would be

[9] It's a good thing that Bentham is already dead. No living (for long) man in Ankh-Morpork can defend mimes, as all mimes are executed, as are, one can only assume, their advocates. It is one of Vetinari's finer qualities.

willing and able to sit upon the throne once more. Or perhaps a council, made up of representatives of all of the distinct populations of the city, with representation determined by what proportion of the city's total population each distinct group made up. The differently-alive would, of course, have the majority, but everyone would have the chance to be heard. Such a scheme could only increase our freedom, and thus, the amount of good in the city.

Yours in undeath,
The late Jeremy Bentham, Guild of Accountants and Usurers
Small Gods' Cemetery

The Good and the Golems

To the Editor:

The late Mr. Bentham contends that I fail to see the necessity of government. He is perfectly right. The thrust of my contention is simply that government is unnecessary. But beyond that, it is also unjustified.

Mr. Bentham claims that the purpose of government is to create the greatest good for the greatest number, and that the Patrician's rule is unjustified because he can't do it. Nor, I believe, would any other government. On the one hand, the standard is too demanding. The gods might be able to secure the greatest good for the greatest number, but no mortal or mortals could ever be expected to.

On the other hand, if the goal as such is the greatest good for the greatest number, why should government be involved at all? It seems to me that if that goal is indeed to serve as our standard of justification for any government at all, we should first show that government is necessary to achieve it. And I see no reason to believe that that's the case. Governments, by definition, get in people's way and use the threat of force to coerce people into compliance. These activities are not in harmony with the goal of creating the greatest good.

What's more, I'm afraid that Mr. Bentham tips his hand in attacks on the golems. Why shouldn't they count as part of the greatest good? I'll even grant Mr. Bentham's contention that they feel neither pleasure nor pain, at least in the physical sense. They still yearn to be free. It hardly seems necessary to argue that they have this longing, since so many of their actions give voice to it. What Mr. Bentham calls their "insidious and subversive revolution" is, in fact, exemplary of the good and decent people they are. Do not forget, Mr. Bentham, that if the golems decided instead on violent rebellion, as is the right of slaves, there is nothing we could do to stop them.[10] Instead, they are quietly and respectfully buying their freedom. The Big Wahoonie would be better off if we were all like the golems. If Mr. Bentham's goal of the greatest good for the greatest number is truly the goal, then surely the good of the golems deserves equal consideration.

But let's assume, for the sake of argument, that Mr. Bentham is right about the amount of detriment the presence of free golems does to our city. Does it follow that they should be kept in slavery, or, as he suggests, buried? It absolutely does not. The golems are intelligent beings, and as such, their freedom cannot be weighed against.[11]

Be clear on this: my praise for the clay men is not based on their obedience, but their consideration. No one should bow before the false authority of the Patrician,

Noli Timere Messorem,
Wolff Paul Roberts
The Shades

---

[10] Seriously, there just aren't enough sledge hammers in the city.

[11] Yes, this includes Corporal Nobbs, who may be questionably human. There is no question that a man(?) who can rob you of your shoelaces in broad daylight while you walk down the street in the shoes is intelligent, or at least smarter than you are.

Learn the Words

Dear Sirs:

The recent debate in this paper about the Patrician's right to rule has been quite revealing, but it has revealed far more about the people of Ankh-Morpork than about the Patrician. We are still suffering the effects of the royal-mania that seems to grip the city from time to time. All of the letter writers, including the contentious Mr. Roberts, expect too much. Mr. Roberts demands that his fellow citizens be angels; Mr. Hobbes and Mr. Bentham wish the Patrician to be a god. They want to be ruled by a man who can cure scrofula with a touch. That man is nowhere to be found (and would have questionable qualifications for the job anyway).

The Patrician is a man with a job to do, and I for one think he does it quite well. Government is a tool, and nothing more. It exists to perform a specific function. Mr. Bentham touches on this, but he identifies the function incorrectly. The function of government is not to make our lives better, but to make our collective life easier. Government oils the cogs of the city, to keep us all working in harmony. It does this by limiting that freedom that Mr. Roberts holds so dear.

But contrary to Mr. Roberts, limited freedom isn't a bad thing. We still have a wide range of choices, just not so wide as we might have without government. Through the threat of force, the Patrician, the Watch, and the Guilds make clear what choices are not available, generally (though not always) because they impose on the liberty of others. People are still capable of making those choices, but through the threat of force the Patrician has placed his thumb squarely on the scales of our reasoning and tipped them in favor making choices that respect our fellow citizens.

This thumb-placement is a delicate procedure, and one that has been made a mess of more often than not in the past. The current Patrician, for all his reputation otherwise, has a light touch. He applies pressure where and when it is needed to keep the great engine that is Ankh-Morpork running smoothly.[12] If he has any fault, it is perhaps in his reluctance to bring force to bear directly where it might help.

The ban on mimes is the one place where Vetinari might go further than is strictly necessary for the order of the city. While I do not share Mr. Bentham's rosy view of these black-and-white nuisances, I consider them harmless. But if this small excess is the price we pay for a ruler who knows what his government is for and uses it wisely, I believe it is worth it. A city wisely governed but free of mimes is far preferable to the alternatives offered by Hobbes, Bentham, or Roberts.

Respectfully,
Raz Josephson, Artificers' Guild
Street of Cunning Artificers

Long Live the Patrician

In his office, Lord Vetinari closed the file and set it aside. He was contemplating it with an air of quiet satisfaction when Drumknott entered a few minutes later, carrying an armload of files.

"Any instructions regarding the contents of the file, my lord?" asked the clerk when he noted the file on the Patrician's desk.

"Hm? Oh, let us see. Vimes has been appraised of Mrs. Webern's complaints and suggestion, has he not?"

"Yes, my lord."

"And how has the Commander responded?" "As I understand it, after a string of colorful oaths, Commander Vimes doubled patrols in Mrs. Webern's neighborhood and ordered that Corporal Nobbs be the only human allowed on those patrols."[13]

---

[12] Occasionally that pressure is applied by the tip of a very sharp knife to a nostril, but we digress.

[13] Sometimes it is just easier to say "human" than "whatever the heck that creepy thing is that is looking at me like it is trying to figure out how steal my knickers, but I can't be sure because I've seen the same expression on my dog when it is having digestive troubles.

"Naturally. In that case, there is nothing further we need do regarding this debate at the moment. Have the clerk in charge continue to monitor the exchange—I'm convinced it will get livelier now that someone has come to my defense. I think we can let it alone for now. I would have preferred it if Mr. Josephson had delayed his defense a bit longer, though. I was rather looking forward to the next volley from Roberts. Do we know anything more about this Raz Josephson, Drumknott? The notes in the file are rather scant."

"Apologies, my lord. I thought it best to keep the notes on the authors' brief, to avoid undue wear on the folder. I have had a full file on each author prepared," said the clerk as he began shuffling through the folders under his arm. "Here is the Josephson file," he said, selecting a slim folder and handing it to Vetinari.

"No need to apologize or explain, Drumknott. Your instincts in the matter of files and folders are unerring as ever," replied Vetinari, opening the file. "Hm. No trouble with law. Not an especially talented artificer, but not incompetent. Wife, children, all life-long residents. Insightful, for one who seems so unremarkable. What do you think, Drumknott? Shall we steer some projects Mr. Josephson's way?"

"As you wish, my lord."

"Anonymously, of course. We can't have people thinking the Patrician plays favorites, after all."

"Of course, my lord."

"And Drumknott?" said the Patrician as the clerk made to leave. "Make a note to remind me, in another month or so, to have Mr. Roberts submit another letter to the *Times*."[14]

"Yes, my lord. Would you like me to draft it?"

"Oh, no, Drumknott. You wouldn't rob me of such a distracting pastime, would you? I will write the letter, when the time is right. We all need our little diversions, after all."

"Of course, my lord. Shall we arrange an inciting incident of some sort?"

"I doubt there will be a need, Drumknott. One will no doubt present itself. They always do. Now I believe I have an appointment with Mr. de Worde regarding today's crossword puzzle. Have someone go and inform him of it."

---

[14] Really the Patrician doesn't need many reminders, but it is important to make Drumknott feel needed now and then.

III

Some Things Are Necessary, Not Personal

11
Can a Leopard Change Its Shorts?

DANIEL MALLOY

> It takes guts to run away, you know. Lots of people would be as cowardly as me if they were brave enough.
>
> —RINCEWIND, *The Last Hero*

The old saying on the Disc claims that a leopard can't change its shorts. The metaphor means something along the lines of "character is destiny." Whatever a being's character is, that's what it is and what it always will be. There's no point in the leopard trying to change its shorts or in other people trying to help it change its shorts or hoping that it will. A leopard is stuck with whatever shorts it happens to be wearing.

The specific leopard we'll be talking about is the wizard Rincewind.[1] The Unseen University dropout is a strange and special character. He is a wizard who can do very little magic and longs for a world ruled by rational, understandable forces. He craves boredom and potatoes.[2] He has a gift for languages, which makes him our ideal guide to Discworld. Along with his travel accessory/companion/pet/bodyguard the Luggage, he's been from one end of the Disc to the other, beyond the Rim, to Dunmanifestin on the top of the Cori Celeste and to the Dungeon Dimensions. And he's run away. A lot. Because of this, Rincewind is often thought to be a coward.

That is the specific set of shorts we'll be looking at: Rincewind's supposed cowardice. Because Rincewind is not a

---

[1] Or "Wizzard," as it says on his official wizard hat.

[2] We all want potatoes.

coward. He may look like a coward and act like a coward and think like a coward and even call himself a coward, but he is not a coward. Rincewind is not a coward because there is no such thing as a coward, just like leopards can't change their shorts because they don't wear shorts in the first place.

What Would Rincewind Do?

Rincewind is not a coward. Having said that, it is true that he often acts like a coward, and thinks like a coward, and even thinks of himself as a coward. But he is no coward. He is more of a wizard than he is a coward, even though, as he says of himself, he is a wizard in the same sense that zero is a number. However, whether we're claiming that Rincewind is something or that he isn't, it is necessary to examine what that "something" is supposed to be.

One of the strange things about a magic-laden universe like Discworld is that it allows for the existence of true opposites. Darkness is not the opposite of light; just its absence. Similarly, silence and cold are not the opposites of sound and heat. They just indicate where sound and heat are not present. The true opposites of light, sound, and heat don't just indicate their absence. They create it. So, when Old Tom marks the hour, it doesn't simply fail to make a noise—Unseen University's clapperless bell sends out waves of anti-sound that silence whatever sounds they encounter.

But we don't need a magic-laden universe to have the kinds of true opposites there are on Discworld. Physical opposites may not exist here, but many would argue that we do have moral opposites. The oldest and most well-known theory of virtue ethics depends on the existence of moral opposites in the strong sense that Pratchett outlines (see Aristotle, *Nicomachean Ethics*).

According to this theory, put forward by Aristotle (384–322 BCE), cowardice is an opposite. But it is not the opposite of courage. Like silence, cowardice simply indicates an absence. For Rincewind to be a coward would mean that he lacks courage. Since courage is a virtue, being deficient in it is a vice.

The opposite of any deficiency or lack is an excess or overabundance. Aristotle tells us that the excess of any virtue can be just as vicious as its deficiency. In the case of courage, the vice of excess is what we call being foolhardy or reckless. The courageous person faces danger, but retains some regard for their safety. To be courageous is not to be free from fear, but to be able to hold it in check and determine when it should guide your actions. The foolhardy, on the other hand, show no regard for their safety. It seems obvious that Rincewind is not foolhardy. His sometime traveling companion Cohen the Barbarian most definitely is. As he and the Silver Horde are described, "they did know the meaning of the word 'fear.' It was something that happened to other people" (*The Last Hero*). Cohen is the man who took on both the entire Agatean Empire and the gods themselves with just the Silver Horde to help (*Interesting Times* and *The Last Hero*, respectively). In the first battle, the Horde was outmanned 100,000 to 1; in the second, Cohen and his friends took on enemies who were cruel, capricious, and infinitely powerful. In neither case was there even a ghost of a chance of survival.

The virtuous path is the middle road between the opposites. Courage is a kind of moderation. Specifically, it is a moderation of fear. The coward has too much fear and too little ability to overcome it. The foolhardy have too little fear. The courageous person has the right amount of fear—not so much as to overwhelm, but not so little that they fail to appreciate genuine dangers or overwhelming odds.

But the moderation of the courageous is not indiscriminate. What the courageous have that the cowardly lack is an ability to see the object or cause of fear in a larger context. Every act of courage involves a risk of some kind. The courageous person is able to weigh the potential gains against the possible loss in a way that the cowardly can't. For the coward, the loss would always be too great. So, Rincewind is behaving like a coward when he tells Pretty Butterfly that there aren't any causes worth dying for "Because you've only got one life and you can pick up another five causes on any street corner!"[3] (Pratchett, *Interesting Times*, 212).

Run Away Another Day

Underlying all talk of virtues and vices is a concept of character. Rincewind is a character, but he also has a character.

[3] And a seamstress, if you are lucky.

Character can be defined roughly as the collection of largely unchanging behavioral traits a person has. When Rincewind is called a coward, the underlying claim is that one of his character traits, or dispositions, is the vice of cowardice. This means at least three things: Rincewind behaves in a cowardly manner, he does so for cowardly reasons, and we expect him to behave similarly for similar reasons in similar situations in the future. Character traits provide descriptions, explanations, and predictions.

The descriptive aspect of character traits is the most obvious. We call Rincewind a coward because he runs away a lot. He is allergic to danger and craves nothing so much as a safe, boring life. When the spells of the Octavo explain why they've chosen him to carry one of them, they tell him it's because "You run away a lot" (Pratchett, *The Light Fantastic*, 66). Running from his destiny again on Fourecks, Rincewind "was not going to be found wanting when duty called. He did not intend to be found at all" (Pratchett, *The Last Continent*, 92). When his guide of sorts on Fourecks points out to him that running away just gets him in more trouble, Rincewind responds "Yes, but, you can run away from that, too. . . . That's the beauty of the system. Dead is only for once, but running away is for ever" (141). That's what cowards do in the face of danger of any sort: they run away.

But just because he runs away is not enough to make Rincewind a coward. Courageous people like Carrot run away too, after all, depending on circumstances. If they didn't run away sometimes, they wouldn't be courageous; they'd be foolhardy and reckless. It takes more than running away to make a person a coward. When we deem Rincewind a coward for running away, we are also offering an explanation of why he ran away. The cowardly Rincewind and the courageous Carrot alike run away from insurmountable odds and certain death. What distinguishes them is that what causes Rincewind to run from overwhelming danger is the same thing that causes him to run from danger that is merely whelming, while what causes Carrot to run sometimes also leads him to stand firm at others. Rincewind is a coward because he acts on cowardly motives. His fear is neither proportionate to what he's afraid of nor subject to his control. As a coward, he is disposed to let fear control him, rather than to control it.

When someone quotes the old saw to him about running away to fight another day, we are told that "Rincewind had always assumed that the purpose of running away was to be able to run away another day" (*Interesting Times,* 227). Saying that Rincewind is a coward doesn't just describe his actions or explain them; it also predicts them. The coward is likely to remain a coward. So, Rincewind will probably run away from dangers, at least some of which don't merit it, in the future because he can't control his fear. Next time he's faced with a danger, he'll run. If Rincewind doesn't run, it's unlikely that it's because he's suddenly become brave. A far more likely explanation of those times when Rincewind doesn't run is that running leads to an even greater danger. For instance, after an initial attempt to run away and abandon Twoflower, Rincewind largely sticks by his side through numerous life-threatening adventures. Why? Because the Patrician made clear that if anything were to happen to the Disc's first tourist, it would be bad for Ankh-Morpork and that "that would be dreadful for you, Rincewind" (Pratchett, *The Color of Magic,* 37).

Rincewind is so reliable on this point that he actually serves as a kind of barometer for others. Twoflower comments that if Rincewind isn't frightened in spite of what appears to be the imminent destruction of the Disc, then there must not be anything to be frightened of (*The Light Fantastic*). And Twoflower is far from alone in that assessment. "Many people who had got to know Rincewind had come to treat him as a sort of two-legged miner's canary, and tended to assume that if Rincewind was still upright and not actually running then some hope remained" (Pratchett, *Sourcery,* 181).

The Patrician, with the expertise of a highly skilled puppeteer, knows that you can't make a coward do anything by encouraging him to be brave or calling on his sense of civic duty. No, cowards are motivated by fear. So, if you want Rincewind to act in one way, make the consequences of not doing so dreadful. Character traits or dispositions are hard to change. For Rincewind to stop running away would require more than just girding himself or bucking up or whatever other platitude we'd like to throw at him. Rincewind runs because he's a coward, as he would be the first to admit.[4] That may not be a trait he's proud of or particularly likes about himself, but it is part of who he is. Brave Rincewind isn't Rincewind.

---

[4] If you could catch him.* (*I CAN CATCH HIM.)

I Know How My Life Works

In *The Last Hero*, Rincewind does something uncharacteristic: he *volunteers*. Specifically, he volunteers for what will almost certainly be a suicide mission, to climb into one of Leonard da Quirm's contraptions and be slingshot under the Disc itself in the hopes of landing on Cori Celesti in time to stop Cohen the Barbarian and the Silver Horde from invading Dunmanifestin.

Even though Rincewind volunteers mainly out of a sense that it is inevitable that he will wind up on the mission no matter what he does—he announces his intention to join the mission by telling the Patrician, "I do not wish to volunteer for this mission"—it is an unpredictable move based on his cowardice.[5] But psychological experiments in the last half century have shown that this is precisely the weakness in the idea of character traits, including virtue and vices: it turns out they don't make very good predictions.

Experiment after experiment has shown that slight changes in our circumstances, such as getting an unexpected cookie or being in a hurry, have more impact on our behavior than our supposed dispositions. Give a person a cookie out of the blue and, regardless of anything else about that person, they become more likely to help others in the near future. The extremely nice person is just as likely as the not-so-nice person to ignore a stranger in need if they are in a hurry. We are all shockingly liable to do things that we would normally consider abhorrent, if we are instructed to by an authority. This sounds like cycnicism, but it isn't. It's what a half century of research about human behavior has discovered. In literature on the topic, it is known as the situationist challenge.

As Gilbert Harman interprets the results of these experiments, they spell doom for virtue ethics (Harman, "Moral Philosophy Meets Social Psychology"). If our behaviors are more heavily influenced by circumstances than they are by character traits or dispositions, then there is no reason to con-

---

[5] Sometimes you just have to accept your fate. I.e. You should not eat Dibbler's sausage inna bun. You are going to eat Dibbler's sausage inna bun. As a result, you will need to call out of work tomorrow—please don't ask why. So you might as well just drink the congealing fat with unidentifiable crunchy bits found at the bottom of your local "Big Al's Fried Meatz Fast Food" *bacon / French fry / "occasional" rat* grill and get the whole thing over with.

tinue to believe that we have character traits at all. Explaining or predicting behavior based on character traits means committing the fundamental attribution error, as it is known in social psychology. If Harman is right, Rincewind is not a coward for much the same reason that you can't paint a sound: the two kinds of things simply do not go together. Worse: the property of "being a coward" simply doesn't exist. It is purely fictional. There are no cowards, just people who find themselves in certain kinds of circumstances.

Now think about the circumstances Rincewind has found himself in: just to start, he is a wizard who is largely incapable of magic. In situations where he becomes important enough to be a target that leaves him defenseless. Now think about all the people (and non-people) who've threatened or actually tried to kill him. It's quite a list: the Patrician, large parts of the population of Ankh-Morpork, the entire continent of Fourecks, Lord Hong and the collective might of the Agatean Empire, the island country of Krull, the Luggage, Trymon and pretty much every wizard in existence, Coin the sourcerer, the Demon King, Fate, and Death himself have all wanted Rincewind dead at one time or another.[6] As he says, "Danger has stared me in the back of the head, oh, hundreds of times!" (*Sourcery*, 62). Through no fault of his own, and certainly not by choice, Rincewind often finds himself in circumstances where very, very powerful beings want him dead and he has absolutely no way to defend himself.

It's all very good for someone like Carrot to condemn Rincewind as a coward—Carrot, who is "rather more than six feet tall and nearly as broad across the shoulders" (Pratchett, *Guards! Guards!,* 28), who carries an unremarkable sword that happens to be always sharp, who has a punch even trolls have learned to respect, who can make D'regs *not* charge (*Jingo*). This is the same Carrot that the Silver Horde, having just stared down the gods themselves and watched them blink, opted not to attack (*The Last Hero*). Meanwhile, you can count the number of things that have backed down from Rincewind without breaking a sweat in the trollish number system.[7] Rincewind faces greater dangers than Carrot—or just about anyone else—with fewer

[6] To be fair Death thinks this about a lot of people.

[7] One. Two. Many. Lots.

weapons. When he faced down Coin the sourcer, who had just removed the gods from Discworld, he did so with nothing more than a sock loaded with a half-brick![8] Then he faced down the Things in the Dungeon Dimensions with his other sock, this time loaded with sand (*Sourcery*). He's not a coward; he's just vastly overmatched by pretty much everything.

The Religion of Cowardice

This conclusion is worrying when we play it out. If Rincewind is not a coward because there are no cowards, and if there are no cowards because cowardice is a character trait and there are no character traits, then that means that there are also no courageous people, or generous people, or honest people. In short, if there are no character traits, then there are no good people or bad people. By implication that means that there is no point in trying to be good. Rincewind's acts of cowardice are not blotches on his character in need of correction, because he has no character at all. Unseen University's Chair for the Public Misunderstanding of Magic could no more be brave than he could taste yellow or sound red.

An even more worrying implication of the situationist challenge is that whether we behave morally seems to depend on the particular circumstances we find ourselves in—circumstances we often have no control over. Taken to its logical conclusion, situationism calls into question not just the existence of character traits, but the entire idea of personal responsibility. Rincewind's cowardly acts are down to the situations he finds himself in, not anything intrinsic about him or even any choices he makes. Things just happen to him.

Against this, virtue ethicists like Christian Miller have argued that the situationist challenge misunderstands the nature of character traits (Miller, "Social Psychology and Virtue Ethics"). Most people, they say, don't really have virtues

[8] Which, true, is a pretty effective weapon, though it will leave one with that unpleasant feeling of having one foot colder than the other.* (*That feeling is likely one of the reasons for the effectiveness of the half-brick/sock combination—The wielder is annoyed at whomever is responsible for his having to take off said sock, the wielder is now also annoyed at the world in general, and the wielder will do just about anything necessary to end this fight quickly and get the damn sock back on his foot before his toes freeze off.)

or vices. Most of us fall in the middle between the two—we are continent or incontinent. A continent person knows the virtuous thing to do, and does it, but for different reasons and with less consistency than the virtuous person. The difference between virtue and continence is the difference between Carrot and Vimes: they usually behave in largely the same ways, but Carrot does so with more assurance and more pleasure than Vimes. Carrot, being virtuous, enjoys acting virtuously for its own sake. The continent Commander Vimes, on the other hand, acts virtuously by keeping his other desires in check. As Vetinari describes him, "He is a thug. You can see his muscles thinking for him. But he overrules them moment by moment!" (Pratchett, *Night Watch,* 157). The guarding dark watches the watchman himself (*Thud!*).

On the other hand, we are not all as lucky as Vimes. Many of us have inner watchmen who aren't quite up to the task. They are the incontinent or akratic; weak-willed people who know what the virtuous action is and would like to take it, but can't quite make themselves. So possibly Rincewind isn't a coward in the sense of having a vice—perhaps he is simply weak-willed. He does have occasional crises of conscience where he tries to override his strong sense of self-preservation for moral reasons.

But there are two problems with the idea that Rincewind is weak-willed. First, his crises of conscience are rare, and often brought on by external influences such as the Luggage (*The Light Fantastic*) or Conina (*Sourcery*). In the absence of such external influences, Rincewind rarely has any problem letting his legs do his thinking. The second problem for the theory that the Assistant Librarian is weak-willed is the fact that when he does have a crisis of conscience, his conscience almost invariably wins out over his cowardice. If Rincewind were weak-willed, then his cowardice should overrule his conscience in most cases of conflict.

This leaves us with the option that not only is Rincewind a coward, but he is a vicious coward. A vicious coward is the mirror opposite of the virtuous brave person. Not only is he a coward, but he doesn't see why he shouldn't be. This describes Rincewind pretty well. He certainly has no shame about it. When Carrot comments "You're just a coward really, aren't you?" the wizard responds, "Yes, but I've never understood what's wrong with the idea" (*The Last Hero,* 238). He goes so far as to describe cowardice as his religion. When Cohen comments that Carrot must be either very stupid or very brave, Rincewind asks in all sincerity "What's the difference?"[9] (251). For the vicious coward, there isn't one.[10]

Running Away Is Forever

Mark Alfano refers to this sort of defense as a dodge, and for good reason (*Character as Moral Fiction*). Like Rincewind, the attempt here is to avoid danger, rather than confront it head on. And, as so often happens to our hapless wizard friend, the attempt to avoid danger just leads to more danger. In this case, the effort to escape the problems posed by the situationist challenge by refining the definition of a character trait leads, in practice, to the same effects as the situationist challenge.

Carrot acts bravely because he is brave. Rincewind acts cowardly because he is a coward. But what about Vimes, Angua, or Igor? How will Ponder Stibbons or Archchancellor Ridcully react to a situation? We can't predict or explain their actions, or those of most people because most people lack character traits. If this answer to the situationist challenge is right, it robs character traits of most of their importance. If our virtues and vices are supposed to explain and predict our behavior, then we must have them. But if most of us don't have them, then they only explain or predict the behavior of certain special people, like Carrot or Rincewind.

Further, if virtues and vices are such rare things, it must be because they are difficult to come by. To be as brave as Carrot or as cowardly as Rincewind would, for your average continent or incontinent person, border on the impossible. And that's just for the folks in the middle. If virtuous courage is such an unlikely accomplishment, a vicious coward like Rincewind would seem to have no hope of attaining it. He can emulate Carrot or Cohen all he likes and he might, by dint of tremendous effort and decades of practice, become a weak-willed cow-

---

9 In the spirit of true, yet short-lived, philosophers everywhere.

10 ONE MIGHT ARGUE THAT THERE IS ONLY THE DEAD COWARD OR THE EVENTUALLY DEAD COWARD.

ard instead of a vicious one—assuming that trying to be brave doesn't get him killed first.

The essence of the problem is that if we define character traits like virtues and vices in a way that avoids the situationist challenge, we end up with the same practical effects anyway: almost no one has virtues or vices, and almost no one can attain them. So their value or disvalue is minimized—the virtues no longer even serve as good ideals, because they are too far out of reach. We may admire Carrot's courage or disdain Rincewind's cowardice, but only in the way that we admire the power of the gods—as something that deserves respect and recognition, but not as something we could acquire or achieve.

But while we can admire a virtue or disdain a vice, we can't realistically praise the virtuous or blame the vicious. Praise and blame require some degree of responsibility. But if virtues and vices are the rare, difficult things we are led to believe, then in all likelihood they are not achieved. Carrot didn't become courageous; it is simply the way he is. So, while we may praise his virtue, we cannot praise him for having it. Similarly, we may think it is a good thing that Carrot is as tall as he is, but it would make no sense to praise him for being tall. He had nothing to do with it. It is just the way he is.

On the flip side, Rincewind may indeed be a craven, vicious coward and we may condemn that fact about him, but we can't condemn him for it. It is just a fact about him—an unfortunate one, perhaps, but a fact nonetheless. It would be more likely for Rincewind to stop being a wizard than to stop being a coward. Rincewind's cowardice is like his small degree of magical aptitude. It's just something he's stuck with.[11]

At this point, the virtues and vices no longer serve their functions. Character traits do not explain; they do not predict; and they do not even serve as helpful signposts for moral behavior. In all but the rarest of cases, people simply don't have them and can't get them. And in those rare cases, they don't really serve a purpose, because their possessors can't do a thing about them and those around them can't usefully look to them for examples. So, there doesn't seem to be much point in maintaining that they even exist. Rincewind is either the rarest of species, a person with a character trait, or he is not. If he is, then even though his

---

[11] Kind of like bunions.

character trait is an undesirable one, there isn't much he can do about it, so the situation isn't helped any by labeling him a coward. If he isn't, then Rincewind isn't a coward.

It's Never Time for a Famous Last Stand

Rincewind's supposed cowardice, along with his magical ineptitude, is one of his defining traits. But that isn't true, because Rincewind is not a coward. It is more accurate to say that he is simply unlucky. "Luck is my middle name. . . . Mind you, my first name is Bad" (*Interesting Times*, 103). Through no fault of his own, Rincewind repeatedly finds himself in situations where anyone who was thinking clearly would behave like a coward. So, he behaves like a coward.

A Rincewind who didn't go to Unseen University, who didn't try to sneak a peek at the Octavo, who never met Twoflower would have led a very different—and much less exciting—life. That Rincewind probably wouldn't find himself confronted by so many forces set on killing him. That Rincewind wouldn't run away so often, because there wouldn't be much for him to run away from.

But no matter how much it does happen, no matter how often Rincewind runs away, or is called a coward, or even thinks of himself as a coward, Rincewind is not a coward. Rincewind is not a coward for largely the same reason that a leopard can't change its shorts. Cowardice is a character trait and there are no such things as character traits, so Rincewind can't be a coward. The reason the leopard can't change its shorts is because he wasn't wearing any to begin with.[12]

---

[12] Well, unless we *put shorts on the leopard*. Which would be a remarkably silly (and suicidal) action. But once having done that it seems unlikely that the leopard could change the shorts. The poor thing would be pawing away at them with big unwieldy claws. Once having removed them (to shreds) the leopard would still be in the unenviable position of having to "change" into new ones as the proverb seems to imply. At which point one can only assume that the leopard would give up and simply eat someone.* (*Rincewind, being far wiser than we give him credit for, would have run away from this scene early on and likely fallen into a hole somewhere.**) (**I said wiser, not luckier.)

12
Becoming Vetinari: Personal Identity on the Discworld

JEREMY PIERCE

Moist von Lipwig was an unrepentant con artist whose life turned around when he happened to get caught and placed into the hands of Lord Vetinari, Patrician of Ankh-Morpork. Vetinari could have executed him for his crimes, but instead he offered him a chance at a new life as the Postmaster General of Ankh-Morpork. Since the alternative was death, Moist took the job, and he thus had a new lease on life. He took on a new identity and task. Well, technically it's not quite a new identity. After all, he had actually been captured under the identity of Albert Spangler. His real name had never become associated with his criminal activities, although Lord Vetinari had discovered it somehow anyway. This allowed him to take on the new identity of Postmaster General as Moist von Lipwig, which just happened to be his real identity. So technically it was just his original but not-very-used identity, which he was now taking up once again. At any rate, it was a different identity than he had been using, and sometimes we say that someone has become an entirely new person when they take on a different identity.

On the other hand, Cosmo Lavish has a different sort of desire. He wants to become Lord Vetinari, not just to be like him but to be him, which is of course impossible. You can't cease to be who you are and become someone else, can you? Cosmo's deepest desire is not just a long shot. It's, in principle, impossible. You can change a number of aspects of what you're like, as Moist did. But could you simply stop being yourself and become some other, already-existing person? How would it still be you that became the other person, if you stopped being yourself and became them? And how would you then be the other person if you somehow became them while they were still alive, and thus presumably they remain someone other than who you are? What makes us who we are?[1]

Staying Moist

Terry Pratchett plays with this concept a little bit when he has one of the Auditors of Reality become an individual. The Auditors are not allowed to be individuals, but one tries it on for size in order to try to stop time. Myria LeJean, once one of indistinguishable Auditors, after not having an individual identity, becomes one. But, if it was originally not an individual, what was it? Should I even be calling it an it? If it wasn't an individual, then there is nothing for it to have been so that it could become an individual. The reason this is so funny is precisely because what Pratchett describes is so clearly impossible.

These examples reveal that we might use expressions like "being the same person" or "identity" in different ways. In a sense, Moist changed identities when he was running various cons. He then changed identities more permanently when he assumed his own name and became Postmaster General and his way of living transformed completely. Yet, in one important sense, Moist is still the same guy all through those changes. We might even say that Moist just is the guy that remains constant throughout all those changes. This is the concept that philosophers call numerical identity. Albert Spangler and Moist von Lipwig are numerically the same, which means that they're just the same guy under different names. But Cosmo Lavish and Lord Vetinari simply are not the same guy in any sense, as much as Cosmo would like that to be true, and his desire could never be satisfied. They are two different men, who are and always will be numerically distinct.

Some cases may seem to blur these lines. For example, Susan Sto Helit, granddaughter of Death, at more than one point has to take over for her grandfather.[2] Does she become

---

1 Read that last paragraph again, slowly. It's even more confusing the second time.

2 SHE IS THE APPLE OF MY SOCKET.

Death? In one sense, she does, because she has to take over the role of being the personification of death. She even develops various abilities and features of her grandfather in doing that. But in another sense she is simply not him. He's still going around doing various things, just not doing his job, which he's left to her. She's not just occupying his role. She has taken on various features of him to do it. But he remains a distinct being. So they still are numerically distinct.

So how can someone go through major changes and yet still be the same person? Must there be something constant to someone across the change that explains why it is still the same person after the change? When Angua turns into a wolf, her entire body transforms. Why do we say that it's still Angua but in wolf form rather than some other creature that has replaced her? When the Librarian of Unseen University was accidentally turned into an orangutan by magic, why do we take him to be the same being he once was when he was still a human wizard? His body and personality have changed significantly. The same questions arise when a lawyer becomes a frog, as happens in the Tiffany Aching novels.

Philosophers have come up with a number of theories about personal identity, but it might be helpful to focus on two main theories and then look at some variations and alternatives. I will discuss psychological continuity and bodily continuity (or brain continuity) before turning to some alternative approaches. The Discworld novels give us many brilliant examples that can illustrate these views and highlight key issues.

Ook[3]

A psychological continuity theory holds that personal identity is grounded in features of our psychology. Although other philosophers had touched on this issue when discussing other questions, the first philosopher to devote an extended treatment focusing on the personal identity question is John Locke (1632–1704), who held a kind of psychological theory. His view is that memory is what explains whether someone is the same

[3] Translation: "On John Locke's Theories On Personal Identity, the Concept of Continuity, and Memory as Constitutive of Identity."

person across some change. As long as we can remember doing something, then we did it.

But Locke himself didn't add in the continuity bit. He just thought it took an actual memory, which later philosophers pointed out isn't going to be fully satisfactory. If I forget doing something, does that mean I didn't do it? Suppose Moist came under the influence of some magical spell that caused him to forget his time as a con artist. He might remember his time as a teenager, before that. And when he was a con artist, he also remembered his time as a teenager. But now he doesn't remember his con artist years. Should we say that Moist now is the same guy as teenage Moist, and Albert Spangler the con artist is also the same guy as teenage Moist, but Moist now is not the same guy as Albert Spangler? That can't be right. But fortunately we do have a friendly fix to Locke's view, offered by Gottfried Leibniz (1646–1716).

Leibniz proposes that Locke could change his view to see memory links from stage to stage as forging an identity across time. If there is continuity between stages, even if not every stage can remember every other stage, then it's still the same person all the way through. If Locke managed to adjust his view in that way, Leibniz tells us, then it at least isn't subject to this objection.

I say this is a friendly fix, but to be clear Leibniz doesn't hold to any of this. He ends up arguing for a dualist view, on which I'll just tell you to keep reading, since we'll come back to him. But even though he's an opponent of Locke on the general approach to this question, it's a friendly amendment to Locke's view in the sense that Leibniz genuinely wants to help Locke improve his view, even though he thinks it's still wrong. Why would he do this? Well, showing that even the better version of Locke's view is wrong makes Leibniz's own view look stronger. So the friendly amendment is still meant to serve the greater purpose of arguing against Locke's view. Lots of good philosophy is done this way, and it might seem like cutthroat backstabbing, but Leibniz really is nice and respectful about it, as the best assassins in Ankh-Morpork would be trained to be.[4]

Further developments in psychological views would modify the view in other ways. There are crucial aspects of what we

---

[4] After all, whether killing a man or his ideas there's no need to be *rude*.

often think of as the core of our being that aren't really about memory. Sometimes we even think of some of them as more central to our being than whether we happen to remember certain things. Our personalities, moral commitments, likes and dislikes, emotional responses, and philosophical convictions might change over time, but there usually is a generally continuous progress or development and not a massive, sudden change in any of them. Often when someone does undergo a huge change in many of those areas, we wonder if it is the same person. Psychological continuity theorists might in fact say that it is not the same person. Moist is still Moist despite his changes, because most of those things remain relatively constant across his life.

The primary motivation for psychological continuity views is that they seem to explain some of our intuitions. They can explain why Angua can be the same person in both wolf and human forms and why the Librarian of Unseen University is still the same guy he was before some stray magic changed him from an ordinary wizard to an orangutan, even if his habits might have changed significantly now that he likes to hang upside down and say, "Ook."

As long as his memories and some of his personality traits, moral commitments, beliefs, and desires have remained constant across the change, a psychological continuity theorist could say that it's the same guy. But matching our intuitions to our theory of personal identity is not so easy once you bring in other kinds of cases. How easily can a psychological continuity view handle golems, who on the Discworld are like robots who simply follow whatever instructions are written and place inside their heads? Golems seem to undergo complete psychological change when their instructions are replaced or, especially, removed entirely. Are they the same golem after such a change? What goes on when Detritus the troll develops great intelligence when his brain gets cold? He begins acting like a completely different person, we might say, but is he someone new? What about Gaspode the dog and Maurice the cat, who become self-aware and intelligent after having not been? Are they completely new beings? If you decide your view on this issue based on your intuitions about cases, you might have a hard time if your intuitions happen to point in different ways.

The most difficult problem for Locke's memory view comes from Leibniz again. He wonders what would happen if someone ended up with a false memory. What if some renegade wizard implanted a false memory into Rincewind the failed wizard, whereby he "remembers" having committed some murder that was actually done by the assassin Teatime. Obviously his memory shouldn't be enough to mean he really did it. We have to have room for the concept of a false memory, but that means memory doesn't determine who the person really is.[5] Leibniz insists that Locke is getting the order of explanation backwards. It isn't that memory determines who you are. It's the other way around. Who you are and what you've done determines whether a memory you have is even genuine. You can't have memories explaining personal identity if you need to know if it's the person who committed the crime to know if the memory is genuine. That would be explaining A in terms of B while then explaining B in terms of A. You haven't explained anything at all with such a circular account. And the same thing can be extended to any psychological feature, since beliefs, desires, hopes, moral commitments, and so on can also be fabricated by any devious enough wizard, witch, or sourcerer who decides to muck around in someone's psychology. (And to those skeptical of whether witches might have sufficient magic for this sort of thing, keep in mind how effective Headology might be at convincing people they have memories, beliefs, desires, or even moral commitments that they might not otherwise have had. As Pratchett's stories about witches have shown, there are many ways to measure power.)

Bodies, Continuity, and Time

Another approach is to take us to be primarily biological entities. What I am is basically an animal, even if (a) human beings and other rational species such as dwarfs, vampires, werewolves, and goblins and (b) magically super-intelligent dogs, orangutans, and frogs are very different sorts of animals from

[5] In fact they've been playing with implanting false memories in rats on Roundworld. After all, what fun is there in doing science if you can't occasionally make a rat think it's a concert violinist ha . . . ha ha ha ha HAAHA-HAHAAH . . . sorry, got carried away.

(c) ordinary wolves, rats, frogs, or even orangutans. Whatever your level of intelligence and whether it's within the normal range for your species or especially elevated, you are still a biological entity, and thus what you are is an animal. One version of a biological continuity view, then, will hold that someone continues to exist as the same being as long as there is a continuing organism that has continuity with the earlier one. In most cases, this is pretty straightforward. Young Moist becomes the con artist calling himself Albert Spangler, who gets captured by Vetinari and then starts calling himself Moist again. The same human organism, with the same human body, continues on. What happens when a body changes species through magic but continues to exist as an ongoing organism? Is it the same body? Is it the same organism? If my Igor keeps replacing my body parts over time gradually, we can see that it's a continuing organism the whole way through, but what if it's a more drastic change?

The Discworld Igors provide a nice example to illustrate the different bodily continuity views. Igors are constantly replacing body parts with new ones. Is it still me if my Igor replaces my brain with an exact duplicate or exchanges my brain with someone else's? The same organism might continue with a completely different brain. A pure organism view of bodily continuity might say that I continue on with a drastically different set of beliefs and memories, while a more brain-based view of bodily continuity might require that the same brain be present for me to continue. But why would someone think the brain is central? It might be an assumption of a psychological continuity view that leads us to believe we need our brain to keep existing. Test your intuitions by imagining a case where your brain gets preserved without your continuing body, but all your memories and personality get replaced.[6] If you really just are your brain, then the resulting person is you, even without the memories and personality.

A bodily continuity view of either sort isn't going to be able to handle an afterlife as a ghost, since the body is dead and gone. The same applies to reincarnating time monks, since those involve a person continuing with a completely new body

---

[6] Or, if you'd prefer, we could try it out. The results, though, could get messy.

(and not just a transformed one like when the Librarian became an orangutan). A Discworld philosopher might therefore dismiss the bodily continuity view out of hand, since those things obviously do occur in the Discworld. Here in Roundworld, we obviously will consider it a more live possibility, at least if we don't believe in ghosts or reincarnation in that sort of way. But some intuitions we have about cases that are outside our ordinary experience might suggest to us that something is wrong with our theory, even if we don't think such cases will ever occur.

So suppose we use the Unseen University wizards' magical teleportation spell to swap my brain with someone else's? The brain view would say we switched bodies. What if we just swapped left hemispheres? Not so clear. What if we swapped half my brain with air? Presumably I'd still be alive, since I could live with just one hemisphere. The same is true if you swapped the other half with air. But what if you swapped my left hemisphere with air and then swapped it with someone else's only remaining hemisphere? Then there are two people running around, each with half of my brain. Do we favor the original body as the one that gets to keep being me? If so, then the brain isn't the only thing that's important, and we no longer have the brain view.

You also can get duplication problems. If one of my hemispheres dies, and you take the other one and put it in someone else's body, the brain view should take me to survive. But if you take both my hemispheres and transplant them each into a different body, I can't be both of the new people, because they're not the same person as each other. If becoming two beings creates problems for the psychological theory, then it also works for the brain view. If we could magically cause all my cells to split in two, resulting in duplicates of my entire body, then we might even have a duplication problem for the bodily continuity view. To be honest, we don't really need magic for this. This is what happens all the time when identical twins split from one organism to two. There really is one organism beforehand, and there really are two afterward. Both do seem to have been the earlier one, and yet they aren't the same being as each other, so they can't both be the original. But it's much more fun to imagine it happening as the result of some accident at the High Energy Magic Building when Rincewind tries to take the trash out, slips on the banana peels being used for conducting magical energy between the keyboard controls and the bees, and inadvertently creates a second version of himself.[7]

As another example, how should we think of Miss Level, Tiffany Aching's witch mentor? Miss Level has two different bodies at the same time, at least until one of them died. She isn't a pair of identical twins, although that's how some people, not having a category for a person with two bodies, thought of her. I think we're meant to see Miss Level as one person, with one unified consciousness, who fully experiences two bodies' perspectives on the world at the same time, even if the bodies are at some distance from each other. Miss Level is in two places at the same time, although she's not wholly present in two places at the same time. Her existence is not spatially continuous. She has two parts that are not necessarily next to each other.

Is this a possible scenario? In Roundworld, we have no mechanism for something like this happening, but that shouldn't rule it out as theoretically impossible. We can certainly imagine someone with a unified consciousness having two bodies in this way. If so, then it suggests that our inner consciousness is more definitive in terms of who we are than anything about our bodies. We also may have no mechanism for how witches borrow the body of an animal, never mind when Granny Weatherwax disperses her mind among the minds of an entire bee hive. Yet there seems to be nothing theoretically impossible about that. Why couldn't a consciousness be movable in that way? Why is it in principle impossible to spread out a consciousness across a larger group of tiny animals? I wonder if our intuitions on those cases better fit the psychological view.

Yet if we accept Leibniz's arguments, the psychological view gets things backward, explaining personal identity in terms of something that really comes later down the line and cannot therefore explain personal identity, since personal identity is what unifies it. And a psychological view would allow for Rincewind to be teleported by magic, where he appears at the other end of the teleportation, presumably to be constructed out of the matter already in that location. Pratchett describes the spell as exchanging masses across distances. One might

---

[7] One can only imagine Death's annoyance at having two Rincewind lifetimers to deal with.

propose that some kind of actual exchange occurs, where the mass actually moves without moving through the area in between, but given that the masses need to be equivalent, it's quite possible that what's going on is that each set of matter gets reshaped to be just like the matter on the other end. The same matter is still present, but now it has the features of the thing on the other end.

Suppose that's what takes place with the wizards' teleportation spell. On a psychological account, it would still be Rincewind afterward, since it still has all his psychological features. On a biological account, it wouldn't be Rincewind. It would be a new person just like him, since his body is no longer around. Even if you think the psychological account has a more reasonable answer, imagine what would happen if you somehow got two of him on the other end. The magic goes wrong, and two duplicates of Rincewind appear. They can't both be the same person, because the same person can't be in two different places at the same time. They end up going off and doing different things. Yet, there seems no reason to prefer one or the other in terms of who is the original. If that's so, then either should be him if the other doesn't appear. But how can the appearance of an additional Rincewind duplicate somehow make the other Rincewind duplicate be someone he would otherwise not be? There's no reason to think a second person just like Rincewind somehow makes the other one not be Rincewind. So psychological accounts have a hard time with that sort of case too.

I suppose I should mention that not all cases of merging or splitting would be like this. In *Thief of Time*, Jeremy Clockson and Lobsang Ludd were once one person and became two at the original person's death but then merged again to become one person. But that is not a case of being just like the person on the other end of a teleportation spell and then having an extra appear. It may be hard to know what to say about the Clockson/Ludd case, but it's not a problem that results because of either a psychological approach or a biological approach.

Going Around

Leibniz argues that we need something more fundamental than our psychological features or our body to explain sameness of self. He says what we really are is our soul, and whether the same person continues is basically whether the soul continues. Miss Level must have had just one soul connected to two bodies (at least until one of the bodies died). The Librarian maintains the same soul across the bodily transformation that leaves him with an orangutan body, and so even though quite a lot of his psychological features change, and his body is thoroughly transformed, there is something that remains constant throughout, and that's his soul. Leibniz could explain ghosts, reincarnation, or any number of occurrences in the Discworld that many of us don't believe usually (or even ever) occur on Roundworld. It also would allow for borrowing, since your soul can become connected to an animal body while still maintaining some connection with your human body.

The strongest argument against basing personal identity on the soul is that a lot of people don't believe in souls anymore. Although a lot of people do believe in souls, it certainly is a downside for those who don't.[8] If you think the other accounts of personal identity don't handle the various cases completely convincingly, and the only alternative is to believe in a soul, which you hadn't already been believing in, then you might be in trouble. We probably shouldn't use a head-counting method to see if a philosophical view is correct, but many people disbelieve in souls because they think there aren't any good arguments for them. The view certainly does stand or fall with the mind-body dualism that it relies on, and if there is no soul apart from our body then I sure hope I'm not the soul that I don't have. The fact that it would solve lots of problems in personal identity doesn't mean it's true anymore than the fact that lots of people disbelieve in souls doesn't mean there aren't any. Nevertheless, it's worth pointing out that those who hold to a dualist view do have an easier time avoiding a lot of the problems that arise for the other views.

But what if you're among those who don't believe in the immaterial, and you're not satisfied with the views of personal identity that we've been thinking through. You might throw up your hands and say there isn't any fact of the matter about personal identity. It just turns out to be a matter of what you mean

---

[8] It's a bit easier to not believe in souls than in the gods . . . less danger of lightning strike.

by the word "person." If you mean it the way the psychological view means it, then one result is correct. But if you mean it the way a biological view means it, then another is correct. There's no further fact of who I really am if my psychological properties get preserved but my body doesn't (or the other way around). There's the psychological me and the biological me, and so on. There's just no me plain and simple. That's not a very satisfying view, but that doesn't necessarily mean it's wrong. Technically speaking, Locke even allows for something like this by distinguishing between the person and the human being, and whether you're the same person might not line up with whether you're the same human being. His memory account really just applies to the person category, not to the human being category. On this view, the Librarian isn't the same human being when he's an orangutan, but he's at least the same person. But there's no fact about whether he's still the same guy in some more basic sense. That does seem an odd thing to say, but I suppose humans turning into orangutans is an odd thing.

Or you could just think there is no continuing self. I cease to exist as soon as any change at all occurs, and some new person begins, someone who happens to have a lot in common with me, but it's an altogether new person nonetheless. David Hume (1711–1776) thought this view might be correct. He didn't think we could know it to be false, anyway. He tended to be skeptical of a lot of things, but he usually didn't take his skepticism to a point where it would affect daily life. He instead took an approach later called pragmatism, where he lived his life as if things are the way they appear, even though we don't know they're the way they appear. One way this works itself out is that I should trust that I'm the same person I think I was a few minutes ago. Hume's view certainly allows for the possibility that no one continues to exist for more than a few seconds, though. That is one way to avoid many of these problems, although I think many will argue that it's taking on even more problems than it's solving.

I should say that not many Roundworld philosophers have been won over to Hume's position, and the ones that have been have not lasted very long, having been replaced by other philosophers immediately afterward. Such a view does not give very much job security or even life security. But a lot of philosophers think there must be some fact about whether I really do survive some radical change. Some have even seen that as an argument for souls, even if they haven't believed in them for any other reason. If you think we have worries enough to hesitate about the other theories, and you're pretty convinced that we do continue to exist through changes, you might then give the idea of the soul more plausibility, especially if you consider the soul a live option. Roundworld philosophers won't always tell you this, but part of doing philosophy is thinking through how willing you are to consider views that you might ordinarily have rejected.

You then have to think through which of the unwelcome options is least bad, because it turns out nothing gives you everything you want. This issue in particular has given rise to some pretty wacky views, or at least some views with wacky consequences, and this chapter only scratches the surface. Contemporary philosophical orthodoxy thinks souls are spooky (that's meant as a technical term for "a view that we should find superstitious and unscientific"). On the other hand, it is a view that most people throughout the history of Roundworld have held, and we might ask how it stands up in comparison to the view that I don't exist or the view that there's no fact of the matter about whether I would survive a successful brain transplant. In that light, arguments that see souls as the least weird option might gain some plausibility.

When All Else Fails, Reid More

There is one other view I should mention, however, but it also has a downside. Thomas Reid (1710–1796) responds to this whole debate by saying that these other views are trying to answer the wrong question. They want to explain what personal identity is in terms of some further, more fundamental thing. Reid suggests that personal identity isn't determined by some other thing at all. It's the more basic concept. Whether I continue to exist can't be reduced to some more fundamental facts about me and my circumstances, whether of psychological facts, biological continuation, or the existence of a soul. According to Reid, the most fundamental fact is not any of those supposed bases of personal identity. Our psychological, biological, and even soul-related properties (if we have any) would be facts about us, and thus they are not as fundamental in any explanation of what's going on as the facts about whether I am present or whether someone else is instead.

The downside of this view is that it does seem to be giving up the game. We might have hoped that we could analyze personal identity in terms of something else, both because it's nice to have deeper explanations of things and because we could then have some criteria by which we could examine any problem cases and then have an answer to whether the Librarian really is the same guy he was before he became an orangutan. On Reid's view, there is a correct answer to that question, but there aren't some more fundamental facts to explain why. That's not all that satisfying, but that also doesn't necessarily mean it's wrong. His view does avoid nearly all the problems of the other views.

It's tempting to come away from all this thinking that philosophy hasn't gotten us very far. After all, it doesn't just show us what the right answer is, the way some other disciplines can. But I expect fans of Terry Pratchett's Discworld stories to know better than that. Something doesn't have to give us all the right answers to be helpful. What does philosophy give us, in this case? It helps us examine what the options are, and on some issues it does give us good reasons to prefer some options to others. With personal identity, it helps us see downsides of every view we might take. That means that, no matter what view we end up with, we're going to have to accept something we might not have wanted to accept. Like Moist when he has a choice to work for Vetinari or die, sometimes we just have to keep moving and see what happens next.

13
How to Be a Dwarf

DANIEL MALLOY

> Racism was not a problem on Discworld, because—what with trolls and dwarfs and so on—speciesism was more interesting. Black and white lived in perfect harmony and ganged up on green.
>
> —PRATCHETT, *Witches Abroad*

Carrot Ironfoundersson is a dwarf—a clean-shaven, muscle-bound, two-meter tall dwarf with flame red hair and biological parents who happen to be human, but a dwarf nonetheless. Cheery Littlebottom is also a dwarf, although unlike many other female dwarfs, she is a she. And Nobby Nobbs is a human being, as far as anyone can tell. He has the paperwork to prove it. The Librarian is an orangutan . . . sort of. Angua is undead, in spite of being alive and well. Reg Shoe is a differently-alive human. Dorfl is a walking clay pot. Wee Mad Arthur is a Nac Mac Feegle who grew up thinking he was a gnome. Rincewind is a wizard in spite of being almost entirely incapable of performing any magic. And, of course, Igor is an Igor.

Each of these identities is more than just a label or a membership. For the beings who claim them, these identities can go to the core of who they are and what their lives are about. Our identities give us a sense of belonging; they help to set our priorities; they define us. Think, for example, of the plight of Wee Mad Arthur: raised by gnomes, he never quite fit. Being tenacious, he made a niche for himself in Ankh-Morpork as its premier exterminator and rat supplier for dwarf restaurants, but he remained alone. He found some companionship in the Watch, but it was only when he discovered his true origins—his true identity as a Nac Mac Feegle—that Wee Mad Arthur became Wee Mad Arthur.[1]

Unfortunately, in most cases the question of identity is more complicated than it was for Wee Mad Arthur.[2] Often, there are politics involved. The politics of identity, or identity politics, center on two main issues: how to define a given identity, and what sorts of accommodations those with different identities ought to make for each other.

Dwarfs, and Trolls, and Werewolves, Oh My!

Discworld is diverse in ways that we here on Roundworld couldn't even begin to cope with. Here we have people eating different foods and speaking different languages and praying to different gods.[3] We are divided by race, religion, sex, gender, sexual orientation, abilities, age, political affiliations, borders, etc. All of these divisions make our world a fairly complicated place. But, here on Roundworld if we stripped all of that away, we would find seven billion nearly identical copies of the same hairless ape. The only biological diversity among these hairless apes, really, is sexual diversity. On Discworld, however, there is a true biological diversity of intelligent species—humans, trolls and gargoyles, dwarfs, goblins, gnolls, gnomes, the various kinds of undead, even the occasional orc or banshee, and Nobby. And then there are the golems, an intelligent species that is in no way biological.

But having a particular biology and having a particular identity are two distinct things. Depending on the identity, biology may play a role in determining whether you can claim it, but simple biology is not enough to assign an identity. Feminist philosopher Simone de Beauvoir (1908–1986) succinctly pinpointed the gap between biology and identity when she said that "One is not born, but rather becomes, a woman" (Beauvoir, *The Second Sex,* 249). Being biologically female and

---

[1] It can be tough when you are raised around peace-loving, cookie-making gnomes when all you want to do is kick someone in the nadgers, steal his wallet, and drink until you can't remember if your feet are supposed to be attached to your legs or actually belong on your head.

[2] TO BE HONEST, SOMETIMES I HAVE TROUBLE TELLING YOU ALL APART.

[3] Or not.

being a woman are distinct things—just as being descended from dwarfs and being a dwarf are distinct things—just ask Captain Carrot.

Here on Roundworld, biology only plays a small role in identity because of the lack of biological diversity among intelligent species. The beings here with social and cultural identities aren't very different from one another biologically: they're all members of the same species, *Homo sapiens*. On Discworld, however, biology can be more decisive, but even in the most extreme cases biology doesn't perfectly determine identity. It would be odd, to say the least, for a troll to identify as a dwarf, but that has as much to do with the longstanding enmity between the two cultures as the biological differences between the species. Really, even that example wouldn't be much more unusual on Discworld than a biologically female human identifying as a man, or vice versa on Roundworld—unusual, but not unheard of.

Captain *Kzad-bhat*, Dwarf

Carrot proudly proclaims his dwarfishness when the opportunity arises. When Lance Corporal Cuddy was recruited to the Watch as part of a diversity drive, Carrot was slightly bewildered, because there was already a dwarf on the Watch—him (*Men at Arms*). But that is common. When Carrot tells people he is a dwarf, they give a reaction that is usual for Carrot—they smile and nod, and walk away wondering whether Carrot is crazy or they are.

The reason for all this confusion is that Carrot isn't a dwarf. He's human. There's no doubt about it. Even his dwarf nickname, *Kzad-bhat*, or Headbanger, isn't in recognition of his appreciation of Music With Rocks In, but of one of the unfortunate and indirect consequences of his being human: because of his height, he had a habit of banging his head in the dwarf mine where he grew up (*Guards! Guards!*). Biologically, *Kzad-bhat* is human. But culturally, Carrot is a dwarf, and is accepted as such by most dwarfs. Even the deep-downers, who have a tendency of declaring other dwarfs *d'harak* or "not dwarfs," reluctantly and begrudgingly accept Carrot's claim to be a dwarf.

The reason for this acceptance, aside from the fact that it is difficult to deny Carrot anything, is that Carrot comes by his dwarfishness honestly. He is biologically human, but he was raised by dwarfs in a dwarf mine. And, in spite of basically every aspect of his physical appearance, he acts like a dwarf.

On the other hand, consider Thomas Stronginthearm, a human who adopted a dwarfish name and a few mannerisms in order to boost sales at his shop (*Feet of Clay*), or Countess Notfaroutoe (a.k.a. Doreen Winkings), who puts on the airs of an old-fashioned vampire even though (1) she isn't a vampire, but is just married to one and (2) vampires are striving to put that past behind them (*Thud!*). Stronginthearm and Notfaroutoe are cultural pretenders—people who appropriate the trappings of an identity without having a genuine claim to it. Dwarfs have been silent about Mr. Stronginthearm, but the Campaign for Equal Heights is quite put out by his pretense. And the Countess seems to be tolerated by vampires, or at least black ribboners, because she is an advocate on their behalf. But toleration is still a long way from acceptance.

So, someone's belonging to a particular group isn't entirely a matter of biology, but also one of choice. However, this choice isn't entirely free. It requires a particular background and authenticity to work. Carrot is a dwarf, but Mr. Stronginthearm isn't.

The choice is also not a one-time thing. Carrot isn't a dwarf because he *ha'lked* his *g'rakha* once, but because he continues to think and act like a dwarf. If Carrot hadn't met the deep-downers in a fashion that exemplified dwarf culture, you can bet they wouldn't have accepted him, even begrudgingly. Identity is not just a matter of choice. It is a matter of performance. We are what we act like.

Cheery's Choice

But there is more involved than just performance. No matter how well Thomas Stronginthearm plays the part, he isn't a dwarf. These identities are social and cultural. It isn't enough to act like a dwarf—you must also be accepted as a dwarf. There are two aspects to this. First you must be accepted as a dwarf by other dwarfs. Second, you must be accepted as a dwarf by non-dwarfs. The latter has been Carrot's primary problem: other dwarfs are skeptical upon meeting him about his claims to dwarfishness, but he quickly wins them over. Humans and others, however, tend to think of Carrot as just a quirky human. Even his closest comrades, Vimes and Angua, still seem to think of his dwarfishness, not as his identity, but as yet another of his little oddities, like his habit of seeing the best in everyone or his obsessive armor polishing. On the other hand, the acceptance of other dwarfs that has proven to be the major stumbling block for the dwarfish equivalent of the feminist movement.

Identity politics is three-sided. There is the identity that you claim for yourself—Carrot and Cheery Littlebottom both claim to be dwarfs. This is why, although Cheery is openly female, the idea of shaving her beard appalls her. Dwarfs wear beards. Then there is that identity as it is understood by members of that group. And finally there is that identity as it is understood by people outside the group.

To make matters even more confusing, none of these identities are stable. They are all constantly shifting. Cheery's personal distaste for certain things and activities generally considered dwarfish, like talking about gold and quaffing, made her uncomfortable around other dwarfs sometimes but never challenged dwarfish identity. Her choice to be openly female, however, flew in the face of dwarfish culture. The dwarfish language didn't even have feminine pronouns (*The Fifth Elephant*). That would be fine and not at all an issue, except for the fact that dwarfish *did* have masculine pronouns. According to dwarfish, everything in the universe is either a "he" or an "it." All dwarf children are sons. There are dwarf mothers and fathers, but that distinction only matters during pregnancy and nursing. As Carrot says when confronted with Cheery, "I've got nothing against females. I'm pretty certain my stepmother is one" (Pratchett, *Feet of Clay*, 181). So, Cheery's choice to try a little make-up and a skirt wasn't just a matter of personal preference; it was a political statement.

It is interesting to note that, although it is implied that Cheery is biologically female, it is never stated outright. That sort of detail would make the Discworld novels a very different sort of series. But the really interesting thing for us is that it doesn't matter what sex Cheery is biologically. She has chosen to be female. In many parts of Roundworld, a biological male choosing to live as a woman or a biological female choosing to live as a man is considered odd, even wrong. Imagine, then, how shocking Cheery's choice really is for the dwarfs of Discworld. This goes beyond a member of one physical sex conforming to the norms of the opposite gender. In deciding to be openly female, Cheery is outright creating a new gender. In Roundworld terms, Cheery's choice would be the equivalent of you or me choosing to be a unicorn.

The negative reaction is hardly surprising. Deep-downers and other traditional dwarfs, including Carrot (at least initially), have a certain understanding of what it means to be a dwarf. That understanding includes distinct sexes, because they are necessary for reproduction, but it doesn't even have a space for distinct genders. In other words, there are male and female dwarfs, but no man dwarfs and woman dwarfs. Regardless of biological sex, all dwarfs are man dwarfs. The deep-downers and the traditional dwarf culture they are trying to preserve practice an odd sort of equality between the sexes. They treat everyone the same—as though they were male. It is oppression in the guise of egalitarianism. Similar approaches to difference and identity are well known here on Roundworld. To ignore difference and distinct identities is not to treat them equally, however. It is to make them conform to the mainstream identity, whatever that happens to be.

As readers, it is easy for us to say, "So? Who cares what a bunch of backward little dictators think?" But Cheery and others like her are in an impossible position. It isn't enough that they be recognized as female—they are female *dwarfs*. Both parts of the equation must be respected. As open females, they share some things with the openly female members of other species—Cheery, after all, gets some of her first tips in womanhood from Angua the werewolf. But when Cheery embraces some feminine characteristics, she isn't rejecting of her dwarfishness. She is in the unenviable position of trying to make the two identities work together.

Take another, rather less tension-filled situation: Gladys the golem (*Going Postal* and *Making Money*). Biologically, Gladys isn't anything—Gladys isn't biological at all. Furthermore, Gladys wasn't constructed with the correct apparatus for anything resembling a biological sex. Golems are typically called "he" because they object to being called "it" and Morporkian, like English, has no gender-neutral pronoun that acknowledges personhood.[4] Nonetheless, in response to the pressure imposed by Miss Maccalariat, Gladys adopts some of the trappings of human women—wearing dresses and answering to the name Gladys. And it isn't long before Gladys is socialized as a woman. At the same time, no one would ever dream of denying that Gladys is a golem. Those two identities, which traditionally have nothing to do with one another, must make accommodations in order to co-exist within a single being. There are certain aspects of womanhood that are simply incompatible with golemhood, and vice-versa.

Returning to dwarfs, the reaction of the deep-downers to the openly female dwarfs (*ha'ak*, as they call them) is that the two identities, dwarf and woman, are not at all compatible. You can be a dwarf or a woman, but not both. To try is to give up your dwarfish identity, to become at least *dr'zka* (not really a dwarf—inauthentic, a pretender, Thomas Stronginthearm) or possibly even *d'harak* (not a dwarf—an outcast).

Still, this looks like a battle that Cheery and her sisters are winning, thanks in no small part to the support of the Low King, Rhys Rhysson. The deep-downers won't go away, and some portion of dwarfs will probably feel as they do for a long time. But mainstream dwarf culture seems to be coming around to embracing dwarf women.

Lawn Ornaments and Gritsuckers

Not that that will eliminate the problems facing female dwarfs. They are still dwarfs, after all, and that brings with it an entirely different set of challenges. To many non-dwarfs, dwarfs are still "lawn ornaments" or *horug*. "Lawn ornament" or *b'zugda-hiara* is a deadly insult among dwarfs, and one often used by humans on Discworld. *Horug* is a troll word for dwarfs, and is generally considered offensive. Aside from the internal struggles in determining dwarf identity, and to say nothing of the personal struggles of non-mainstream dwarfs, there are also external struggles that any social and cultural identity encounters. It is these external struggles that tend to produce stereotypes of various sorts, and attitudes toward those with this identity based on those stereotypes.

---

[4] And, moral beings though they are, no one wants to annoy a golem.

The dwarfs of Discworld are supposed to be short (by human standards), hairy, well-endowed, greedy, obsessed with gold, rat-eating, drunken, hard-working, and borderline asexual. When non-dwarfs interact with dwarfs, they tend to expect some or all of these traits. When they encounter a dwarf like Cheery, or Carrot, or Casanunda, non-dwarfs have trouble understanding them. This is because many non-dwarfs, like the deep-downers, engage in essentialism.

Essentialism is the theory that a thing's essence or nature dictates its properties. It is a reasonable theory when dealing with things, but it is woefully inadequate when dealing with people.[5] People of various sorts have the ability to define themselves and as such have to be dealt with on a case-by-case basis. Treating Angua the way you would any werewolf you ran across would be doing her a grave injustice.[6]

The trouble is how to allow room for individual self-definition while retaining any kind of group-identity. Angua may be the exception, but for most people, including Cheery, pure self-definition, a life without any kind of group-identification, is inconceivable. That's part of the reason Cheery's path is so difficult. The last thing she wants is to be declared *d'harak* and cast out from dwarf society all together.

This problem is just as tricky from the outside as it is from within. On the one hand, there has to be at least some acknowledgment of a person's individuality. On the other hand, group identity can sometimes impose expectations of behavior. You don't approach a vampire in all situations in the same way as you approach a dwarf.

Take Cut-Me-Own-Throat Dibbler. Dibbler is as free from prejudice as any intelligent being could possibly be. A true salesman, when Dibbler looks at another intelligent being, be it human, troll, dwarf, undead, goblin, or anything else that might have money, all he sees is an opportunity. But he must make accommodations for the various identities. Trolls, after

---

[5] And some things—like the Luggage. But then, what can deal with the Luggage?

[6] Similarly, most orangutans take no notice when some uninformed individual calls them "monkeys," but many a patron of The Mended Drum has discovered, quite unpleasantly, that you shouldn't use the m-word when referring to the Librarian.

all, have no interest in Dibbler's standard fare of meat pies; and most dwarfs would prefer a good rat. So, old Throat needs to have some standardized ideas about the different group identities he's likely to encounter. But at the same time, and again to his credit, he has no problem shifting gears at the drop of an Ankh-Morpork dime.[7] If this particular dwarf isn't taken by rats, Throat will have no problem finding something else to sell him (whether he owns the thing or has any right to sell it is a matter best left to the Watch).

The reason Throat can get along with anyone[8] is because of the identity he imposes upon them. For Throat, the world is really only made up of two groups: Throat and his customers. Everyone who is not Throat himself is a customer waiting to happen. Beyond the fact that customers have money that rightfully belongs to him, Throat has very little interest in them.

Like Throat, most people are essentialists of some sort because it is easier to enter encounters with new people or groups with some ideas of what you can expect from them. Where Dibbler has the advantage over many people is in his ability to adjust when his expectations are dashed. Many people, both on Discworld and here on Roundworld, cling to their expectations even in the face of contrary evidence. Such a person will find an unconventional member of a group, like Cheery, Carrot, or Casanunda impossible to deal with. They do not fit the mold. Typically, such a person, like Lord de Worde, or Fred Colon, will simply cling that much harder to his expectations.[9]

Old Fred Colon is actually a very good example. When the Watch first began recruiting non-humans, no one was more opposed than Fred. In fairness to the old sergeant, it should be said that this had more to do with Fred being rather stuck in his ways than out-and-out prejudiced. Nonetheless he gradually came to accept the non-human recruits. But he's never quite given up his prejudices. He tends to think of the non-human members of the Watch as exceptions. Non-Watch

---

[7] Which, like any money dropped in Ankh-Morpork, moves *very* fast indeed.

[8] Except for previous customers, of course.

[9] Like Lord Rust, they will simply not acknowledge the existence of what does not conform.

dwarfs are still, in Fred's mind, greedy, thieving little buggers. Non-Watch trolls are still brutal thugs with the brains of a rock. He'd be the first to defend Detritus or Cheery,[10] but that's because they are, in his mind, some of the "good ones." All non-Watch non-humans are presumed guilty of something. But then, Fred is a Watchman to the core, so that goes for pretty much everyone. Especially Nobby. The difference is that Nobby is presumed guilty of some low degree theft based on past performance. Non-Watch dwarfs, in Fred's mind, are presumed guilty of being scheming little chiselers; non-Watch trolls are presumed guilty of being unthinking engines of violence. Not because of performance, but because of race. Fred Colon is Ankh-Morpork's leading racial profiler.

The Campaign for Equal Heights

Beyond the simply prejudiced and the simply lazy, there are also those who profess to respect members of other groups and even go so far as to speak up for them. To some extent, this is a fine and even admirable instinct. But it can be taken too far all too easily.

The Campaign for Equal Heights is the most prominent such group in Ankh-Morpork. The Campaign is a group comprised mostly of humans who are determined to protect the rights and dignity of dwarfs, whether dwarfs want them to or not. The trouble tends to arise from the fact that the members of the Campaign seem to know very little about dwarfs and have even less interest in learning. Like the deep-downers and Fred Colons of the world, Campaigners have an image of what dwarfs are, and little to no tolerance for dwarfs who don't fit their mold. Carrot, for instance, simply offends them.[11]

The central problem with the Campaign for Equal Heights and other such groups, both on Discworld and Roundworld, is that while the members like the groups they are trying to protect, they don't actually respect them very much. Campaigners tend to treat dwarfs as children who need adults (humans) to

---

[10] Well, okay, not the *first*, strictly speaking, but that's down to cowardice and obesity. He'd definitely try to help out, as soon has he was sure there was no danger and he'd managed to catch his breath.

[11] No one else would care, but I'm sure this worries Captain Carrot.

look after them—never mind that dwarfs live longer than humans and rarely need any more protection than is provided by the standard dwarfish attire of helmet, chainmail, and battle ax.

To get an idea of what Campaigners really think of dwarfs, compare their actions to those of Lady Sybil and her dragon-breeding friends. The Campaigners may not be quite as overbearing, but the attitude is analogous: these precious little darlings need someone to look after them. That may be true, to an extent, of an accident waiting to happen like a swamp dragon, but what most dwarfs need is to look after themselves. And, happily, they are quite well equipped to do so.

A better idea of how to do what the Campaign claims to want to do is given to us by Mrs. Cake. Aside from being a slightly clairvoyant terror of all religions and the post office, Mrs. Cake is also the proprietor of a boarding house that welcomes all comers, but caters especially to Ankh-Morpork's growing undead population. Mrs. Cake treats all of her tenants with respect, which means respecting their differences and accommodating their distinct needs as well. She refreshes the gravel in the coffins of her vampire tenants and leaves windows open when need be and has door handles that can be easily opened by a paw. She has her rules, as any landlady must, but understands that the world isn't one-size-fits-all.

Better Vampyres and the Überwald League of Temperance

It's never stated as a rule of Mrs. Cake, but it seems to be the case that the vampires she rents to are members of the Überwald League of Temperance, or black ribboners. The black ribboners represent an interesting problem for identity politics, and one that isn't so easy to illustrate using the dilemmas facing Discworld dwarfs. Individual black ribboners surely have their own motives for renouncing the sweet red stuff but the overall motivation of the League is assimilation. The founders of the movement, like Lady Margolotta, see the way the world is going, and that way is human. Vampires as a species seem to face an unsavory choice between assimilation and extinction. In a way, this is similar to the rift in dwarfish culture—all the things the deep-downers loathe about their fellow dwarfs are really all the different ways they perceive dwarfs assimilating to humans. Their response is to become more dwarfish than dwarfish.

In like manner, the Magpyrs, the vampire[12] family in *Carpe Jugulum*, tried to preserve some parts of vampire culture—blood drinking and domination over human beings—by ridding themselves of the vulnerabilities that humans could exploit. The old Count is about the only representative of the old vampire ways we see in the Discworld novels. The Magpyr family attempted to resist assimilation—no blood sausage and sing-songs around the piano for them. Instead, like the deep-downers, they doubled down on their identity. The way to resist humanization, as it were, is to become more of a vampire, a better vampire. As the younger Count says, "Every day, in every way, we get better and better."

But, as we see in the reactions of the old Count and in various dwarfs like Rhys Rhysson, to double down on one's identity is often to change or even deny that identity, just as much as assimilation is. We can certainly argue that the Magpyrs gave up more of the defining traits of vampires than any black ribboner. Black ribboners give up drinking blood—that's all. Lady Margolotta hasn't given up dominating humans by any measure—she's just found less direct and far more interesting ways to do it, like politics. The Magpyrs, on the other hand, have renounced the vampire's weakness to garlic, aversion to running water, fear of holy symbols and holy water.

Even their treatment of humans is decidedly un-vampire-like. There is no game, no seduction, no romance—in short, no respect. Humans, instead, are treated like cattle, herded and penned to be fed upon as needed. The old Count understood the rules; the new Count tried to change them to suit his new breed of vampyres. Their fate in *Carpe Jugulum* is thus poetically appropriate. When they feed upon Granny Weatherwax she turns the tables on them—rather than her becoming like them, they become like her. As she puts it, "I ain't been vampired. You've been Weatherwaxed." In attempting to preserve their vampire identity, the Magpyrs sacrificed it completely.

The black ribboners, on the other hand, respect the rules. So long as a vampire doesn't feed on a human, the vampire doesn't

---

12 Or, rather, *vampyre*, as the Magpyrs prefer to be called.

get staked through the heart. Is that too far? Is a vampire that refrains from feeding on humans still a vampire? How far can an identity bend before it breaks?

Concerns like this assume something that simply isn't the case: namely, that identities are stable. In the case of vampires, there is a certain rigidity in the identity that isn't as prominent in human identities or even dwarfish identities. This is caused by two factors: first, unlike most human or dwarf identities, vampire identities are rooted in biology. Vampires are a species as well as a social and cultural identity. While they may not need to feed on human blood to survive, they do have compulsions that are far more deeply ingrained than any ritual or tradition. The second cause of the rigidity in vampire identity is simply the fact that individual vampires live so long and are so hard to kill. This is also why dwarfish identity, while not as resistant to change as vampires, is slower to change than human identity. When compared to vampires and dwarfs, humans have a rapid succession of generations and each new generation seeks out some way of defining itself that contrasts with the one before it.

Change has gradually caught up to vampires. Maintaining their old ways is a path to extinction. So, they are forced to adapt. They are presented with two contrasting approaches: assimilation and domination. Assimilation is harder, and seems to involve giving up more of the old identity. But domination is the far riskier bet, especially, as the Magpyrs learned, if Granny Weatherwax is in the vicinity.[13]

We Can Rule You Wholesale

The internal struggles of the vampire and dwarf communities are mirrored by similar struggles only hinted at among other intelligent beings on Discworld. In his own way, Angua's brother Wolfgang was attempting the same thing as the Magpyrs and deep-downers (*The Fifth Elephant*). All of these struggles are inspired, in various ways, by the close proximity of differing species and differing cultures. At this point, it

---

[13] The few who have tried to oppose Granny's will are generally found arms around knees, rocking themselves gently while dribbling in a corner humming a reassuring tune. Encounters with Death tend to be less terrifying.*

(*THOUGH MORE MORTIFYING . . . JUST A LITTLE HUMOR.)

seems that the major source of change on Discworld is humans. Other species are either adopting human ways, or adapting their own ways to be compatible with them. This pressure to assimilate, to conform to a predominant culture is the core of identity politics.

Humans themselves aren't immune to the pressures of assimilation. Humans across Discworld are being coerced in subtle and not-so-subtle ways to conform to the standards set by Ankh-Morpork. Klatch, Four-Ecks, the Counterweight Continent, Djelibeybi, Omnia, Borogravia, and Zlobenia are all being influenced, directly and indirectly, by the culture of Ankh-Morpork. And on the Sto plains, not only are their mail and klacks and railroads originating from Ankh-Morpork; law enforcement officials are as well (*Night Watch*).

Like the other species, all of these cultures are divided to some degree by the promise of Ankh-Morporkian commerce and profits, on the one hand, and the desire to preserve their ways of life unchanged on the other. Some degree of change is inevitable, but how much is acceptable and how much is too much is something that each culture, and indeed each individual, must decide for themselves.

And what of the other side? Should Ankh-Morpork and its human population do anything to encourage assimilation further? Or to preserve the cultures threatened by it? Should each culture on Discworld have its own version of the Campaign for Equal Heights? Perhaps unsurprisingly, the present ruler of Ankh-Morpork, Patrician Havelock Vetinari, is setting a good example for the people he rules. After all, it seems that it was he who opened up Ankh-Morpork to permanent non-human residents. The Patrician's approach to cultural assimilation and integration seems to be much the same as the ancient city's response to invaders: open the gates and let them in. Buy anything they have that's worth having and sell them whatever they can pay for. The Patrician, in general, neither encourages nor discourages any aspect of any particular identity. He accepts all comers, provided that they do not threaten the workings of the city. If you can make your identity work in Ankh-Morpork, and can stand the smell, then you are welcome. But if you interfere with the city's workings,[14] then it's the scorpion pits for you.

---

[14] Or are a mime. Tolerance has its limits, after all.

The virtue of the Patrician's ruthless indifference, or perhaps his pragmatism, is that it leaves the question of identity to the people who actually have to choose and perform their identities. Like Cut-Me-Own-Throat Dibbler and Mrs. Cake, the Patrician respects people enough to make their own way. Or, perhaps more accurately, the Patrician realizes that his job is complicated enough without worrying about what people call themselves or how they act when they're not interfering with one another. "Free men," he says, "pull in all kinds of directions. It's the only way to make progress" (Pratchett, *The Truth,* 313). So, the only way for the Patrician to keep the intricate mechanism that is Ankh-Morpork working is, often, to stay out of its way, which means letting people figure things out for themselves—especially when the things they're trying to figure out are themselves.

14
Being One's Me: (Witchy) Personal Identity on the Discworld

TRIP MCCROSSIN

"She's gone funny in the head," Granny Weatherwax says of Magrat Garlick, early in *Witches Abroad* (19). Granny, Gammer Brevis, Nanny Ogg, and Old Mother Dismass are atop Bear Mountain, discussing the "increasing shortage of witches" in the wake of Desiderata Hollow's recent passing (17). Winding their way through candidate successors, Old Mother Dismass suggests Magrat finally, but Granny objects. "Funny in the head" she's gone, wanting "to relate to herself," but then she "wouldn't listen" to Granny's explanation (20). "Simplicity Garlick was your mother, Araminta Garlick was your granny," she'd explained, "Yolande Garlick is your aunt and you're your . . . you're your *me*" (19–20). And hearing it again, she "sat back, with the satisfied look of someone who has solved everything anyone could ever want to know about a personal identity crisis" (20).

Granted, *a* personal identity crisis is not *the* personal identity crisis, as it figures in the history of philosophy—John Locke's perspective on personal identity, that is, from the 1694 edition of *An Essay Concerning Human Understanding*, and the controversy that it sparked, which persists today. Still, while Magrat "wouldn't listen," we can, and should (20). In the context of *Witches Abroad* being a "story about stories," about "what it really means to be a fairy godmother," and finally "also, particularly, about reflection and mirrors" (5), Granny's "you're your *me*" may indeed help to move us closer to solving everything anyone could ever want to know about *the* personal identity crisis.

Sticks and Bristles

To better understand the problem Locke was responding to, first of all, consider for a moment Granny's troublesome broomstick. Getting it airborne, we're told, "always required a great deal of galloping up and down," as it never seemed "to get the message until it was being shoved through the air at a frantic running speed" (48). Faced with the "intractability" of her broomstick, "dwarf engineers everywhere confessed themselves totally mystified by it," given that they've "replaced the stick and bristles dozens of times" (48). But here's the problem. What is there to a broomstick but its stick and bristles? And so, while the engineers are rightly mystified by it, given that they've replaced its stick and bristles dozens of times, what's the *it* that's doing the mystifying? If they've done so dozens of times, that is, why hasn't Granny had *dozens* of different broomsticks in the process?

The "sun was well up" when Nanny and Magrat "spiraled into the sky," setting off with Granny for Genua, as per Desiderata's posthumous instructions, to prevent Granny's sister Lilith from manipulating Ella into marrying the Duc (48). As usual, though, they waited on Granny, as she coaxed her temperamental broomstick aloft. And as she did so, no doubt cursing it to the heavens, perhaps she pondered, in a philosophical moment, is *this* broomstick I've recently gotten back from the dwarfs, having taken their latest crack at repairing it by replacing its stick and bristles, in fact *the same* broomstick I gave them in the first place?

It appears to have the same design, yes, but that design now provides form to altogether different material—an altogether new stick and altogether new bristles—and so while it may indeed *appear* to the same broomstick, is it *really* now the same *identical* broomstick? Perhaps, she might wonder, those wretched dwarfs don't *repair* broomsticks at all! Perhaps they've simply a big old warehouse filled with sticks and bristles, which they assemble into equally intractable broomsticks, and which they then simply *pass off* as repaired! But if this doesn't seem like such a serious worry, as applied to broomsticks and such, it *would* seem be if the same applied to us!

Were Granny to worry about her broomstick's identity, that is, she might well also worry about *her own*. Witches on the

Disc describe themselves as human, albeit of special witchy variety, and also as persons. The same goes for Granny herself then. Like the rest of us, though, over a certain period of time, all the cells of her body come to be replaced with new ones. Still, she's no less convinced that she's *the same witch*, and so *the same person*, she was earlier on, even though her body, taken cell by cell, is in fact different material.[1] But if there's a worry about *broomsticks*, why not, as for the rest of us, also for *witches*?

Grannies and Glods

To better understand Locke's own perspective now, consider that he would want Granny to *relax*. Who she *is* as a *person*, he'd propose, however witchy a one, is *not* a function of her body *at all*. Rather, as "a thinking intelligent being, that has reason and reflection, and can consider itself as itself the same thinking thing in different times and places," her personhood is a function of her "consciousness, which is inseparable from thinking," and "can extend to actions past or to come," and can do so, it seems, independently of what becomes of her body (Perry, *Personal Identity*, 39–40).

To hone in a bit more precisely on Locke's perspective, let's think now about a more fanciful example than Granny's broomstick. What would we say, for instance, if we found that Granny and Nanny, different as they are, mysteriously exchanged bodies for a time—as a result of a bit of "headology" or "body borrowing" run amuck—each remembering, all the while, doing only those acts otherwise associated with what is now the other's body? And what if at least some of these acts were either praiseworthy or blameworthy? Would we want to direct our praise or blame to the one who remembers the praiseworthy or blameworthy acts, but whose current body is not associated with them, or the one who has no such memory, but whose current body is so associated? Locke urged us to choose the former, and to do so for primarily *moral* reasons.

We routinely invoke the idea of personal identity, Locke thought, because it's a *tool* that we routinely *need* in address-

[1] I feel confident in saying that if we pointed this out to Granny she would likely swat us a good one upside the ear and point out that we have no business discussing her cells or any other "delicate" matters of personal privacy.

ing the moral dimensions of our daily lives. "In personal identity," he tells us, "is founded all the right and justice of reward and punishment" (Perry, 46). This means that we judge Granny and Nanny each morally accountable *only* for behavior they are *conscious of*—regardless of what others may sincerely testify, as to the bodies otherwise associated with the same behavior. That no one may recognize either Granny in Nanny's body, or the Nanny in Granny's, is in this sense simply irrelevant. Our job, Locke thought, is to uncover the persons *truly* accountable for what we praise and blame, being those sincerely conscious of doing the corresponding acts.

Locke's perspective was hotly debated throughout the eighteenth century. And after a lull during the nineteenth century and the first half of the twentieth, it was hot again beginning in the second half, in both philosophical literature and popular culture, including *Witches Abroad*. In both periods, concern over Locke's perspective is primarily fourfold.

First, if personal identity is exhausted by continuity of consciousness, as Locke suggests, and our best lead to the latter is remembering being ourselves in past circumstances, then what if Granny recalls now something she did when Magrat was a young girl, and at the time recalled something she did when she was herself a young girl, but hasn't now the latter memory? Wouldn't the older witch be, then, unlike what we imagine, a different person from young Esme?

Second, if memory can be parceled out, then why not personhood? While we have the illusion of being persisting things, that is, perhaps we're rather more transient things instead, succeeding and replacing one another in time, similar enough in the process to escape notice?

Third, if Granny remains herself precisely as far back as she remembers, on what basis does she have such memories, if not by being the same person in the first place? But doesn't this seem oddly circular?

Finally, what if by the grace of God, or in more recent times some surgical technique or science-fiction technology, a person's memories were to persist not in the single body, but in multiple bodies? Here we have the strange case of Glod, "a small dwarf from a mountain community hundreds of miles away who found himself magically dragged to the kingdom and relentlessly duplicated," as a result of which "the people of Al-

Ybi are renowned for being unusually short and bad-tempered," several thousand of whom would be the same person as the original dwarf dragged from afar (6).[2] And of course we eventually have Granny and Lilith multiplied a billion times as a result of "mirror magic," Lilith without a body any longer it seems (332–36). But don't such cases, apparently conceivable on Locke's picture, pose a problem? As two distinct things can't be the same as a third, aren't such cases at odds with the laws of logic?

The last two concerns have taken center stage in the personal identity debate, generally speaking, and in particular in *Witches Abroad*. Better yet, the storyline would appear to have us, with Granny's help, respond to the latter in terms of how we respond to the former, which appears then to add something genuinely new to the long conversation.

Granny *v.* Locke

The circularity concern is most often associated with Joseph Butler. Locke's "wonderful mistake," Butler thought, was in not realizing that while "consciousness of what is past" *reveals* our personal identity to us, it does so only because we were there in the past *in the first place* (Perry, 100). Instead of trying to define personal identity in terms of other personal properties, then, he thought it best just to think of it as basic and indefinable. If Butler were listening in, as we are, on the conversation that night atop Bear Mountain, about whether Magrat had gone "funny in the head," he'd likely have been pleased as punch with Granny's "you're your *me*" analysis of how Magrat can best "relate to herself."

When we ask Locke's question, "wherein personal identity consists," Butler thought, we can't help but find that "all attempts to define, would but perplex it," even while "there is no difficulty at all in ascertaining the idea" (Perry, 99). To paraphrase Granny, we can define how we relate to our various relatives, as she defines Magrat as someone's daughter, another's granddaughter, and still another's niece. Likewise, we can

[2] Dwarfs notoriously do not get along with other dwarfs . . . imagine how much trouble they'd have getting along with themselves. One figures it would be like a sack full of wet cats.

define how they and others relate to us, as Gammer Brevis does when she recalls her "slightly watery-eyed expression of hopeless goodwill wedged between a body like a maypole and hair like a haystack after a gale," a "relentless doer of good deeds," a "worrier," and so on (20). But when it comes to defining how we relate to *ourselves*, there's really "no difficulty," as each of us is to ourselves simply "our own *me*."

And if memory depends on personal identity, Butler thought, and not the other way around, then this must mean, contrary to Locke, that personal identity needs the persistence of bodies in addition to that of consciousness. Where else do memories come from after all? Granny doesn't appear to go so far as this, but she doesn't resist overtly either, other than her resistance to "tu'penny-ha'penny psychololology" (132).

To better understand Granny's "you're your *me*" perspective on personal identity as "Butlerean," as it were, we look now to her eventual confrontation with Lilith, involving as it seems to the duplication worry raised by the Glods of Al-Ybi. Doing so seems also to shed welcome light on a historical curiosity in the personal identity debate. While Butler is generally thought to originate the above line of resistance to Locke, he hints that he's very likely indebted in this to views expressed several decades earlier by Samuel Clarke, who was among the first, if not the first to raise the fourfold concern (Perry, 283–314). The curiosity that's been left unaddressed in the process, though, is why Butler was not similarly moved then by Clarke's concern regarding duplication.

One Witch's Happy Ending, Is Another's . . .

Witches Abroad is a "story about stories," the narrator tells us early on, where stories are understood on the Discworld in a very particular way (5). "People think that stories are shaped by people," we learn, but rather "it's the other way around," and if one knows this, as Lilith does, then "the knowledge is power" (2). What this comes to is a provocative bit of theory that's known on the Discworld (and one wonders whether it might apply equally well *off* it) as the "theory of narrative causality" (2).

> Stories, great flapping ribbons of shaped space-time, have been blowing and uncoiling around the universe since the beginning of

> time. And they have evolved. The weakest have died and the strongest have survived and they have grown fat on the retelling . . . stories, twisting and blowing through the darkness. And their very existence overlays a faint but insistent pattern on the chaos that is history. Stories etch grooves deep enough for people to follow in the same way that water flows certain paths down a mountainside. And every time fresh actors tread the path of the story, the groove runs deeper. [. . . A] story, once started, *takes shape*. It picks up all the vibrations of all the other workings of that story that have ever been. This is why history keeps on repeating itself. (2–3)

"It takes a special kind of person to fight back," the narrator concludes, "and become the bicarbonate of history" (4). The problem is that there are *good* bicarbonates, like Granny, but there are also *bad* bicarbonates, like Lilith.

"Nothing stood in the way," now that Death had claimed Desiderata, "of what Lilith liked more than anything else," which is a "happy ending" (15). They'd long struggled over the fate of Genua, in particular who would rule it. Now, from her perch in the "highest tower in the palace," Lily's imposing on the city various overlapping stories—variations on those of Cinderella, Little Red Riding Hood, Sleeping Beauty, and The Wizard of Oz, among others—to produce together the overall ending she desires, which is that Ella "have beauty and power and marry a prince" (11–14).

Witches Abroad is also a story about "what it means to be a fairy godmother" (5). As such, the storyline is a broad allegory designed to have us think, in light of what transpires in Genua, about the different forms of social and political organization available to us, and the different ways authority is expressed as a result. Part of this is considering the relative merits of being "the kind that gives people what they know they really need," like Granny, "not what we think they ought to want," like Lilith (310). From our perspective, Granny's surely the good fairy godmother, and Lilith's the bad, but we're also moved to consider what it means that they think of themselves somewhat differently.

Granny's been "the good one" only because, she admits, when Lilith was kicked out of the house at thirteen for being "wanton," and went off and "had all the fun," Granny simply "had to be." Lilith, on the other hand, ever disdainful of "inefficient good intentions" (295) is convinced that *she*'s "the good one," and Granny the "wicked witch."[3] While she's "feeding people to stories," as Granny objects, "twisting people's lives," she's doing so for the sake of the "happy ending" she envisions for them, whatever their desires may be otherwise (330). "You can't go around building a better world for people," Granny objects, because only "people can build a better world for people. Otherwise it's just a cage" (298). "What will that matter in a hundred years' time?," Lilith asks, rhetorically of course, if she can make Genua into "a great city" after all (294).

To this end—arriving finally at the idea of *Witches Abroad* as "also, particularly, about reflection and mirrors" (5)—Lilith is perched in the highest tower in a particular way. She's standing between two mirrors "set almost, but not quite, facing one another," so that she can "see over her shoulder and watch her images curve away around the universe inside the mirror," can "feel herself pouring into herself, multiplying itself via the endless reflections" (4). Her point being, "if images can steal a bit of you, then images of images can amplify you, feeding you back on yourself, giving you power" (49)—the power, that is, to *make* a happy ending, by which she means an ending that *she* finds happy.

Our point being that there seems to be, interestingly, more going on here than mere reflections. When Lilith would move out from between the mirrors, we learn, "the effect was startling. Images of Lilith hung in the air behind her for a moment, like three-dimensional shadows, before fading" (14). And it's not just startling, but worrying, as Magrat frets as she looks down at the mirror-like glass slippers she's wearing, "because the person that walked away might not be the same person," as if "you were spread out among the images, your whole soul was pulled out thin, and somewhere in the distant images a dark part of you would get out and come looking for you, if you weren't very careful" (257).

Which is how we come back around to the duplication worry we identified earlier, in the case of the many Glods of Al-Ybi.

---

[3] Such disagreements based on perspective are not uncommon among sister witches. The disagreement usually being settled by whomever is a faster hand with the hemlock.* (*Which also explains why there aren't that many witches who have sisters anymore.)

Who's the Fairest . . .

"You broke my mirror!," Lilith wails. Mirror magic being Lilith's method of choice, what better way for Granny to stop her, than to destroy the mechanism—her mirrors, one of the two at least, which is what she does. "You have to break both to be safe," Lilith wails again, "you've upset the balance" (329–30). The consequences are sublimely disastrous for Lilith, and for Granny, and also interesting for us.

"Image after image shatters," we learn, "all the way around the great curve of the mirror world, the crack flying out faster than light," to its "furthest point and curves back, speeding down the countless worlds," returning "towards its point of origin, carrying with it the fleeing reflections of all the mirrors" (329–30). Reaching it, Lilith's reflection "turned around, smiled beatifically, and reached out of the frame to take [her] into its arms," and with a single utterance of her name, "Lily!," all the mirrors "shattered, exploding outwards in a thousand pieces from the top of the tower so that, just for a moment, it was wreathed in twinkling fairy dust" (331). And here's where things get weirder still.

"Where the maze of mirrors had been were empty frames," Nanny and Magrat find, and on the glass shards covering the floor lay "a figure in a white dress" (331). At first they think it's Lilith, but Nanny realizes soon enough that it's Granny. But Lilith's body's nowhere to be found. Perhaps they assume that she was altogether consumed by the explosion, which Granny was perhaps far enough away from to be spared, though nonetheless unconscious. What they don't know, but we do, is that Lilith didn't perish, though in what sense we're not sure. Nor are we so sure in what sense precisely Granny is unconscious.

What Nanny and Magrat don't know, that is, but we do, is that Granny and Lilith are now trapped in a distinct portions of the "mirror universe," each in limbo along with "a billion" of their seemingly indistinguishable reflections. "Where am I?," they each ask. IN THE MIRROR, Death answers. "Am I dead?," they then ask. THE ANSWER TO THIS, according to Death, IS SOMEWHERE BETWEEN NO AND YES. "When can I get out?," they ask finally. WHEN YOU FIND THE ONE THAT'S REAL, Death tells them (332–33). And isn't *this* precisely the challenge at the heart of the duplication worry.

This One!

Let's take for a moment a simpler, more conventional example. Not Granny and Lilith as they are in the storyline, each in their respective portions of the mirror universe, one among a billion and one versions of themselves. Let's take just one of them, Lilith say, and have her duplicated just once. Just as all the other mirrors explode, in the last remaining one, Lilith's reflection "reached out of the frame to take [her] into its arms," and so in the mirror universe we have two Liliths as a result, each competing, from our perspective at least, to be "the one that's real" (331). In the case of amoeba, we're generally comfortable determining "the one that's real," as both new amoeba are real, and each is new, and so distinct from the original, which no longer exists. As Lilith's a person, though, what does this do to her personal identity over the span of time in question?

Conventionally, there are three competing ways to describe such a situation. First, *both Liliths* survive *as the same person* who stood before the exploding mirror. Second, *neither of them* does, in the sense that, like the dividing amoeba, the competing Liliths are persons not only distinct from one another, but distinct also from the witch who stood before the exploding mirror. Finally, *just one of them* does, the other being somehow a lesser competitor, in the sense at least that for one of the Liliths in particular, the "one that's real" question seems to be distinctly more heartfelt.

How to choose? The first alternative seems initially appealing, at least in the limited case where we have just Lilith and her one duplicate. But because two distinct things can't be the same thing as a third, it would seem also at odds with the logic of identity. The second alternative is more in keeping with the logic of identity, but seems also more at odds with the two-Liliths example. If neither is identical with Lilith as she stood earlier before the mirror soon to explode, then *that* Lilith no longer exists, and duplication is effectively a form of death. But then why would Death entertain the "the one that's real" business in the first place? The third alternative, finally, seems relatively in keeping with both the two-Liliths example and the logic of identity, but still it's not at all unproblematic. It nicely communicates greater legitimacy to the "one that's real," yes, whichever one this may be, and so is in keeping with Death's challenge. But what if in "reach[ing] out of the frame to take [Lilith] into its arms," she perished in the process, then the reflection would have been Lilith—the last one standing, as it were. But can being the same person over time really be just a matter of there not being a better candidate competing for the title? Is there anything further in the storyline that helps us here?

What do we know? We know that Granny and Lilith are in their respective portions of the mirror universe. We know that each is there along with a billion duplicates. We know that each is in the same conversation with Death, about how to "get out." We know that Nanny and Magrat have found Granny's unconscious body, but not Lilith's, who we can imagine they imagine is dead. And we know that Granny and Lilith are each unaware that the other is also in the mirror universe. We *also* know, though, that *we* have a perspective that none of the rest of them have.

We know, that is, that the billion and one Grannies are associated with a living body, in some witchy way, but that the billion and one Liliths are not, or at least appear not to be. And this together with what we hear when we hear them, out of one another's earshot and also Nanny's and Magrat's, responding very differently to Death. And the difference not only serves the "good and evil" storyline, but the related personal identity storyline as well. Lilith, in response, "ran on through the endless reflections," and was lost. But Granny, by contrast, "looked down at herself" and said simply, "This one," echoing it seems her earlier "you're your *me*," and was freed.[4]

If Butler had come along with us from atop Bear Mountain to where we are now, looking in on Granny and Lilith as they struggle with Death in the mirror universe, wouldn't he likely say that he's just as pleased (as punch, that is) with Granny's "This one," as he was with her earlier "you're your *me*"? And mightn't he want to add that this is why he never felt the need to worry as Clarke had about the whole duplication business? Let's say, he'd offer, as he reminds us of his view, that we're prepared to see personal identity as a basic and indefinable part of the human condition. And let's also say, he'd go on, that this is so because we "relate to ourselves," as Magrat aspires to do,

[4] THERE IS NOTHING MORE REAL THAN ME, AFTER ALL.

through the bodies that house us. Then to be sure, he'd conclude, the successful response to Death's challenge is going to be Granny's, as she "looks down," and not Lilith's, who doesn't. "Perhaps I should have written this down after all," he might say, regretfully, "something to the effect, 'I'm not worried as Mr. Clarke is because . . . etc.' or such like, but unfortunately I didn't —*thank goodness* Mr. Pratchett wrote *Granny* down for us!"[5]

---

[5] I'd like thank John Perry and Carol Rovane for all that they taught me, personally and through their writing, about the nature of personal identity. Neither bears any responsibility, of course, for what I've done with their insights and encouragement. I'd like to thank Howard Ducharme for his seminal essay on Clarke's perspective on personal identity. Finally, I'd like to thank William Uzgalis and Ezio Vailati, from whom, in conversations with John Perry, which I had the good fortune to be part of, I learned much about Clarke's views and their place in the long conversation about personal identity.

IV

Ye Canna' Ken What Ye Canna' Ken

15
The Serious Monk's Guide to Re-writing History

JOHN V. KARAVITIS

On a quiet evening in late summer, a citizen of Ankh-Morpork might find himself lying on a field of grass, looking up at the stars, reflecting on the world and life within it. *This world is our home! And what a wondrous world this is,* he might say to himself.[1] And what a wondrous world Discworld truly is. The Disc that is all the known world is supported by four elephants, which in turn stand upon the shell of the Great A'Tuin, an unbelievably large Giant Star Turtle that traverses the vast emptiness of space. At the edge of the Disc, the waters of the ocean fall over into unseen darkness.

This description of Terry Pratchett's Discworld is mentioned numerous times, so it must be true, right? The Discworld anthology of more than forty novels chronicles the events of that wondrous, fictional world. But these novels aren't just a series of stories of an elaborate fantasy world where magic is writ large, and its inhabitants struggle with the same mundane issues that afflict all of us in our little nook of the universe. The novels that make up the Discworld anthology are also at the same time the *history* of its events. With each novel, we experience Discworld's history from a different angle—from stories of individuals struggling from one day to the next, to stories of influential cities and powerful kingdoms, and even the unknown, uncharted lands in between.

This is, I think, an interesting way of looking at a forty-volume anthology of a single world full of magic and fantasy. Of

[1] Assuming one can find any grass in Ankh-Morpork.

grandmotherly witches and more-than-slightly-unhinged kings, of guilds of assassins and thieves,[2] and underpaid and underworked city night watch guards.[3] But if the Discworld anthology is also a history of Discworld, maybe if we're daring, like a brave guard of the Ankh-Morpork Night Watch, we might learn a thing or two about what history really is.[4] Maybe everything we've thought about what history is has been wrong! Maybe our view of history, of *our own* world, is upside-down!

What's that, you say? You already know what "history" is? You don't need to read some dull, boring essay about the philosophy of history, and all that? Well . . . I suspect that when most people are asked what "history" is, they may very well roll up their eyes and refer to the mind-numbing sequences of dates and associated boring and useless facts about people and places and events that they were forced to learn about in school.[5]

Nothing could be further from the truth.

You *are* interested in *the truth,* aren't you? Isn't that why you picked up this book? Well . . . Perhaps I could tell you a story. Yes. *A story that will explain everything . . .*

If You Fall into the River of History, You Will Get Soaked!

By the peach fuzz on the chin of the Great A'Tuin! thought Initiate First Class Pleece Tellusmore. On his way back to the great temple to take his final exams, which would mark his transition from a monk-to-be to a full-fledged monk, Tellusmore had inadvertently slipped and fallen sideways into the cold current of the stream that ran alongside the outer edge of the temple grounds, bumping his head on a large, slick stone. His yellow

---

[2] Licensed to do business, annual dues paid up front, of course, thank you very much.

[3] But who do manage to save the world, on an as-needed basis, but only *as* needed, you understand.

[4] The Ankh-Morpork Night Guards' *Official Unofficial Cheat Sheet for Historical Matters* specifically references four Discworld novels: *Wyrd Sisters* (1988); *Guards! Guards!* (1989); *Small Gods* (1992); and *Thief of Time* (2001).

[5] That's just the Teachers' Guild doing what *it* does best—making learning boring! (But don't tell my grammar school teachers I said that! Because I obviously didn't!)

robe, which he had worked hard to earn the right to wear, was now soaking wet, and a little muddied, too. Picking himself up, wet sandals clacking and squeaking as he progressed, Tellusmore crossed over the ornate red and yellow lacquered wooden bridge and hurried to the temple grounds. He stood next to one of the low braziers to both dry his robe and warm himself. A short distance away, over by a row of massive, rotating cylinders right outside the temple wall, a custodian glanced over at him, took in his sorry state, and chuckled briefly to himself, before resuming his quiet and methodical sweeping.

As Tellusmore was trying to dry off, a group of four young children came over. More than likely a self-appointed reconnaissance group from a school field trip to the temple, they pointed and laughed as they approached him.

Look! said one, pointing with exaggerated emphasis. *That monkey is wearing a yellow robe!*

And of course what he said was absolutely true. Initiate First Class Pleece Tellusmore was indeed a monkey. But no ordinary monkey, mind you. An intelligent, articulate, and studious *monk-to-be*, who was very soon going to be a full-fledged *monk* (the first in his family!), and Defender of History and of All Things Historical.

Chee chee chee! screeched Tellusmore, his tail snapping to and fro. *Yes, you are correct!*

It can TALK! exclaimed another child.

Of course I can talk! replied Tellusmore indignantly. *If the Librarian at the University can be an orangutan, then . . . Shouldn't you be with your teacher, you rapscallions?*

Teacher shmeacher! School shmool! the first child replied. *They brought us here to learn about history, and how the monks here "protect" it! BO-RING!* The three other children briefly looked at one another, and then they all vigorously nodded in agreement with what had been said.

Tellusmore sighed inwardly. Exactly the kind of anarchistic attitude that the Teachers' Guild managed to instill in its charges with hardly any effort at all. How *did* they accomplish that so effortlessly?[6] And exactly the kind of attitude that a monk of his order had to be on the lookout for, to fight against

---

[6] Please refer to the prior footnote about the Teachers' Guild. You *are* reading these footnotes, aren't you?

and correct. History must be protected at all costs! It tells us how our world came to be, and why things are the way they are. It shows us how to act properly, in the stories of great heroes and holy men. And to know where we're going, we need to know whence we came! It's always been about *history*!

Tellusmore took a quick glance at his wristwatch. 11:37 AM. Plenty of time for what he knew he had to do.

Children, said Tellusmore. *Let's head off to the temple's library. I've got a story to tell you . . .*[7]

History—It's What People Are Told It Is

The first story that Tellusmore tells the children is *Wyrd Sisters*. This is the story of the murder of a king, the theft of his kingdom by his killer, and retribution and justice being brought to the land in the end. Now, of course, the "story" is a bit more involved than this. I've just given you the 10,000-foot view. To fill in the blanks, I'd have to mention the three witches whose efforts helped bring about the return of the kingdom to the rightful heir, especially how they threw the entire kingdom of Lancre fifteen years and two months into the future, all by the power of magic.

Although fate, destiny, magic (it "glues the Discworld together"), and the various gods are all important, it is Destiny that takes center stage. Destiny is an inescapable fact of life. Death, when speaking to the recently-departed King Verence, acknowledges that even He can have no knowledge of anyone's destiny. The three witches frequently get involved in heated discussions among themselves where they focus on Destiny's impact on the affairs of people. From listening in on their arguments, one would think that what will happen was going to happen regardless of one's efforts to the contrary. Granny Weatherwax notes, "You don't have to search for people when destiny is involved, you just wait for them in Ankh-Morpork" (*Wyrd Sisters*, 223). But apparently even something like Destiny isn't the final arbiter of events on Discworld. "Destiny gets it wrong half the time" (267), Hwel the dwarf playwright tells his boss Olwyn Vitoller, who is the

---

[7] Honestly, if I hear anyone refer to this literary device as a *mise en abyme*, I swear I shall surely scream! Editor Michaud, I do believe that I am looking in *your* direction!

owner of the traveling troupe of actors. Hwel thinks of Destiny as "funny stuff" that one cannot trust, and that one cannot control.

Belief in destiny runs deep in Discworld, and this belief colors the way people see their world and the events within it. But even more powerful than Destiny is the power of *words*. We see the power of words affecting the way that people view the world in a conversation between the Fool and the Duke and the Duchess. "Words can change the world," the Fool informs them. The Duchess challenges the Fool, and tells him that she believes that "Strong men and their deeds" change the world. In the ensuing argument, the Fool explains how words can change the past. "Because the past is what people remember, and memories are words. Who knows how a king behaved a thousand years ago? There is only recollection, and stories. And plays, of course" (187). Incredulous, she asks "You tell me history is what people are told?"

Taking the Fool's counsel, the Duchess decides that a play is to be written that would present the death of the King of Lancre in such a way that neither she nor the Duke would be implicated—in effect, re-writing history. The Fool is then charged with finding a playwright who could write such a play. (This turns out to be Hwel the dwarf.) This play would be revisionist history, and history would become what people were told it was. On the way to the castle, to attend the performance of this play, Granny Weatherwax voices her displeasure with the theater and actors. "As if the world weren't full of enough history without inventing more" (295).

It looks like history is a narrative that seeks to explain what happened and why. As such it is a human creation; and the past, that is, *history*, is what people are told it is. And typically, what people are told is what they believe to be true.[8] But enough of that. Let's get back to Tellusmore and the children, and see how that story is progressing.

Beware of Libraries! Therein Lie Dragons!

Oh, wow! Great! What a story! A "wyrd" story, ha ha ha! Wait, that's history? Does this mean we're historicals, too? No, you

[8] So, rest assured, you will believe everything that you read in this essay. Especially that little monkeys in yellow robes can talk and become Defenders of All Things Historical! I shall write it, and you shall believe it!

gloopy, you mean histori-ANS! The four children, sitting on the library floor at the feet of Tellusmore, and thus face-to-face with him, all chimed in at once, their exclamations crashing into one another's in a discordant din. Tellusmore carefully replaced the aged, well-worn volume of *Wyrd Sisters* back into the empty slot on the library shelf, its creaky binding rebelling loudly at the tight fit among the other volumes. He allowed himself the luxury of a smile. *You see!* he thought to himself. *With a little bit of presentation skill, and knowing your audience, history—*

And then what happened? What happened after that?[9] The children peppered the monk-to-be with their demands. *Tell us more! Tell us more! Tell us more!* they chanted.

Initiate First Class Pleece Tellusmore, monk-to-be of the order that protects History in All Its Forms, flicked his tail; did that oh-so-cute thing that monkeys do when they wipe their face; took a deep breath; and began yet another story . . .

The next story that Tellusmore pulls out is *Guards! Guards!*[10] It is a story full of magic, dragons (both big and small), the gods (duh!), destiny, chance ("who can sometimes overrule even the gods") (346), conspiracies, dungeons, and yes, that happily-ever-after mushy stuff you typically find in stories that have dragons in them, where people fall in love at the end, and everyone lives happily ever after. Should I stop there?[11] Have you had your fill? No? Okay then . . . details you too shall have.

A secret brotherhood seeks to overthrow the Patrician, who is the current ruler of Ankh-Morpork, and install a king in his stead. This king would, of course, be under the control of the secret brotherhood. They plan to take over Ankh-Morpork by summoning a huge dragon, and they can do this because the leader of the secret brotherhood stole a dragon-summoning book from the Library of Unseen University. Along the way, the guards of the City Night Watch, the Librarian of Unseen University (an orangutan!), and Lady Sybil Ramkin (a duchess

---

[9] Kids! Just can't get them to *shut up already*! Sorta like readers who wonder "Are we at the end of this essay yet? Are we there yet? Are we there yet?" Good grief! Stop that! (What have I gotten myself into here?!?!)

[10] As noted in the Ankh-Morpork Night Guards' *Official Unofficial Cheat Sheet for Historical Matters*, of course!

[11] You *do* know that this is *me* talking here, and not Initiate First Class Pleece Tellusmore, right? You are *not* a monkey, and I am *not* your uncle! *Chee chee chee* indeed!

of Ankh-Morpork, and breeder of small swamp dragons) manage to discover who the leader of the secret brotherhood is, and eventually Ankh-Morpork is restored to its proper state—with the Patrician back in power, and the city free of big, property-value-obliterating dragons.

Destiny also has a role to play in this novel, and it's the same role it played in *Wyrd Sisters*. Destiny is seen as inescapable. Cut-Me-Own-Throat Dibbler tells Captain Vimes "When a stranger comes into the city under the thrall of the dragon and challenges it with a glittery sword, weeell, there's only one outcome, ain't there? It's probably destiny" (*Guards! Guards!* 196).

But as with *Wyrd Sisters*, *destiny* takes a back seat to *history*. Throughout *Guards! Guards!*, there is an expectation that events have to occur in a certain pattern, and then be placed in proper *historical* perspective. When the Librarian went back in time one week to discover who had stolen the dragon-summoning book,[12] he knew that he had to be very careful. The third rule of the Librarians of Time and Space states "Do not interfere with the nature of causality" (253). If one were to interfere with the course of history, "Time could bifurcate, like a pair of trousers" (253), and terrible things could happen. At the end, as the Patrician and the Council are expressing their gratitude to Captain Vimes and the members of the City Night Watch, Vimes reflects on the purpose of the ceremony. "It was, of course, vitally important that there be a ceremony like this. Then the whole thing could be neat and settled. And forgotten. Just another chapter in the long and exciting history of eckcetra, eckcetra" (388). And that's how the events that transpired in *Guards! Guards!* will be written down, in the *historical* record of Discworld.

And yes, you read correctly—past events can be forgotten. But if past events are forgotten, then they cease to be history. Events occur, but they have to be recorded to be remembered, to become history. From the father of history, Herodotus (484–425 BCE), to the founder of modern history, Leopold von Ranke (1795–1886), historians[13] have for the longest time sim-

[12] Books sure do seem to play a huge role in this essay. Maybe children are onto something with their dislike of reading books.

[13] Boring old fuddy-duddies who are long since dead. Which means that you can confidently ignore what they said about anything, let alone historicals and other such stuffings. So, move along, gentle reader. Nothing to learn here.

ply reported the past "as it actually happened," and for the most part without any interpretation or analysis of events. We write down what has happened, and this becomes history.[14]

People Had Forgotten the Days of the Gods . . .

Whoosh! Weeee! I'm a dragon! No, I'M a dragon! I'm gonna breathe my flame onto you! No way, I want to be like Captain Vimes, Hero of Ankh-Morpork, riding a dragon! The four children all jumped up just as Tellusmore finished his story, and started to run around, arms stretched out like dragon wings, whirring and purring like wound-up toys with the spring just released. Tellusmore was positively bursting with pride. He was now more than ever glad that he had decided to enter the Order, and aspire to become a monk. *See how important defending history is?* he thought to himself. But by now, his robe had almost completely dried, and he had more pressing—

And then what happened? asked the first boy.

Chee chee chee! screeched a surprised Tellusmore. *Wait, what?* he asked, his tail flicking to and fro. *What do you mean, 'And then what happened'?*

What happened after that? the first boy asked.

Tellusmore looked up at him, then stared off into space, and then started to nervously prance around in cute little circles, now wondering quite what he had gotten himself into. He began to mutter a soft, nearly-silent prayer to the gods, whichever would listen to him, as he tried to decide which volume of Discworld history he could use to silence these rambunctious rapscallions once and for all. His eyes fluttered nervously to-and-fro along the dusty library shelves . . .

Tellusmore settles on reading from *Small Gods* to the children. The great god Om realizes one day that he is trapped in the body of a tortoise, and that he is powerless. Apparently only one church novice, Brutha, can still hear him, which is the only reason that Om hasn't vanished into oblivion. (Gods need to be believed in, in order to exist—just like history!) The religion based on Om has simply been chugging along on its own

[14] You wouldn't want us to end up in the wrong Trouser of Time by accident, would you?

momentum, not because anyone else still actually believes in Om. To regain his power, Om must command the recognition of as many followers as possible. Om succeeds in regaining his godly powers, and Brutha becomes the Eighth Prophet and reforms the church. The next one hundred years are a time of peace.

Small Gods presents the idea of forgetting history, and what this means to people. In the past there were many small gods, and they grew in power with the number of their believers. Those gods who lost believers lost power, until eventually they became whispers in the wind. Forgetting their gods also means forgetting the past. The many different gods of the past once provided explanations for how the world works, which is also a function of history.

The idea of forgetting history is also presented by the novice Brutha. Although illiterate and uneducated, Brutha has a photographic memory. Earlier, while the soldiers are busy trying to burn down Ephebe's Great Library ("Crammed with useless and dangerous and evil knowledge"), Brutha races to memorize as many of the library scrolls as he can. But the library scrolls are themselves a collection of philosophical ideas about how the world works, which is also a function of history.

Brutha's photographic memory implies that his mental record of the scrolls, which becomes the surviving repository for the history of the world, is absolute, static, and objective. But with human memory, this can never be. Psychologists have demonstrated not only that there is no such thing as a true photographic (or "eidetic") memory, but that every time we access a memory, we change it. There is no true objective remembering—at least for very fine details. Brutha's memory can never provide an objective record of history. Rather, his memory of the knowledge of the library scrolls is vulnerable to his eventual forgetting of details, and of course his inevitable death. So history will eventually be forgotten, unless someone writes it all down.

And it's not just that history has to be recorded in order to be remembered. Early on we are told by the sacred text that history has to be observed and controlled. "Otherwise it's not history. It's just . . . well, things happening one after another. And, of course, it has to be controlled. Otherwise it might turn into anything." At the end, we meet Lu-Tze the History Monk for the first time in the *Discworld* anthology. We learn that the century of peace really should have been a time of war and bloodshed, but that Lu-Tze had decided otherwise.[15]

By this point, gentle reader, you should be convinced that the way history is treated in the stories that monk-to-be Tellusmore is using to educate the children remains consistent. History is what we say it is. And what we say it is, is what we write down. And it's only the stories that we write down that we can possibly remember.

History—A Lie You Can Understand

Lu-Tze! Lu-cy! Loose-E! Goose-y! Moose-y! Mess-y! Messy messy messy!!! sang the children. Monk-to-be Tellusmore was exasperated. And exhausted. Where was the children's teacher? There was no way he could keep doing this. By now, even a full-fledged card-carrying monk of the Order would have—

Tell us more! Tell us more! Tell us more! they chanted.

Tellusmore scrunched his little monkey face, flicked his tail once, twice, thrice. When molding young minds, one must be careful not to leave any fingerprints. *All right then. One last story. You will then officially be "Students of Discworld History," and back to your class you will go! You can go write your own stories after this!*

Now! Now! Now! Now! they chanted, little fists furiously pumping in bloodthirsty unison.

Tellusmore walked a few steps to a nearby shelf, and scampered almost to the very top shelf where the volume *Thief of Time* resided.[16] It must have heard him coming, as it began to try to fling itself off the shelf as Tellusmore approached . . .

In *Thief of Time*, the Auditors of Reality, whose job it is to make sure that the physical laws of the universe operate as intended, decided that human beings are simply too messy and unpredictable. So they set in motion a plan for the creation of a perfect clock which, once working, will cause all time to cease.

---

[15] I guess you *can* interfere with the course of history and not have horrible things—like bifurcated trousers—happen, after all!

[16] More like "had been napping" instead of finding something useful and honest to do with its time. But you know books. Lazy things and such, spending all day long stuck in one place, being of no use to anyone most of the time.

Lu-Tze, the History Monk we first met in *Small Gods*, is tasked with preventing this perfect clock from being created. (He had faced this challenge before, in Überwald, and "succeeded," if only by chance.[17]) Together with Lobsang Ludd, formerly of the Ankh-Morpork Thieves' Guild; Susan Sto Helit, the granddaughter of Death; and Myria LeJean, a renegade Auditor in human form, the perfect clock is destroyed; and time is unfrozen.[18]

In *Thief of Time* we learn about the creation and purpose of the History Monks. Founded by Wen the Eternally Surprised, the purpose of the Order of the History Monks is to "see that tomorrow happens at all." Wen's philosophy is that there is just the present moment, that is, "now." He believes that the universe is created second by second, and the past is what we remember it to be.

The last time that history shattered (the "Big Crash"), the History Monks had to rebuild it from scratch. "We stitched it up as best we could . . . filling up the holes . . . It's a patchwork, really"[19] (*Thief of Time*, 182). The History Monks do the same the second time around. Their spinning cylinders, the Procrastinators, are simply tools that they use to control the flow of time, and thus affect history. "But their biggest ally was the human ability to think narratively" (206). Which is how people learn and talk about the world—by using stories.

There is resistance to the idea that history is constructed. Death claims that "EVERYTHING THAT HAPPENS STAYS HAPPENED" (145), and Lobsang Ludd initially rejects Mr. Soto's assertion that he no longer exists in the Thieves' Guild's records. "You can't rewrite history!" This resistance feels like an argument in favor of destiny in human affairs. However, Lu-Tze and the History Monks interfere with and rewrite history all the time. Lu-Tze uses a witch's broomstick to travel to Ankh-Morpork, even though it's "'absolutely forbidden,' said Lu-Tze. 'cos it's

---

[17] Or was that destiny? Hard to tell sometimes... By the gods, is it written down somewhere?

[18] A lot of other things happened along the way, of course, but when you're covering history, you have to be picky with your focus and the details. Please, rest assured! I'm a professional!

[19] Yes, and explain that to all the codfish who "helped" patch up time. What? You don't see what codfish have to do with . . . Eh, just trust me on this.

Interfering With History'" (241). History is repaired after the first glass clock burst its metal spring, and the glass clock is (almost) surgically removed from history. History is repaired yet again after the second glass clock is destroyed. While in the library of the Guild of Historians, Death's granddaughter, Susan, realizes the History Monk's purpose. "Around her, historians climbed library ladders, fumbled books onto their lecterns and generally rebuilt the image of the past to suit the eyesight of today" (207).

You see, people don't just want history. They *need* it. But it has to be a collection of stories that are both meaningful and coherent. Stories that explain and that help us make sense of things. Events do not occur in isolation, and history involves meaning. As contemporary philosopher of history W. H. Walsh (1913–1986) noted, history reconstructs the past in a narrative that is intelligible. There are connections between historical events, and historians make these clear. This emphasis on a narrative imbued with meaning makes the History Monks true historians.

I think that people unconsciously know that the messy details and the focus of the stories that make up the past are best left to professionals. To the historians.

It couldn't be any other way.

Epilogue, or the Beginning of yet Another Story

Monk-to-be Tellusmore finished the last story. His shoulders sagged, and as he closed his eyes, he drew a deep breath. When he opened them . . . the children were gone!

Chee chee chee! he screeched in terror, and began to run around himself in circles. *Where could they be?* And just then, at that moment, Tellusmore's head dropped, and he caught a glimpse of his watch.

11:38 AM.

Only a minute . . . ?!?! That's not poss—

And in fact his yellow robe had dried, and he felt as warm as toast. Looking around, he caught sight of the custodian, who was, as he always seemed to be, just sweeping. He thought of asking if . . . and then quickly decided that he should hurry along to his final exams.

As Tellusmore scampered away into the bowels of the great temple, ready to take the final step of his journey from monk-to-be to full-fledged monk (and Defender of All Things Historical, of course), he wouldn't have seen the custodian look up his way and smile.

"I know you're going to do just fine."

At Long Last, the End of This Essay

The Discworld anthology is a narrative that is also its own history. Its stories are based on parodies of historical events and well-known works of fantasy and literature. In the same fashion, part of this essay has been written as a parody of Discworld.[20] Within this essay, I've written a story of my own where the history of Discworld is told to a group of young children. Although many might feel that teaching history to children is a waste of time, and that the same history will have to be re-told to them once they've grown up a bit, American historian H. Stuart Hughes (1916–1999) would have disagreed. His position was that history can't just be a sterile collection of dates and facts. Given its narrative form, the historian has to choose an angle and write his story with passion and imagination. It's this emotional content that will encourage us to use history to shine a light on the events of our current world. Teaching children history takes on an added importance because it could stir their imaginations, and get them interested in the subject. The same way Hughes was, when, as a child of eight, his family took him on a trip to France after the First World War.

It should be apparent by now that history is constructed—by people. More to the point, we can say that history is "performative." That is, history is what we say it is. Words are performative when uttering them creates their reality—like saying "I do" makes a marriage official, or "I bet" establishes a wager. Sure, we learn new facts about the past all the time. We get evidence from archaeological digs, re-discovered manuscripts and scrolls, eyewitness testimonies, unsealed government files,

---

[20] Well, okay, if you want to believe that adorable little monkeys in yellow robes can speak and study history, please, don't let me stop you! I want to believe, too!

even surprising pictures from Google Earth. These new facts either reinforce or call into question our current view of history. Details are important. But we also have to look at the big picture. History can change when we look at the past from a different angle. What we decide to focus on is as important as the details. It's the story of the trees and the forest. From one angle, all we see are trees. From another, we realize that there are roads cutting through the forest. When it comes to constructing the narratives that define our past, the trees and the forest both matter.

In both *Small Gods* and *Thief of Time*, we come across the phrase "like opening a box with a crowbar that's inside." It sounds curiously like a Zen riddle, but I believe that here author Terry Pratchett is winking at us, and hinting at his philosophy of history. Obviously, a box is opened with a crowbar already in hand. But if the crowbar is *in* the box, you can *still* use it to open the box. Just pick up the box and drop it from a great height. The weight of the crowbar will break the box open.[21] (Yes, I know. *Messy messy messy!!!*) Likewise, historians construct a box called "history" that has all of our stories inside. So in a deep sense, it has all of us inside it, too. And there's only one way to create or change history.

We are the crowbar.[22]

---

[21] I FIND CROWBARS . . . UNNECESSARY.

[22] Yes, yes, I know. The most profound philosophical conclusion EVER. Thank you, thank you very much. But now you know what history is. Please send all of your heartfelt thanks and appreciation, or, in an alternative version of history, any vituperative criticism and demands for a full-refund (what do *I* care, *my* job is finished!) for the inclusion of this essay to the book's editor, Mr. Nicolas Michaud, EdD, Department of Philosophy, Unseen University, Ankh-Morpork, Discworld, "*eckcetra, eckcetra* . . ."

16
Getting at the Truth

DOUGLAS JORDAN

> "Do you think I used magic?"
> Esk looked down at the queen bee. She looked up at the witch.
> "No," she said, "I think you just know a lot about bees."
> Granny grinned.
> "Exactly correct. That's one form of magic, of course."
> "What, just knowing things?"
> "Knowing things that other people *don't know,*" said Granny.
>
> —Terry PRATCHETT, *Equal Rites*

Discworld is a place where it seems no one has much of a right to be sure of anything. It is a world in which the truth can be changed by writing, a world in which even the most powerful wizard cannot be sure his spell will work, and the wisest witches know that what people believe is often more powerful than what they know. Discworld is, simply, magical. So we are comfortable saying it doesn't need to make much sense, and anything the characters claim to know might well be wrong. Good thing we live in a far more sensible world . . . where we can be sure of what we know. The funny thing is, in our world without magic it took only one little three-page paper from a relatively unknown philosopher to turn everything we knew about knowledge into, well, bunk.

"What is knowledge?" According to classical definitions, which have lasted until the middle of the twentieth century, knowledge is a true, justified belief. Ancient Greek philosopher Plato (424–348 BCE) was the first to define it as such. This perspective of knowledge has three components. The first is that a person must believe a statement. The second is that the person must be justified in believing the statement. The third is that the statement must be true. Under the classical account of knowledge, if one part is missing, knowledge does not exist.

The statement that is alleged to be knowledge must be true. A false statement cannot be knowledge, no matter how much the speaker wants it to be. If a Wizard were to claim that there are only three elephants holding up the Disc, that the turtle's name is not A'Tuin, or that dwarfs are taller than trolls, then these claims would not be knowledge. We all know them to be false. There are four elephants holding up the Disc. The turtle's name is A'Tuin, and trolls are taller than dwarfs.

The statement must be justified. There must be good reason to believe that the statement is true. There are many theories upon which justification can be based. The most common justification for belief in any principle, fact, or idea is that the person providing the information is an expert or authority on the subject. The justification from authority is first set forth by Plato of ancient Greece. Coherentism is a theory of justification that entails when a belief is in line with other pieces of knowledge, it is reasonable to believe it. This occurs when multiple pieces of evidence converge to produce greater reason to believe in the truth of a statement.

Archchancellor Mustrum Ridcully is an authoritative figure on magic.[1] Hailing from the Unseen University, his years of experience and rank make his statements on magic well believed. A person would be justified in believing a statement made by him. However, it is important to note that just because a person is an authority on something does not make him an authority on everything. You would be hard pressed to find the Archchancellor to be an expert on the nature of world-holding elephants and turtles. But his areas of expertise, physics and magic, are probably best not questioned. It is also good to consider whether or not the statements made are true. Mistakes can happen, as well as lies and accidents. If, while drunk, the Archchancellor were to incorrectly explain a level one wizard spell, his expertise will not save him.

---

[1] Though most of his authority comes from being an imposing figure with a loud voice . . . like most authorities now that I think about it.

Coherentism is seen in the physics of Discworld. It relies on this type of justification. The particle thaum is composed of sub-particles. Each of these sub-particles—up, down, sideways, sex appeal, and peppermint—has properties ascribed to it. Each of these particles has a relation to the other. By understanding how one works, a wizard can figure out how its opposite functions. This is because all of the particles are compatible with each other, and their function is coherent.

The person claiming knowledge must also hold the claimed knowledge as a belief. A belief is similar to a statement. The only trait the belief, or statement, must have it is that it can carry a truth value. The truth value of a belief or statement is that it must be able to be either true or false, not both or neither. Every statement uttered by the characters of Discworld is a belief. Every sentence written in the lore of Pratchett qualifies as well.

There are many combinations of these factors that do not amount to knowledge. These combinations are a justified truth, a true belief, a justified belief, a justification, a belief, and truth. However, unless all three elements are present at the same time, for the same statement, knowledge cannot be claimed.

A justified truth by itself cannot be knowledge. This is because it is not held by any individual, but is merely a free-floating truth. It takes the belief of a person to become knowledge. In addition, knowledge is an attribute of a person, not a concept floating through space and time. Consider Lady Ysabell, Duchess of Sto Helit. When she was a little baby, she did not have knowledge of any commonly held facts. She did not know Rincewind existed, or that he was not actually dead. These two facts were true and justified. However, because she did not have any belief about these facts, she had no knowledge of them either.

An unjustified true belief is not knowledge. This is designed to eliminate lucky guesses and coincidences from the category of knowledge. Scientists and wizards have both calculated the odds of patently absurd events occurring. The scientists say that the odds are millions against, while the wizards say that these events are almost certain to occur. In the event that the wizards happen to be right, it is hard to see how they can claim knowledge. Their luck and guess happened to become true. For this reason, unjustified true beliefs are not knowledge.

A false, justified belief is not knowledge. A lie or falsehood cannot be knowledge. No matter how strong the justification is, it can never meet the standard. If Archchancellor Mustrum Ridcully were to tell a first-year class of wizards the wrong incantation of a spell, there would be no knowledge. It does not matter what the motives of Archchancellor Ridcully are. He could have misspoken; he could have been trying to fool them, or might have been tired. Despite how much the students believe him, the fact that he is wrong,[2] and his statement untrue, makes knowledge of this lesson impossible.

Any of the elements by themselves, a truth, a justification, or a belief, cannot amount to knowledge. All three pieces of the puzzle must be there. That being established, we can know that the Disc is resting on the backs of four elephants. It is knowledge, though not necessarily common, that their names are Berilia, Tubul, Great T'Phon, and Jerakeen. What is not knowledge, at least at this time, is what the universe is expanding into, what Great A'Tuin is thinking, or the origins of the universe.

Begettiering a Problem

In 1963, Edmund L. Gettier published a paper entitled "Is Justified True Belief Knowledge." He wrote the paper in an attempt to satisfy academic publishing requirements enforced on him by the university he was working at. It was a three-page paper that he was very apathetic about. He had a student translate the paper into Spanish, and it was subsequently published in a South American academic journal. Gettier makes a very basic argument in the paper which challenges the definition of knowledge.[3] He shows how accidental, though well-guided justification, can meet the knowledge requirement. But if that justification is accidental, how can it be said that one actually has knowledge?

The argument that Gettier makes is that there are circumstances that will arise where a statement can be made, the

---

[2] I suggest *never* being the student to suggest to him that he made an error, unless one feels like being a pair of smoking shoes and a pointy hat.

[3] I imagine Gettier teaching class and thinking to himself when dealing with snarky students, "I destroyed a 1000-year-old commonly held philosophical belief forwarded by the greatest philosopher ever to have lived in three pages, and I still have to deal with this? . . . Well shit."

statement will be held as a belief, it will be justified and true, but will not be knowledge. This will arise because of little known facts, deception, or improper justification. Imagine that there is a man at the Unseen University. He is not a wizard. However, he tells people that he is a level seven wizard. This man's goal is to fool other people. He carries a fake staff; however it is painstakingly carved to replicate those carried by other level seven wizards. He wears the same clothes, and talks in the same manner as other wizards. To all the level zero and level one wizards, he is undetectable from a true level seven wizard. Sadly, one day the fake wizard is killed. A young wizard sees it happen and goes around telling people that a level seven wizard was killed. It is the talk of the University. However, unbeknownst to the young wizard, another level seven wizard was assassinated so that a level six wizard could take his place. The real wizard that was killed was not known to anyone. He was a hermit, hiding in the Ramtop Mountains. So when the young wizard tells everyone that a level seven wizard was killed, it is in fact a true statement. In fact, it is also a justified statement, since he can give good reasons namely the pointy hat and staff. In this case, a statement such as "a level seven wizard was killed," would be a true, justified belief. However, it is hard to see how such a statement could be categorized as knowledge as the statement is based on deception, and is a mistake of facts.

The statement made by the young wizard was that a level seven wizard was killed. However, it is hard to see how this can be knowledge. The problem is that it fits the classical definition established by Plato. The statement is true. A level seven wizard was killed, although it was not the one the young wizard thought it to be. The statement is justifiable. Everyone thought the fake wizard was real. He put on a really good show. There was nothing to cast doubt that he was not a real wizard. Lastly, the young wizard had the belief.

There the young wizard stood. He had a true, justified belief that was not knowledge.

That's Novel. I'll Soon Fix That

The young wizard is not alone in his concern. Many philosophers have tried to reconcile the argument posed by Gettier with the classical idea of knowledge. Harvard philosopher Robert Nozick, along with Rutgers philosopher Alvin Goldman attempt to repair the damage done by Gettier. The other response primarily used to solve Gettier problem is specificity.

Nozick uses the traditional idea of knowledge, and adds what he calls a truth-tracking function. The truth-tracking function entails that if a proposition or statement is in fact true, then the person would believe it. Conversely, if the statement is false, then the person would not believe it. The goal of Nozick's truth-tracking function is to rule out accidental knowledge. Using the wizard assassination case from earlier, this would mean that if the fake wizard was known to be a fake, and the wizard in the Ramtop Mountains was known to exist, then the statement about the wizard's death would not count as knowledge.

Goldman uses a causation function to dismiss the Gettier cases. The causation function means that the truth of the proposed knowledge causes the person to believe it. The object of the causation function is to rule out accidental knowledge. Imagine that a man is walking next to the River Ankh in the city of Ankh-Morpork. He is bumped by a dwarf. The dwarf and man apologize for walking into each other. Several minutes later, the man sees Reacher Gilt ahead of him on the street. After passing by Reacher Gilt, he pats his pocket and notices that his wallet is missing. The man cries out that someone stole his wallet. The man thinks that Reacher Gilt, the known criminal and conman, stole his wallet. However, unknown to the man, the dwarf that he bumped into was the one who picked his pocket. Is this knowledge? The man had justification to think that the criminal stole his wallet. Why wouldn't he?[4] Suppose Reacher Gilt was just released from prison days earlier. The man's statement was true. Someone did steal his wallet. Lastly, it is clear that he holds the belief. This was witnessed by the emotion in which he cries out while making his claim. Under the traditional paradigm, this would qualify as knowledge. However, the Goldman causation function dismisses this statement as not being knowledge. Had the man

---

[4] That's how you know that Gilt isn't that great a thief. Had it been Moist von Lipwig, you never would have thought to blame him . . . paragon of virtue that he is.

had insight that his wallet was stolen by the dwarf instead of Reacher Gilt, then he would not have claimed the wallet to be stolen by Reacher.

Specificity is when a statement is made more clear and exact. It is the opposite of vagueness, which a Gettier problem thrives on. The difference between specificity and vagueness can be shown with a quick thought. It is after all a bit vague to say, "A level seven wizard died." Which seems to be part of the problem." Imagine the speaker had said, "That wizard was just killed," pointing at the now dead impostor.[5] This would no longer be a case of knowledge, because the corpse is not, and was never, a wizard. Those people surrounding him, and within earshot, would understand what the speaker was referring to. It would be a statement that people understood the meaning of, though it would be a lie. As the statement refers to a non-existent wizard, it could not be true. Therefore, it would be knowledge.

Looking at the second case of the stealing dwarf, specificity again makes the statement not knowledge. It is clear that the speaker intends people to understand that it was not just anyone, but Reacher Gilt who stole his wallet. If he spoke his intentions, there would be no Gettier case, as there would be no claim to knowledge. Reacher did not steal the wallet, so the truth condition is not met.

There's the Rub

The problem is, of course, that although those two ideas help, they don't solve the problem. In the case of truth tracking, how does one actually "track truth?" We start having to say things like, "Well if I had known . . ." But that sounds like a common knowledge problem we have anyway. The problem is really a matter of good justification. Are we saying that the only way we can have knowledge is if our justification is one that cannot lead to a false conclusion? If so, how do we know when that is the case? How can we tell when we have a "truth tracking justification" or one that just "seems to track truth?"

Similarly, does specificity actually make the Gettier problem go away? What about a case in which Reacher Gilt does steal my

---

[5] SERIOUSLY, MY JOB WOULD BE MUCH EASIER IF YOU ALL COULD BE KIND ENOUGH TO WEAR NAME TAGS.

wallet, but my justification is mistaken. I assume he stole my wallet because he bumps into me. But what if he had stolen it an hour earlier when I was buying a sausage inna bun? I would be correct when I said "Reacher Gilt stole my wallet." But the specificity requirement would require that I say, "I don't know he stole my wallet" because my justification would be wrong—"He bumped into me." But it is true that he stole my wallet!

So, what we realize is this, maybe our world doesn't have much more knowledge than Discworld. In fact, perhaps the occupants of Discworld are a little closer to knowledge than we are. After all, we think that we know lots of stuff . . . but the inhabitants of Discworld are a bit more flexible to how wrong they can be because weird stuff happens there all the time. Maybe the fact that they aren't quite as certain as we are makes it easier for them to let go of false "knowledge" while our round world often takes centuries to let go of bad ideas like slavery, the Earth as center of the universe, sexism,[6] and fanny packs.

---

[6] Let's be honest, that one is still going strong. Heck, even the dwarfs of Discworld seem more open to the idea that women and men are equal than we are. But then again, we don't have Granny Weatherwax around to remind us how *very* foolish "isms" are.

17
Sin, My Young Man, Is When You Treat People as Things

KAMIL KARAŚ

It is human nature that we ask questions. Some of them are easy to answer, some are not, and some need to be based on something more powerful than mere human being, like one divinity or another. Without a proper god you can't even make an honest living these days. That's why people believe in gods—or God—be it Yahweh, Allah, Currency, the New World Order, the Flying Spaghetti Monster, Quetzalcoatl, or Anoia. And because gods tend to be pushy (all those commandments of "don't do this, do that, smite the unbeliever, eat ramen, tear their living hearts from their chests") and like showing their followers what pleases them and what doesn't, people invented a word which, after some time, became extremely popular. Actually, even the non-believers, atheists or agnostics use the word a lot. This word is "sin." The concept of sin seems to permeate all known universes, the one we live in and the Discworld included.

Sin

The term has made a great career. "It's a sin to miss such an occasion," they say. "It would be a sin to let her go away," they say. Well, sometimes they are right, sometimes they aren't. Funny how well it fits in the speech of people who declare themselves free from the chains of religion. The fact that the word "sin" is readily used even by the staunchest atheists shows that there are different senses of the word.

So, what is sin? There are several answers to this question—from Samuel Beckett's (1906–1989) "the only sin is the sin of being born" and Martha Graham's (1894–1991) "the only sin is mediocrity," to Dean Koontz's (born 1945) "in self-defense and in defense of the innocent, cowardice is the only sin" to the simply profound answer given by Granny Weatherwax "Sin . . . is when you treat people like things." Each of them, it seems, covers different areas of human thought. However, we can find yet another approach to the question—the religious one.

"A wound in man's inmost self. In the light of faith we call it sin: beginning with original sin, which all of us bear from birth as an inheritance from our first parents, to the sin which each one of us commits when we abuse our own freedom," we read in St. Pope John Paul II's (1920–2005) *Reconciliation and Penance*. What he calls a sin is breaking the covenant between God and men. Having started with the original sin in the Garden of Eden, it continues as a constant part of people's lives. It's a willful act which severs the connection between God and man. In other words, sin happens when the following cause-effect relationship is fulfilled: god → commandment → transgression of the commandment → sin.

We can definitely speak about sin in connection with the Discworld. Yes, but now you will say—How come? There is no God there! Oh, well, actually there are a lot of gods, both great big fishes and small ones. Each of them tries to get as many believers as they can to secure their power base. In a world where the divine power depends on the quality of faith—vide the case of Om, where the whole country claimed to believe in their almighty god and yet the one in question could function only as a small and rather irritated tortoise—all this because of the quality of faith. This happens when you believe rather in red-hot-rod-pushing (they did not invent pens right then) bureaucrats known as the Quisition of the Church of Om.

It is very interesting, because, although most of the gods (with the exception of Nuggan and Om) don't give commandments, they are very eager to express their extreme dissatisfaction with any disbeliever they meet. On the Disc, the gods have "a habit of going round to atheists' houses and smashing their windows" and are "not so much worshipped as blamed" (*The Color of Magic*). Being an atheist in Ankh-Morpork gives you an anticipated lifespan of a lone Ku Klux Klan member in the middle of Bronx in the dead of night. The only character able to discuss atheism with the gods is Dorfl the golem, a thunderboltproof creature of clay. So, does discussion of sin in a world with so many gods make sense?

Well, first of all, the creatures described by the author on the Disc are, without doubt, of (mostly) human(ish) nature, but even those who are not technically human act like it in a way we can understand. What's more, they don't stand and only passively observe their own world—many of them actually comment on what sin is. Probably the most important and acknowledged moral thinkers on the Disc are Lord Patrician Havelock Vetinari and Esmerelda Weatherwax, a witch better known as Granny Weatherwax.

Lord Vetinari, the Patrician of Ankh-Morpork, has his own opinion on sin and evil, which he doesn't hesitate to present to his Captain of Watch, Samuel Vimes, in *Guards! Guards!* To his mind, people are only bad—there really aren't good and bad people fighting, but, simply, evil men—often on opposite sides. For him, the sin is clearly a sum of all low deeds, of not saying "No" to evil. It's really hard not to notice that Lord Vetinari expresses a very cynical and negative opinion of the people he rules. It is also easy to understand, that, for the Patrician, sin is simply not saying no to evil—this being very close to eighteenth-century philosopher Edmund Burke's (1729–1797) "the only thing necessary for the triumph of evil is for good men to do nothing." What is also noticeable, is that Captain Vimes tries to defend the people of Ankh-Morpork from Vetinari's harsh cynism, but Vimes lacks ideas of how to do so: Vimes knows Vetinari is right.

Esmerelda Weatherwax is an extremely powerful, but also deeply moral, witch. She also has her own vision of people and sin. As she says to Mightily Oats, a young, Omnian priest who tried to justify his religion to her, "sin, young man, is when you treat people as things. Including yourself. That's what sin is. . . . People as things, that's where it starts." Oats tries to reply, "Oh, I'm sure there are worse crimes." But Weatherwax points out, "But they starts with thinking about people as things" (Pratchett, *Carpe Jugulum*, 313–14). Oats, here, utters a loud (though only spiritual and not verbal) cry—a desperate cry of a person trying to understand difficult matters, like why the world isn't the way theology describes it. His mentor, Granny Weatherwax, proves to be a genius philosopher/theologian, showing the right way in short, concise words. She is also a deeply empathic person who, as a witch, unceasingly struggles to help people in life.

Looking Inward

The letter to Romans in the Bible tells us that even the unbelievers, the Gentiles, have their own law in their hearts (2:14–15). It seems like many of us believe that there is a voice inside us telling us right and wrong. This voice is an emanation of the so-called natural law, which tells us "perform good, avoid evil." It's called conscience, intuition, however you may call it—it's important that it can be found and functions in such a way we can be sure that we are bad men (or women). In other words, that we are sinners. And yes, even the non-human characters on the Disc, like dwarfs or trolls, have their own natural law which tells them what is good and what is evil. Similarly, people tend to be religious and get their own gods.

But can all that be rational? Well, yes, according to novelist, literary scholar, and popular theologian C.S. Lewis (1898–1963). He has wondered and written about the topic of the natural law functioning within humankind. He was able rationally to categorize and name what has always been inside every human being. In his paper called *The Moral Law Is from God*, he refers to a certain set of rules (a standard of behavior) that, Lewis claims, all people share and know about. This law, called the Law of (Human) Nature is one every person has inborn and doesn't need to be taught—but can always choose whether he or she wants to obey it or not. In this the law is different from the rest of laws of Nature, like gravity or laws of physics—for they cannot be disobeyed.

People all around the world realize this Law in an almost unchanged way. Of course, they may have certain differences—like, say, who we can lie to, or who deserves to be treated selfishly—but in general, says Lewis, the norms of behavior are strikingly similar through the ages. If we compare several cultures, like the ancient Chinese, Greeks, or citizens of the Roman Empire, the similarities become evident. This fact alone should raise suspicions about the possibility of the existence of a certain moral matrix from which humankind was once created. Another factor standing for the already mentioned suspicions is that the Law is reciprocal—it works both ways. You can break your word given to me and it's simply okay with you—but if I break my promise to you, you will complain about suffering unfairness from my side. Such bilateralness is evidence of universality of the Law.

Someone would say that the evidence I just mentioned is nothing other than the effect of cultural upbringing—in other words, that the natural law is simply a product of culture, a human invention. Lewis says that nowadays people take for granted the possibility of learning something from their parents. This is as true in my time as it was in his. However, children learn two kinds of truths in their lives—things that are real, unchangeable truths (like mathematics or physics) and, using Lewis's phrase, "mere conventions" (like the side of the road we drive on, fashion, the colors of flag etc.[1]). The former are quite similar within humankind (despite the differences which will naturally occur due to the uniqueness of every single person) and we can separate a single, model rule out of it. The latter may differ severely among people—in some countries pink may be fashionable and in other countries wearing pink may be punished with prison, etc.

Of course, some changes must be applied to certain laws in the course of the progress of humankind. Lewis claims that if it weren't for those changes, we people would never have changed for the better—and changes for the better are necessary for morality to develop wisely. It is a well-known fact that some moralities are better than others—Lewis gives a good example of the Nazi morality compared to the Christian one. And the very fact that we actually compare moral values shows that there must be a standard, a model, against which different versions are put. Certainly, Pratchett appeals to that law throughout Discworld, reminding us constantly that treating others, whether trolls, dwarfs, or even goblins as things just doesn't feel right. This standard is what we would call Natural Law—higher than any human-invented restriction.

One more thing—if such a Law actually exists, who or what created it? Lewis claims there are at least two possible answers. The first is the materialist one. It means that everything happened to exist out of sheer luck, by chance or

---

[1] Though sometimes fashion can be contentious as in the case of Ankh-Morpork dwarfs who want to wear chainmail dresses.

because of an incomprehensible whim of the universe.[2] Those who believe in this version say that the law is just a by-product of the self-creation of everything—there was no aim and nobody knows why the law exists. The other option is the religious one. The advocates of this answer say that there is something standing behind the creation and that something is conscious, with a certain reason—a mind struggling to create beings in his favor. That "something" is completely undiscoverable by the means of science. However, it created people and made them capable of observing not only their external world, but also their internal selves—I mean what they feel and how they perceive themselves. Being a person, says Lewis, makes me or you able to observe and realize that each and every one of us remains under the moral law, which we did not create, we cannot forget even if we tried, and which we may obey or disobey at our pleasure. The fact that each of us has that shared knowledge of sin, thinks Lewis, is evidence that something made humanity with a shared moral intuition.

Lewis asks if there is a chance of determining whether the world exists on a whim and without aim, or there is a mastermind plan behind it. His answer is accurate—we cannot observe such a mastermind in any way other than in ourselves, for the creating power surely would not reveal itself in different, observable fragments of reality—such power itself would be the entire reality. As people, we possess an ability to conclude the wholeness from fragments. Each of us is such a fragment. Thus, if even one human finds in him- or herself a law that tells him or her wrong from right, we could conclude it must be repeatable, it must happen in different people, too—and that there must be Someone or Something that gave us both the law and the ability to recognize it. Since we cannot give such powers to ourselves, and the only other thing we know that exists is matter (and Lewis finds it unimaginable for a piece of matter to give anything or anyone powers or even instructions), the only power that could do this to us must be God.[3]

---

[2] A "cosmic sneeze," if you will.

[3] Note, additionally, that such thinking also provides the added benefit of reducing the need for lightning-resistant underwear.

The Wages of Sin (Are Pretty High)

According to the Roman Catholic faith, sins are broadly divided into two kinds—mortal and venial. St. John Paul II says in *Reconciliation* that for Doctor of Church like St. Thomas mortal sin is the sin which certainly leads to eternal punishment in Hell; whereas venial sin is the sin that is punished with a punishment much shorter and possible to serve while alive or after death in purgatory. All those (or at least a huge part of them) who are Christian learn from the very beginning (from 1 Corinthians 6:8–9) that "know ye not that the unrighteous shall not inherit the kingdom of God? Be not deceived: neither fornicators, nor idolaters, nor adulterers, nor effeminate, nor abusers of themselves with mankind, nor thieves, nor covetous, nor drunkards, nor revilers, nor extortioners, shall inherit the kingdom of God." Truly, there's nothing as ingrained in human nature, as sin.

"The wages of sin is death," says the Bible, "but so is the salary of virtue, and at least the evil get to go home early on Fridays," adds Terry Pratchett in *Witches Abroad* (176). This is so true, especially in a world where the main proof for the existence of gods is lightning aimed straight at the sinner. But wait a moment—can we ever speak about the "wages of sin" on the Disc? Pratchett doesn't give us direct examples of a god repaying someone for bad deeds (we just need to remember that actually not believing in gods is not a very evil deed)—one of the very rare cases is the moment Dorfl is struck by thunder after declaring the Gods do not exist. Also, you can find a dispute among the most powerful priests in Ankh-Morpork, ending with a divine attack on Hughnon Ridcully, the Chief Priest of Blind Io. The bolt doesn't strike the target because Io, being the more powerful deity, protects his servant. But Pratchett does appeal to our shared moral intuition, and in doing this he makes Lewis's point.

For example, in *Witches Abroad*, Granny Weatherwax, Nanny Ogg, and Magrat Garlick meet a magically changed wolf and they realize it has been cruelly violated and made to behave like a human—only that they who did it left the wolf with the animal instincts. So the animal is trying to talk, walk on two legs, and is clearly mad and dying from hunger since its human nature prevents it from feeding in its natural way.

Someone must have played with the creature using magic. However, those who cast the spell making the wolf think it was a human being, did not perform the act correctly. The animal's hind legs are barely strong enough to let the wolf walk on them and its paws are completely unprepared technically for catching anything or preparing food. Also, the wolf's larynx and trachea are not suitable for human speech, which the enchanted wolf tries to imitate. Even worse, the animal's brain is changed in such a way that it demands its owner (the wolf) behave like a human—which, in the unchanged lupine form, clearly is torture for the animal. Since Granny says there is no help for the animal, the wolf chooses to die by the hand of a woodcutter. At the moment of death the creature is more human than animal. It is sentient enough to ask for death, to be freed from the pain.[4] Granny honors the wolf with a human-like funeral, instead of skinning and discarding the meat and bones.

The scene comments on at least two notions. First of all, experimenting on animals and people—when they are in charge of the doctors/researchers of all kinds, who want to experiment on a living specimen and never worry about the consequences. Consider, for example, Nazi "doctors" like Josef Mengele or his fellow torturers from the "medical facilities" of the concentration camps during WW II. They performed absolutely cruel and ruthless experiments (like sewing glass into wounds, amputating limbs, and injecting pregnant female inmates with toxic substances), very often killing the objects of their research, in order to (as they claimed) develop medical science.

Another thing Sir Terry is possibly commenting on here is the difference between our treatment of terminally ill animals and humans. People easily decide to kill an animal to "shorten its pain," even if it can be cured—but are reluctant to let an incurably ill person die (or to let a person in a coma be unplugged from the medical equipment) on his or her own accord. This is all much more important if we remember that Pratchett himself was an advocate of "assisted death." What he fought for was to give people certain rights—to finish their own lives when their pain became unbearable or their existence would be a nuisance for their families. What he is using to

[4] INTERESTING. GENERALLY I VIEW SENTIENCE AS BEGGING FOR MORE LIFE.

make his case, though, isn't a commandment so much as moral intuition. We see the plight of the wolf, and we seem to share a sense of its wrongness. That shared intuition of right and wrong, even when applied to fantastically imaginary situations on Discworld is Lewis's point. If we have a shared feeling of wrongness at the plight of a fantasy wolf in a world populated by walking luggage and nice Orcs, then maybe Lewis has a point, maybe we do have shared moral intuitions.

Killing Us Softly

What Granny so boldly defines as "treating people as things" (and what for Lord Vetinari is "not saying no to evil") is nothing more than a "social sin"—a sin which, committed by one man, stays in society and develops into something more, what St. John Paul II calls "the structures of sin." In *Sollicitudo Rei Socialis* he claims that those "structures" "are rooted in personal sin, and thus always linked to the concrete acts of individuals who introduce these structures, consolidate them and make them difficult to remove. And thus they grow stronger, spread, and become the source of other sins, and so influence people's behavior." The once-committed sin goes around and creates structures, which, in fact, have a tremendous impact on our lives.

There's no need to deny it—the Disc is an extremely dangerous place to live on. Natural and preternatural cataclysms (like invasion from the Dungeon Dimensions), the hardships of rural life, or adventuring can all shorten your life. You can die or get dead on the Disc in many ways—especially if you come to a city like Ankh-Morpork. There are places there, like the Shadows, where they will kill you for what you wear and an 'orrible and bloody murder happens so often the event becomes something common.[5] But that's not what I'm looking for. That's simply a violent way of living, illegal and frowned upon by the Watch. There is something much more interesting in the higher spheres of society. If you happen to be rich, or at least earn a certain sum of money per annum, you can get killed in a stylish and sometimes surprisingly expensive and

[5] But as the citizens of Ankh-Morpork will tell you, always an event worth taking the time to watch while eating a sausage inna bun.

inventive manner by one of the gentlemen of the Assassins' Guild.

Founded by Sir Gyles de Munforte as the *de Munforte School for Gentlemen Assassins*, the organization soon evolved into a Guild and became a pillar of society. They were given certain rights, namely they could kill whomever they wanted, as long as they paid taxes to the city. As they created their own rules of conduct, the Assassins' Guild decided not to kill without a huge sum of money (as shown in their motto—*nil mortifi sine lucre*—'no killing without payment'). Additionally, only people earning more than twenty thousand Ankh-Morpork Dollars per year could be inhumed (as the Assassins call it), since if you earn that much, you can at least hire bodyguards—meaning that you are able to defend yourself. Codified to the top, the way the Assassin acted during his mission gave his or her "client" (or simply, the future victim) a chance to defend him- or herself. So if you had a lot of money and knew how they worked, you could be pretty safe from the Guild's agents.

There are many famous Assassins on the Disc. From the Patrician Lord Vetinari, through Teppic (the protagonist of the *Pyramids*) to Mr. Jonathan Teatime (the unlamented psycho from the *Hogfather*), the (almost) unstoppable Gentlemen and (after a few years) Ladies of the Guild act as executioners for the rich. From their beginnings they have killed many nobles, even the rulers of Ankh-Morpork—for example, young Havelock Vetinari inhumed, or rather spooked to death, Lord Winder the Patrician. Found in *Night Watch*, it's probably the best described inhumation in the whole Discworld series. An Assassin comes into the ballroom through doors guarded by two Palace Guards, kills them skillfully with dual pistol crossbows, and then turns his attention to Lord Winder. The Patrician freezes, unable to react. He is completely shocked, for the way the Assassin behaves breaks every rule of conduct provided for an inhumation of a noble.[6] He can only utter a short cry—a question about the Assassin's identity—but his nemesis does not answer and, instead, raises his sword as if to hit. However, before he is able to strike his victim, Lord Winder dies because of suffocation—he chokes on the cake he's eating. Then, the Assassin says "boo" and leaves the place. The corpse

6 But let's be honest, we wouldn't have our Havelock any other way . . .

of the late and unlamented Patrician stays in the ballroom, cooling slowly.

Fantasy aside, the abhorrence people have of murder isn't just a taught religious thing; atheists also feel the inner and innate prohibition concerning killing another human being. The inviolability of another person's body is probably the oldest and one of the most deeply ingrained rights. The sin the Assassins commit is more terrible because it is sanctified by contract and city-state laws. Killing people, even if sanctioned by city laws, is one of the most terrible sins. It is dangerous to feel that human life can be priced, dangerous to treat people as things. However, before we condemn Discworld for that, we should remember that the Assassins' Guild is probably an ironic reflection of the existence of sanctioned killing in the world we live in as in the case of war and "collateral damage."

There are many examples of structural sin—ones of the worst kind in the Discworld series books. Taken from this angle, the Discworld seems to be a place steeped with hatred and lack of respect for one's neighbor's life and property, a place where the structures of sin already created the culture of evil in the fullest. But this should not be something strange to the reader. All in all, the Discworld is an almost perfect reflection of our own reality, with every single absurdity and evil taken sometimes quite literally.

V

Probably Quantum

18
Fate on the Discworld and Roundworld

JEREMY PIERCE

The sweeper worked his way from one end of the room to the other, making sure he got every scrap that wasn't supposed to be there. As his day wore on, he was looking forward to completing the daily chores and curling up with the philosophical tome he had been working his way through, but it was not meant to be. He detected something around him that wasn't quite right, and he turned around to see what had changed.

LU-TZE, the skeletal figure intoned.

The sweeper immediately knew who it was. "Is it time for this already? I've messed with time so much that I've lost track of how much time I have left."

I HAVE NOT COME FOR YOU,[1] said Death. I SEEK CONVERSATION.

"Why would one of the anthropomorphic forces of the Discworld want to discuss anything with a lowly sweeper?"

WE BOTH KNOW THAT YOU ARE ONE OF THE WISEST AND MOST POWERFUL AMONG THE HISTORY MONKS, EVEN THOUGH YOU PRETEND NOT TO BE ONE OF THEM.

"Technically, I'm not one of them. They pay me to sweep the floors. Most of them don't even know my name, and that suits me fine."

THEY KNOW YOUR NAME. THEY JUST DO NOT KNOW THAT IT IS YOURS. THEY KNOW WHAT LU-TZE IS CAPABLE OF. THEY JUST DO NOT KNOW THAT YOU ARE LU-TZE. BUT YOU DODGE THE ISSUE. YOU HAVE A LEVEL OF UNDERSTANDING I COULD NORMALLY ONLY FIND AMONG THOSE I WOULD RATHER AVOID.

---

[1] YET.

"You mean the Auditors of the Universe?" Death shuddered both at the mention of their name and the reminder of their attempts to meddle.[2] "I don't blame you for wanting to avoid them," Lu-Tze continued. "They did try to wipe you from existence once, and they create a whole lot of work for both of us every time they involve themselves."

I WAS THINKING MORE OF THOSE BEINGS WHO CALL THEMSELVES THE GODS, WHO ARE CONSTANTLY PLAYING GAMES. YOU KNOW HOW OFTEN FATE CHEATS, FOR EXAMPLE. DO YOU KNOW THAT HE HAS ADMITTED TO USING LOADED DICE? THEY ALWAYS TURN UP 7. DOESN'T HE KNOW THAT YOU CAN'T CHEAT DEATH? DO YOU REMEMBER THE FAILED WIZARD WHO COULDN'T WORK ANY MAGIC BECAUSE OF THAT SPELL IN HIS HEAD? FATE HAD THE GALL TO COMMAND ME TO TAKE HIS SOUL JUST BECAUSE THE LADY LIKED USING HIM AS A PAWN.

"Yes, I remember Rincewind. He's created some temporal problems that needed to be sorted out, so the History Monks have had to keep an eye on him. His time-traveling once shorted out some Procrastinators at the temple. Well, I guess I'm not getting back to my book, so what did you want to talk about?"

FATE, ACTUALLY.

"What about him?"

NOT THE GOD NAMED FATE. I MEAN THE THING HE TAKES HIS NAME FROM.

"Don't say that around him. I hear he likes people to think that it's named after him."

HE IS NOT TO BE CONFUSED WITH ANYTHING THAT MIGHT RIGHTLY BE CALLED FATE. YOU KNOW FULL WELL THAT PEOPLE CAN ALTER THEIR FATE. REMEMBER THAT 500-YEAR WAR THAT YOU REPLACED WITH A PERIOD OF LASTING PEACE? HE COULDN'T STOP YOU.

"Not in that case, no. I hate to remind you of that apprentice you took a while back, though. What was his name, again?"

MORT. THAT WOULD HAVE BEEN EMBARRASSING IF I WERE NOT ME, BUT I DID GET A GRANDDAUGHTER OUT OF IT.

"I'm sure I don't need to remind you of the reason he stopped being your apprentice. He tried to change someone's

---

[2] Which is an impressive thing to see on someone who is all bones.

fate, and it created an alternative timeline within the bubble of influence that his interference created, but it eventually bounced back."

MOSTLY.

"Yes, mostly. But that means the attempt to change fate didn't really work."

ARE YOU ABOUT TO LECTURE ME ON NARRATIVE CAUSALITY?

"You know we don't use that term among the History Monks. But the Disc is rich in narrativium.[3] Some stories just have to be told, and some patterns just have to be realized."

THAT IS ONE KIND OF FATE.

"And it's demonstrably present throughout the history of the Disc. Whenever something is a one in a million chance, it's nearly guaranteed to happen, especially if the hero actually says it's a one in a million chance."

YES, ALTHOUGH THE LADY CLAIMS TO BE THAT MILLION TO ONE CHANCE.

"And there are all sorts of story types that the narrativium ensures will be fulfilled."

IT IS TRUE THAT CERTAIN STORY TYPES ARE BOUND TO MANIFEST THEMSELVES WHENEVER THE RIGHT DETAILS ARE IN PLACE. YOU DO KNOW THAT SOMETIMES THAT'S BECAUSE WITCHES ARE MEDDLING, THOUGH, RIGHT? I'M SURE YOU REMEMBER THE TIME THOSE WITCHES IN LANCRE INSISTED THAT THE RIGHTFUL PRINCE BE THE ONE TO OVERTHROW THE DUKE, SO THEY STOPPED TIME FOR FIFTEEN YEARS TO ALLOW THEM TO SKIP TO THE BOY'S COMING OF AGE.

"That one certainly took some sorting out. I acknowledge that in that case they sought to help things out, but I have to wonder if their meddling is what made it turn out that the story wasn't properly fulfilled."

---

[3] Narrativium, according to the science of Discworld, is the most common element on the Disc. It is responsible for narrative causality, that quality of Discworld that ensures that, as stories require, that heroes escape the vile clutches of villains when it is impossible, that if you run into a disheveled young woman with really mean step-sisters be nice to her because she will become queen of something, somewhere, and that if you put an even number of socks in the wash, you will have an odd number when you pull them out.*) (*Although there is no narrativium on Roundworld, for some reason the damn socks rule still holds . . . Proving that some things are more powerful than the elemental forces binding the universe together and those things are really obnoxious. It probably has something to do with lawyers.)

OF COURSE IT WASN'T PROPERLY FULFILLED. NEITHER BROTHER WAS THE RIGHTFUL KING. BOTH BROTHERS WERE SONS OF THE FOOL. PEOPLE ONLY ASSUMED THEY WERE BOTH SONS OF THE KING, BECAUSE THEY KNEW THEY HAD THE SAME FATHER. THE WITCHES JUST LEFT OUT THE CRUCIAL DETAIL ABOUT WHO THE FATHER REALLY WAS, AND EVERYONE ASSUMED THEY WERE BOTH SONS OF THE KING. IT HAD NO CHANCE OF BEING FULFILLED.

"But it would have fit the narrative better if the one believed to be the long-lost heir had gotten the throne. Instead, the fool became the king."

YOU KNOW THAT THEY GOT A BETTER KING AS A RESULT.

"Yes, but was that because of fate or because the witches intervened?"

WHY CAN'T BOTH BE TRUE? WHY CAN'T FATE WORK THROUGH THE ACTIVITIES OF THE WITCHES? ARE THEIR CHOICES LESS RATED THAN ANYONE ELSE'S? AT ANY RATE, THAT'S NOT THE KIND OF FATE I MEANT TO DISCUSS WITH YOU. HAVE YOU BECOME ACQUAINTED WITH THE ROUNDWORLD PROJECT AT UNSEEN UNIVERSITY?

"I know of it."[4]

I HAVE HAD THE OCCASION TO VISIT ROUNDWORLD AND LEARN OF ITS UNUSUAL PROPERTIES. DID YOU KNOW THAT THERE IS NO NARRATIVIUM THERE? ALSO, TIME MOVES AT THE SAME RATE EVERYWHERE, EVEN WHEN PEOPLE SEEM TO BE EXPERIENCING TIME AT DIFFERENT RATES. WELL, I SUPPOSE IT CHANGES WHEN YOU APPROACH THE SPEED OF LIGHT, BUT THERE'S NOTHING LIKE THE POCKETS OF TIME HERE MOVING AT DIFFERENT RATES.

"There would be no need for the History Monks there, then."

IT IS A WORLD THAT SIMPLY OBEYS LAWS OF CAUSALITY.

"They have no stories? That sounds rather dull."

THEY HAVE STORIES. THERE JUST IS NO NARRATIVIUM, SO THE STORIES DO NOT MAKE THEMSELVES HAPPEN. A MILLION TO ONE CHANCE REALLY ONLY HAPPENS ONE TIME OUT OF A MILLION.

"That would be different."

WHEN THE ROUNDWORLD PHILOSOPHERS SPEAK OF FATE, THEY DO NOT MEAN A BEING LIKE THE ONE WHO LIVES AT CORI CELESTI. THEY ALSO DO NOT MEAN NARRATIVE CAUSALITY.

"Do you mean determinism? Do they all think their laws of causality will determine everything that happens from the

---

[4] He really didn't.

moment of Roundworld's creation onward? Some Überwaldian philosopher named Vonmausberger said something like that, right?"[5]

I BELIEVE THE ENTIRE BONK SCHOOL OF ÜBERWALD HAD SOMETHING LIKE THAT IN MIND. SOME OF THE ROUNDWORLD PHILOSOPHERS WOULD AGREE WITH THE VIEW. SOME OF THEM WOULD NOT.

"The thesis is obviously false for our world because of the narrativium, except perhaps for golems with those instruction cards they have to follow that are implanted inside their clay heads, but it must be a live option for them. Do you know enough to know if their world really is like that?"

KNOW THAT SOME OF THEIR BEST PHYSICISTS BELIEVE THERE TO BE RANDOM EVENTS THAT HAVE NO EXPLANATION.

"Well, that would make the deterministic thesis hard to believe."

INDEED. BUT A ROUNDWORLD PHILOSOPHER NAMED EPICURUS (341–270 BCE) ONCE PUT FORWARD A THEORY EXPLAINING FREE WILL IN TERMS OF SUCH RANDOM EVENTS. HE WAS AN ATOMIST. HE THOUGHT EVERYTHING WAS MADE UP OF INDIVISIBLE ATOMS THAT NORMALLY JUST OBEYED THE LAWS OF NATURE, BUT UNLIKE EVERY OTHER ATOMIST HE WANTED TO AVOID DETERMINISM.

"Why does he have all those numbers and letters following his name?"

WHO?

"Epicurus (341–270 BCE)."

HIS NAME IS EPICURUS. THE NUMBERS AND LETTERS ARE HIS ROUNDWORLD LIFESPAN IN ROUNDWORLD YEARS. MY VISIT TO ROUNDWORLD SEEMS TO HAVE LED TO MY ABSORBING THEIR CONVENTIONS OF LISTING DATES WITH AUTHORS' NAMES THE FIRST TIME I MENTION THEM.[6]

"That's going to get annoying. So it doesn't sound like Epicurus was making it easy for himself when it comes to free will, if he's got to fit it to a deterministic set of laws of nature."

---

[5] As is the case with most madmen in Überwald, it was really Igor who did all the work. But imagine how hard it would be to teach that history course . . . So Igor developed an idea further developed by Igor, whose results, much later on were put to practical use by Igor, but only really understood recently because of the writing of Igor . . . * (*A less well known fact is that really most of the work is done by an Igorina, but sexism is rampant everywhere.)

[6] Proving that even Death is subject to bureaucracy . . . again, lawyers. . .

NO, BUT HE DID AVOID THE PROBLEM BY POSTULATING A SWERVING ATOM. EVERY ONCE IN A WHILE, AN ATOM WOULD SWERVE OUT OF ITS PATH AND DO SOMETHING UNCAUSED. THESE APPARENTLY WERE SUPPOSED TO COINCIDE WITH FREE CHOICES.

"I'm not sure that will work, though. If their choices are caused by random events, how are they responsible for them? Wouldn't random occurrences be just as outside their control as the determinist causes would be?"

THAT WAS HOW EPICURUS'S TWO MAIN OPPONENTS RESPONDED. TWO GROUPS, THE STOICS AND THE SKEPTICS, WERE CONSTANTLY CHALLENGING EPICURUS AND HIS FOLLOWING.

"You know, these names sound a bit familiar to me. Didn't Didactlyos of Ephebe list these schools as influences on him?"

DIDACTYLOS CLAIMED TO BE INFLUENCED BY GROUPS CALLED CYNICS, STOICS, AND EPICUREANS, YES. BUT THE DISCWORLD EQUIVALENTS OF THESE GROUPS WERE DIFFERENT.

"How so?"

THEY ARE MORE HUMOROUS, BECAUSE OF THE INFLUENCE OF NARRATIVIUM IN OUR WORLD. THEY ALSO HAVE FAR LESS-DEVELOPED VIEWS, MOSTLY BECAUSE IT HAS BETTER COMIC EFFECT IF YOU DON'T HAVE TO WADE THROUGH TOMES OF PHILOSOPHICAL TEXT TO UNDERSTAND THEM AND CAN JUST SKIP TO THE HILARIOUS THINGS THESE PEOPLE DID. REMEMBER DIDACTYLOS'S SUMMARY OF THOSE VIEWS AS HE COMBINED THEM.

"I was just reading that, in fact. 'You can't trust a bugger any more than you can throw him, and there's nothing you can do about it, so let's have a drink. ' I assume the Roundworld philosophers are less funny, then?"

LESS INTENTIONALLY FUNNY, AT LEAST.

"Ah. So back to the topic. So how did Roundworld Epicurus's opponents respond to him, then?"

THE STOICS, PROBABLY BEST REPRESENTED BY CHRYSIPPUS (279–206 BCE), PREFERRED TO THINK OF FREEDOM AS COMPATIBLE WITH BEING PREDETERMINED. THEY TOOK THE EPICUREAN VIEW AS INCAPABLE OF EXPLAINING HOW SOMEONE'S CHOICES CAN COME FROM THEIR OWN BELIEFS, DESIRES, AND MORAL CHARACTER. THEY PREFERRED TO SAY THAT THEIR CHOICES WERE CAUSED BY THOSE THINGS, SINCE THAT WOULD MEAN THOSE THINGS LIE BEHIND THEIR CHOICES. AN EPICUREAN WOULD HAVE TO SAY THAT NOTHING CAUSED THEIR FREE CHOICES, AND THE STOICS FOUND THAT TO BE A FAIRLY UNSATISFYING APPROACH.

"But how did they explain that being predetermined is compatible with being free? Wouldn't it still be true that their choices are entirely caused by things that are completely out of their control? If the state of the world at a time before they were even born basically caused them to make all the choices they make, how could they possibly be in control? They have no control over the state of the world at that time, and they have no control over the laws of nature. So how do they have control over their current choices that are caused by such things?"

AH, BUT THE STOICS DID NOT EXPECT TO CONTROL ALL THE CAUSES OF THEIR ACTIONS, JUST THE MOST IMMEDIATE ONES. IF YOUR BELIEFS, DESIRES, EMOTIONS, AND THOUGHTS ARE THE IMMEDIATE CAUSE OF YOUR ACTIONS, THEN YOU STAND BEHIND YOUR CHOICES IN A WAY THAT YOU DO NOT STAND BEHIND OTHER EVENTS THAT OCCUR. THIS IS SO EVEN IF YOU DO NOT STAND BEHIND THE MORE DISTANT CAUSES OF YOUR ACTIONS.

"I guess that does feel more like it comes from me than anything like a random occurrence in my brain would."

THAT IS THE IDEA.

"But this shouldn't be all that satisfying for someone who wants to avoid determinism. If these were the only options, I assume an anti-determinist would just throw up their hands and say that we must not be free."

THAT IS NOT WHAT THEY IN FACT DID, HOWEVER. IN A STRANGE TWIST OF FATE, THE SCHOOL OF THOUGHT KNOWN AS THE SKEPTICS PROVIDED A THIRD APPROACH.

"The Skeptics? People who didn't trust anything? They sound like the sort of people who would spend their time arguing against everything. They don't sound like they would make any effort to try to find better versions of theories that they like but that had failed. How did they end up rescuing Epicurus from the Stoic arguments?"

THESE SKEPTICS PRIDED THEMSELVES ON RESISTING VIEWS, YES. SOME OF THEM SEEM TO HAVE GOTTEN A KICK OUT OF SAYING THEY DID NOT BELIEVE ANYTHING. BUT THE PARTICULAR SKEPTIC I HAVE IN MIND WAS NAMED CARNEADES (214–129 BCE). UNFORTUNATELY, MOST OF THEIR INFORMATION ABOUT HIM HAS BEEN LOST TO TIME, AND THEY HAVE NO HISTORY MONKS TO INVESTIGATE THINGS PROPERLY. BUT FORTUNATELY A SKEPTICALLY-MINDED THINKER NAMED CICERO (107–44 BCE) HAS PRESERVED SOME COMMENTS ON CARNEADES'S APPROACH. IT IS FORTUNATE FOR ROUNDWORLD THAT

CICERO WAS OUSTED FROM HIS SEAT IN THE SENATE OF ROME, ONE OF THE GREATEST EMPIRES THEIR WORLD HAD SEEN TO THAT DAY, BECAUSE IN HIS DAYS OF EXILE HE SPENT HIS LATTER DAYS COMMENTING ON PHILOSOPHY.

"He was a politician, then? Are you sure we can trust him? Are politicians in Roundworld any better than the Discworld ones?"[7]

HARDLY. BUT CICERO IS ONE OF THE BEST SOURCES ROUNDWORLD HAS FOR SOME OF THE UNPRESERVED WRITINGS OF THE EPICUREANS, STOICS, AND SKEPTICS.

"Wait, you said the Skeptics prided themselves on not having beliefs. How could Carneades defend an approach at all?"

IT IS NOT CLEAR THAT HE BELIEVED THE APPROACH TO BE TRUE. PERHAPS HE JUST INDICATED IT AS AN OPTION. THE SKEPTICS LIKED TO HOLD OUR MULTIPLE OPTIONS AND THEN SAY THAT THEY COULDN'T KNOW WHICH WAS TRUE. THAT'S HARD TO DO IF YOU THINK EPICURUS'S OPTION IS NOT VIABLE.

"Ah, I see. So they wanted another option so they wouldn't have to take a stand, and Carneades came up with it?"

THAT IS POSSIBLE. BUT IT MIGHT JUST BE THAT CARNEADES WAS NOT AS RADICAL AS SOME OTHERS WHO TOOK THE NAME OF SKEPTIC. MAYBE HE WAS WILLING TO HAVE VIEWS BUT WAS ESPECIALLY SUSPICIOUS OF VIEWS THAT WERE PRESENTED TO HIM, AND HE SPENT MOST OF HIS TIME ARGUING AGAINST OTHERS. THIS CERTAINLY WAS IN THE CONTEXT OF ARGUING AGAINST BOTH THE EPICUREANS AND STOICS.

"But did he actually put it forward as a view?"

UNCLEAR. CICERO PRESENTS HIM AS DOING SO.

"The politician. Right. Maybe we should be more skeptical of Cicero. So what was this view, anyway? I suppose I don't care as much about who believed what as I do about what the views are and whether they make any sense."

CARNEADES CALLED IT A VOLUNTARY MOTION OF THE MIND.

"How is that different from the swerving atom?"

THE SWERVING ATOM HAS NO CAUSE. THIS HAS A CAUSE.

"If it has a cause, how is it different from determinism?"

DETERMINISM HAS PRIOR EVENTS CAUSING THINGS. THE CAUSE OF THIS IS THE PERSON THEMSELVES.

---

[7] It seems a silly question, but hope springs eternal . . . and dies in the winter of reality.

"Wait, I thought I had a good handle on how non-narrative laws of causality are supposed to work. One set of events causes another set of events. Stuff that happens in my brain can cause further things in my brain, eventually causing me to do various things. What is Carneades proposing that goes beyond that?"

HE IS NOT PROPOSING EVENTS IN SOMEONE'S BRAIN AS THE CAUSE. THE PERSON IS THE CAUSE. THE PERSON IS NOT THE COLLECTION OF EVENTS IN THE BRAIN BUT SOMETHING ABOVE AND BEYOND THE BRAIN.

"Is this about souls? Did your journey there involve any soul-reaping? I have no idea how they work in Roundworld."

NOR DO I. I WAS THERE ONLY AS AN OBSERVER. BUT SOME INVOKE THAT NOTION TO EXPLAIN WHAT CARNEADES IS GETTING AT. OTHERS DO NOT. THE IDEA IS THAT YOU ARE MORE THAN THE SUM OF THE EVENTS THAT TAKE PLACE WITHIN YOU. YOU ARE MORE THAN YOUR BELIEFS, DESIRES, EMOTIONS, THOUGHTS, AND SO ON. WHETHER THAT IS A NON-PHYSICAL SOUL MIGHT BE A SEPARATE QUESTION.[8]

"Well, it does seem like this avoids both the unwelcome Epicurean view that someone's choices are a result of random chance and the full-blown determinism of the Stoics. You can still say that every event has a cause, even. It's just that some causes are events, which have further causes themselves, while other causes are simply people, who are not themselves caused to cause it."

BUT IT DOES RAISE A QUESTION: YOU ARE NOT CAUSED TO CAUSE YOUR CHOICE, BUT YOUR CHOICE IS STILL CAUSED BY YOU. YOU CAUSE YOUR CHOICE. IS YOUR CAUSING OF THE CHOICE CAUSED? IF SO, THAT SEEMS TO LEAD TO DETERMINISM. IF NOT, IT SEEMS TO LEAD TO EPICURUS.

"How does Carneades resolve that?"

CICERO DOES NOT TELL US OF THAT.

"I was beginning to like that view, too. I suppose he could just say *that* there is no such event as the causing of his choice."

THAT SOUNDS RATHER DESPERATE, THOUGH.

"I'm going to have to think about this more. You've given me a task that has caught my interest. There's got to be a way to make this view work. Where did you end up on the question?"

I RATHER LIKE THE STOIC APPROACH MYSELF.

---

[8] To which Death knows the answer, but refuses to share, the bastard.

"Ah. That would explain why you were insisting on fate working through the witches' free choices. You really think their choices would be free if fate were behind things? It didn't occur to me to apply this to our own case. I was so absorbed in how this affects Roundworld that I didn't realize the same issues apply to us. If narrative causality or gods calling themselves Fate and the Lady are constantly manipulating our destinies, I suppose the same questions arise."

SOMETIMES CONSIDERING THE ISSUES IN A CONTEXT REMOVED FROM OUR OWN HELPS CLARIFY THINGS IN A WAY THAT LOOKING AT OUR OWN WORLD MAY NOT. THAT IS WHY I READ FICTION.

"I suppose so. But it makes me wonder. If the gods have worked out a plan for how things are going to go, doesn't that threaten freedom in a different way? I mean, I spent all my time messing with time, and sometimes it's to ensure that a predetermined future will happen. It's not predetermined by causes, but it's predetermined by narrative causality, gods, and the History Monks. Or me, since I'm technically not a History Monk."

YOU ARE BOTHERED BY THE NOTION THAT SOMEONE MIGHT KNOW AHEAD OF TIME WHAT YOU WILL DO? IT HAS NEVER BOTHERED ME. I HAVE THE BOOKS OF PEOPLE'S LIVES, ALONG WITH THE LIFETIMERS THAT CONTAIN THEIR ALLOTTED TIME.

"Right, but you bend the rules. I know about that wizard you've got stashed away. His lifetimer would have run out centuries back if you hadn't pulled him out of time and made him your servant. Oh, the stuff we had to do to adjust for that!"

I DO NOT NORMALLY BEND THE RULES. HE IS A RARE EXCEPTION. MOST PEOPLE'S LIVES ARE LAID OUT IN FRONT OF THEM TO BE LIVED IN A WAY THAT IS FOREORDAINED.[9]

"But this isn't the same as that Roundworld determinism we were talking about. There's no worry about laws of nature guaranteeing what will happen here. Narrative causality won't allow that, and we've got all these gods playing dice with people's lives."

AND CHEATING.[10]

"Yes, and cheating. So it doesn't seem like the threat here is determinism. It's something else."

---

[9] If Death seems flustered at being caught bending the rules, he isn't. Death does what he wants (as long as the Auditors don't find out).

[10] Death holds a grudge.

I HAVE ALREADY REGISTERED THAT I AM COMFORTABLE WITH DETERMINISM.

"But this is a different issue. This seems to be an issue about time itself. If the future is already settled, then there's nothing I can do to change it, right? That creates a problem even apart from determinism."

THE ROUNDWORLD PHILOSOPHERS DISCUSSED THIS AS WELL.

"I imagine the Epicureans didn't like the idea."

NO, THEY DID NOT. THEY PROPOSED THAT THE GODS THEY BELIEVED IN COULD NOT KNOW THE FUTURE, OR ELSE NO ONE WOULD BE FREE.

"And did the Stoics have a response? You do seem to like them."

THEY HAVE GOOD THOUGHTS ON MANY ISSUES. THEY SUGGEST AVOIDING EMOTIONS. I CAN ATTTEST TO THE DISASTROUS OUTCOMES THAT RESULT WHEN I GET TOO EMOTIONAL. MUSIC WITH ROCKS IN, FOR INSTANCE.

"Hey, back to the issue. What did they say about gods knowing the future?"

THE STOICS BELIEVED IN ONE DIVINE BEING ABOVE ALL OTHERS. THEY IN FACT BELIEVED ROUNDWORLD ITSELF TO BE A GOD.

"What, the sphere they lived on? Didn't they know it was just a rock?"

NO, I MEAN THE ENTIRE POCKET UNIVERSE THAT THE ROUNDWORLD ROCK OCCUPIES. THEY SAW THEIR ENTIRE UNIVERSE AS AN INTELLIGENT DEITY WHO HAD PLANS FOR THE DIRECTION OF ITS OWN DEVELOPMENT.

"Something like narrative causality? I thought they didn't have any narrativium."

THEY DO NOT. BUT MANY PEOPLE IN ROUNDWORLD HAVE BELIEVED IN A DIVINE CREATOR WHO CAUSED THE VERY EXISTENCE OF THEIR UNIVERSE.

"Wasn't it really created by that Ponder Stibbons fellow and the other wizards as way of siphoning off energy when they first split the thaum?"

THEY HAVE NO AWARENESS OF ITS ACTUAL CAUSE. THEY HAVE TAKEN THEIR WORLD TO BE GUIDED ALONG BY AN INTELLIGENT AND CARING DEITY WHO INTENDS THINGS TO WORK OUT IN THE END. UNLIKE NARRATIVIUM, IT HAS A MIND BEHIND IT. NARRATIVIUM JUST WORKS TO FULFILL ITS PURPOSES WITHOUT BEING CONSCIOUS.

"But the Stoics are taking a different approach, it seems. They see the universe itself as intelligent and developing itself according to its purposes?"

THAT IS THE IDEA. IT WOULD EXPLAIN WHY ROUNDWORLD BEHAVES IN SUCH ODD WAYS. THE UNSEEN UNIVERSITY WIZARDS HAVE NOT HAD MUCH SUCCESS IN FIGURING IT OUT. IF IT IS INTELLIGENT AND CARRIES OUT ITS OWN HIDDEN PURPOSES . . .

"Yes, I get the idea. So how does this solve the foreknowledge problem? Doesn't it just make it worse? The Stoics were determinists. If their divine universe is directing itself toward certain ends, why does that somehow allow for people to be free?"

THE STOIC VIEW IS COMPATIBILIST ABOUT FREEDOM AND DETERMINISM. THEY ALREADY HAVE AN ACCOUNT OF HOW THAT WORKS.

"Right, but how does it help with this question?"

IF FREEDOM IS COMPATIBLE WITH BEING PREDETERMINED BY UNCONSCIOUS CHOICES, WHY IS IT NOT COMPATIBLE WITH BEING PREDETERMINED BY CONSCIOUS CHOICES?

"Ah. So they just apply their compatibilism about freedom and determinism here. If the divine universe has purposes for how it will develop as a universe, and I have my own purposes for what I do, both can coexist and be free choices."

THAT IS THE IDEA.

"Hmm. I'm not happy with either approach. I don't like Stoic determinism, but I'm not happy with the Epicurean idea that truth about the future means I'm not free. Did Carneades, by any chance, happen to have a mediating view on this issue as well?"

INDEED HE DID. PERHAPS NARRATIVE CAUSALITY DOES HAPPEN SOMETIMES ON ROUNDWORLD.

"Or maybe he's just following his own tendencies to seek out mediating views as options."

YES, THERE IS THAT.

"So what did he say?"

HE DISTINGUISHED BETWEEN CAUSATION AND TRUTH. CAUSATION INVOLVES BEING CAUSED BY PRIOR EVENTS. TRUTH SIMPLY MEANS THE THING WILL HAPPEN. IT MIGHT NOT BE CAUSED BY PRIOR EVENTS.

"Okay, but isn't it still guaranteed to happen? It may not be caused by prior events, but the problem is that it's set in stone. We don't mind the past being set in stone, because it's already happened, but if the future is set in stone, doesn't that threaten our freedom? It seems as if its mere truth is the problem."

YOU OF ALL PEOPLE SHOULD SEE THE PROBLEM WITH THAT LINE OF REASONING. HAVEN'T YOU IN FACT CHANGED THE PAST?

"I try to maintain the timeline. That Sam Vimes fellow in Ankh-Morpork once ended up in his own past, with the prospects of the whole timeline being changed. I steered him to take on the role of his former mentor, who had just been killed by the murderer Vimes had been chasing before the time-storm took them back. My efforts prevented the timeline from being altered too much."[11]

YES, BUT YOU HAVE BEEN KNOWN TO MEDDLE. MUST I REMIND YOU AGAIN OF THE 500-YEAR WAR THAT YOU REPLACED WITH A LENGTHY PEACE?

"Okay, I admit to meddling on occasion. How is that relevant?"

IF THE PAST IS NOT SETTLED AND CAN BE CHANGED, THEN IT IS NOT DIFFERENT FROM THE FUTURE. AND YOU ARE HAPPY TO SPEAK OF THE PAST WITH STATEMENTS YOU CONSIDER TO BE TRUE. IS THERE TRUTH ABOUT THE PAST? IS TRUTH ABOUT THE FUTURE ANY DIFFERENT FROM TRUTH ABOUT THE PAST?

"You know it isn't always like that. Dios the high priest in Djelibeybi traveled back in time and became the very origin of the city and high priestly system that had led to his going back in time. And that Rincewind fellow turned out to be the origin of all life when he tossed his sandwich away in prehistoric times."

IT DOESN'T MATTER IF ALL CASES OF TIME TRAVEL ARE LIKE THIS. ALL WE NEED IS SOME. AND YOU HAVE CHANGED THE PAST.

All right, but now we're talking about something that isn't settled, and I'm interested in the view that the future is settled, so maybe we should avoid our world entirely, since even the past isn't settled here. Let's switch back to Roundworld, since they don't have any time-traveling or changing of the past."

FINE. IN ROUNDWORLD, THERE IS TRUTH ABOUT THE PAST, CORRECT?

"Of course."

IS THE FUTURE ANY DIFFERENT FROM THE PAST?

"You tell me. I have no idea what the rules are there. Didn't you just say it's a fixed timeline, without any ability to change the past?"

THAT'S RIGHT. IN FACT, THEIR BEST PHYSICS CONSIDERS SPACETIME TO BE ONE ENTITY. TIME IS NOT A THING IN ITSELF BUT A CONSTRUCT

---

[11] Another rule of narrative causality . . . sucks to be a mentor.

OF PEOPLE'S EXPERIENCE. SPACETIME IS THE GENUINE ENTITY, AND THAT INVOLVES ALL EVENTS IN SPACE AND TIME LAID OUT IN ONE ARRAY, WITH EVERY POINT IN SPACETIME BEING EQUALLY REAL.

"Hmmmmm. The History Monks have shown that our time is unreal as well, but that's because only the present is real."

THAT APPROACH WOULD NOT FIT WELL WITH THE SPACETIME OF ROUNDWORLD. THERE IS NOT EVEN A COHERENT NOTION OF SIMULTANEITY THAT FITS WITH THEIR PHYSICS. SOMETHING IS ONLY SIMULTANEOUS WITHIN A FRAME OF REFERENCE. AS I SAID, TIME IS A CONSTRUCT. ALL THE POINTS IN SPACETIME ARE EQUALLY REAL.

"But doesn't that mean all the events in spacetime are equally real? How is that supposed to help with the foreknowledge problem? And haven't we gotten a bit off track from Carneades?"

ACTUALLY, NO. CARNEADES SAYS THAT THE FUTURE IS LIKE THE PAST IN THAT THERE ARE TRUE STATEMENTS ABOUT BOTH THE PAST AND FUTURE. WITHOUT THE ASSUMPTION OF THE FUTURE BEING CAUSED BY THE PRESENT, CARNEADES IS COMFORTABLE RECOGNIZING THAT THERE ARE TRUTHS ABOUT THE FUTURE, BUT THEY MIGHT NOT ALL BE CAUSED BY WHAT'S HAPPENING NOW.

"How are these truths true without being unchangeable? Wouldn't that mean there isn't any possibility of things going in a different direction from the one they will go in?"

CARNEADES DISTINGUISHES BETWEEN TRUTH AND NECESSITY. SOMETHING CAN BE TRUE WITHOUT BEING NECESSARY. SUPPOSE THE PAST IS FIXED, AS IT IS IN ROUNDWORLD. THAT MEANS ALL OF CARNEADES'S CHOICES ARE NO LONGER CHANGEABLE, SINCE THEY ARE NOW IN THE PAST. BUT THAT DOESN'T MEAN HE DIDN'T HAVE REAL CHOICES AT THE TIME HE MADE THEM. SO IT IS FALSE TO SAY THAT HIS CHOICES ARE NECESSARY. THEY DID NOT HAVE TO BE THE WAY THEY WERE. BUT THEY WERE THE WAY THEY WERE. THERE IS A TRUTH TO THEM BUT NOT ANY NECESSITY.

"Okay, that makes sense for the past, but what about the future?"

IF SOMETHING CAN BE TRUE WITHOUT BEING NECESSARY, THEN THE SAME CAN APPLY TO THE FUTURE. IF THE PAST CAN BE TRUE WITHOUT BEING NECESSARY, THEN SO CAN THE FUTURE. ROUNDWORLD OCCUPANTS MANY NOT KNOW WHAT THE FUTURE WILL BRING, BUT THERE CAN BE TRUTHS ABOUT THE FUTURE WITHOUT THE FUTURE BEING NECESSARY.

"But how can that be? If it's true now, what's going to make it be true? Doesn't determinism have to be true for the future to be guaranteed?"

THAT IS MISSING THE POINT. HE DOES NOT SAY THAT IT IS GUARANTEED IN THAT SENSE. IT IS NOT NECESSARY. IT IS JUST TRUE.

"But what makes it true? If there's something now that makes it true, it seems as if we're back to determinism."

YES, BUT THAT IS NOT WHAT HE SAYS. THERE IS NOT ANYTHING NOW THAT MAKES IT TRUE. WHAT MAKES IT TRUE IS WHAT HAPPENS IN THE FUTURE.

"I see my problem. I'm reading our own world's condition into Roundworld. In our world, only the present is real, so the only way to guarantee the future is with determinism or fate of some other kind. But there might be truth about the Roundworld future in the existing future. Or, rather, in the points of spacetime that are future to us as we experience time."

EXACTLY. I SHOULD POINT OUT THAT IN OUR WORLD, WHERE ONLY THE PRESENT IS REAL, THE PAST IS ALSO NOT FIXED, AS YOU WELL KNOW. THAT MAKES IT MORE DIFFICULT FOR THERE TO BE TRUTHS ABOUT THE PAST.

"Yes, I've taken advantage of that, as you well know. It does seem as if Roundworld's unusual properties can explain how there can be truth about the future without it being predetermined or fixed in a problematic way. So truth about the future isn't a problem after all, for them at least. Is this enough to solve their foreknowledge problem, then?"

REMEMBER THAT THE STOICS DID NOT NEED IT SOLVED. THEIR COMPATIBILISM ABOUT FREEDOM AND DETERMINISM LEAVES THEM WITH NO SUCH PROBLEM. SOMEONE COULD KNOW THE ENTIRE HISTORY OF THE WORLD WELL INTO THE FUTURE WITHOUT THREATENING THE KIND OF FREEDOM THAT THE STOICS BELIEVED IN.

"But what about the freedom that the Epicureans and Carneades favored?"

SOME OF THEIR PHILOSOPHERS DID NOT THINK CARNEADES'S SOLUTION ALLOWED FOR THE FOREKNOWLEDGE, CICERO DID NOT, FOR EXAMPLE. HE DID NOT THINK A DVINE BEING COULD KNOW THE FUTURE WITHOUT DETERMINISM BEING TRUE.

"Why not?"

HOW WOULD A BEING LIKE OFFLER THE CROCODILE GOD KNOW WHAT YOU ARE GOING TO DO TOMORROW? DOES HE PREDICT BASED

ON YOUR CURRENT STATE AND THE LAWS OF NATURE? THAT WOULD ONLY WORK IF DETERMINISM IS TRUE.

"I see. But didn't you say some of the Roundworld philosophers believed in a divine being who created the entire universe? Wouldn't such a being exist outside this spacetime thing you were talking about?"

THAT WAS A COMMON VIEW. A PHILOSOPHER NAMED AUGUSTINE (354–430) SEEMS TO BE THE ONE WHO INTRODUCED IT, BUT HE DIDN'T CONNECT IT TO THE FOREKNOWLEDGE ISSUE. HE INSTEAD SOUGHT TO EXPLAIN GOD'S KNOWLEDGE OF PEOPLE'S CHOICES IN TERMS OF PREDICTING WHAT THEY WILL DO FROM THEIR CURRENT DESIRES.

"So he was like the Stoic determinists, then?"

NO, HE EXPLICITYLY REJECTED THAT VIEW. HE DISTINGUISHED BETWEEN BEING CAUSED TO DO SOMETHING AND DOING SOMETHING BECAUSE YOU DESIRE AN OUTCOME. HE SAW THE FIRST KIND OF EXPLANATION AS A CAUSE THAT PUSHES YOU TOWARD SOMETHING ELSE AND THE SECOND AS A GOAL THAT ATTRACTS YOU TOWARD IT. HE DID NOT LIKE THE IDEA OF FREE CHOICES STEMMING FROM CAUSES OF THE FIRST SORT. HE PREFERRED TO SEE CHOICES AS EXPLAINED BY OUR BEING ATTRACTED TO SOMETHING.

"That distinction makes sense, but the second kind avoids determinism by not guaranteeing the future, right? If I have various things attracting me, and I can choose any of them, then how does God know which one I'll go for?"

AUGUSTINE THOUGHT PEOPLE WOULD ALWAYS CHOOSE THE THING THEY MOST DESIRE. GOD CAN SEE WHICH THINGS PEOPLE DESIRE AND HOW MUCH THEY DESIRE THEM, SO GOD CAN PREDICT WHICH CHOICE PEOPLE WILL MAKE. BUT CHOICES DO NOT CAUSE IN A DETERMINISTIC WAY, SINCE THEY DO NOT PUSH PEOPLE TO DO THINGS. THEY JUST ALWAYS DO IN FACT DO THE THING THEY MOST WANT. SO IT IS PREDICTABLE WITHOUT CAUSING IN THE BAD WAY.

"You know, maybe I've found a model of freedom that I like even more than the one Carneades presented. I knew if I kept thinking about it I'd hit on something better."

YOU DID NOT HIT ON IT. I PRESENTED IT TO YOU.[12]

"Yeah, yeah. Details. So you said Augustine didn't think of applying his view of God as outside the entire universe to the foreknowledge problem. Did anyone later on think to do that?"

---

[12] There are philosopher Stoics, and then just stoics . . . Death apparently is one of the latter.

INDEED. AN AUGUSTINIAN THINKER NAMED BOETHIUS (480–524) DID. HE USED AUGUSTINE'S VIEW AS A WAY TO THINK OF GOD AS HAVING ACCESS TO EVERY MOMENT IN TIME, ALL AT ONCE, SO TO SPEAK.

"So if God has access to what's future to Boethius, then God can see what will happen to Boethius, all without there being any deterministic order to cause, from what was true in Boethius's own time, everything that would later happen. I see how this is going to go."

IT DOES SOLVE THE PROBLEM OF HOW GOD WOUD KNOW THE FUTURE WITHOUT DETERMINISM BEING TRUE.

"You know, I need to get ahold of some of these Roundworld philosophers' books. This has been a fascinating discussion."

THANK YOU FOR BEING MY SOUNDING BOARD. I CAN'T IMAGINE THIS GOING WELL IF I HAD APPROACHED OM OR BLIND IO FOR A CONVERSATION OF THIS NATURE.

"No, but if you ever find me unavailable, there's always Bilious, the god of hangovers!"[13]

I WILL KEEP HIM IN MIND.[14]

And with that, Death mounted his horse Binky and rode off to wherever his next appointment was, leaving Lu-Tze pleased that fate had led Death to him to have that conversation, which promptly led him to wonder if he should really be attributing such things to fate after all or even wondering which sense of fate he must have had in mind when he thought that.

---

[13] Philosophical conversations are a lot like a long night of drinking . . . Loud, headache-inducing, and you never know who you are going to either (a) hit with a chair or (b) wake up with in the morning.

[14] Death doesn't have a sense of humor.

19
The Alchemy of Flat Worlds

CHRISTOPHER KETCHAM

It's an ancient classroom theater—you know the type with wooden desks bolted to the floor on cement risers that soar like a Greek amphitheater. And way down front before a wall of dusty green chalkboards next to an aging oak lectern is a diminutive looking professor, bespectacled, wearing a black robe and a billowing chartreuse bow tie. The students at these desks squirm and chatter and their desks creak and groan.

"Settle down, settle down," rumbles the professor and he turns to the blackboard and writes in great white letters . . . Prof. Moby Dickens Melville, Phy. 433, Philosophy of Worlds (which he underlines with a flourish) and places the chalk on the lectern. The class settles down a bit, but the quietude is punctuated by a book falling off a desk. Blam!

Professor MDM (what the student body calls him . . . such is the influence of texting these days) looks up towards the risers and sees that there are perhaps the same number of wizards as Flatlanders in the class. It appears that the diversification efforts of the university have born some fruit, though he thought such an effort would fail.

Faithful narrator here. We are now seeing two worlds, Flatland and Discworld. These are two very different kinds of "flat worlds." In a flat world like Flatland there are only two dimensions. By that, we mean there is only length and width . . . no height! So if you were to turn Flatland completely on its side, we would not be able to see it at all, because it wouldn't have any height at all. Think of it like a piece of paper. You can see it easily like this . . .

But as you turn it it gets thinner and thinner . . .

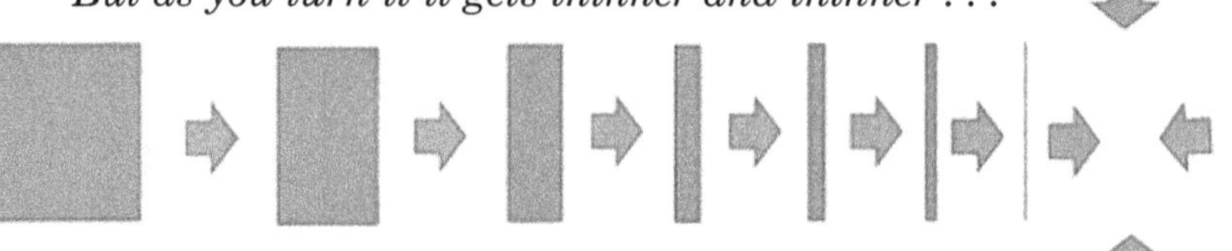

Just like a sheet of paper would as you turn it towards its edge. But in a true two-dimensional world, when it was perfectly on the edge, it would appear to completely disappear because of the complete lack of height.

However, in a flat world like Discworld there are three possible dimensions and there are questions that need answering! And, thus, the Discworld / Flatland "Transformational Learning Adventure began."[1] *Would a Flatlander pop (like explode) in a three-dimensional world? Would a Discworlder (wizard) capable of three dimensions deflate on a two-dimensional Flatland, squishing organs into unusable mush? It only makes sense that to increase diversity, concessions had to be made and that was to create an unseen university that can accommodate both types of flat worlds. And yes, think of this, Unseen University (UU) can now accommodate round worlders too! Sorry, Congress has not approved loan legislation for UU so you will need a rich uncle to pay your tuition. But think about it, isn't UU true diversity in the making?*

MDM is still unsure about all of this . . . in UU he can see, but his mind does not yet see how he will communicate with these alternate-world beings. He is also concerned how these students will be able to reconcile their differences, their significant differences in how Flatlanders and Discworld wizards live their lives, their cultures, and their dimensional orientation.

---

[1] Like at all universities, this kind of jargon basically just means that the school is going to pay a bunch of money to develop some new program, tell students that they are going to get some sort of "Life-changing experience only offered by our institution," charge students more tuition, and get bored with it two to five years later when the next shiny initiative comes along.

And it was with some trepidation the professor recalls that he listed Physics 433 in this year's catalog because it requires that he navigate between the two known flat worlds: the wizards' Discworld I (See Pratchett, Stewart, and Cohen, *The Science of Discworld*) and the Flatlandian Flatland (see Abbott, *Flatland*). While UU may have opened the floodgates to diversity the old prejudices still loom large on the respective worlds and his trepidation is that these have been solidified in student minds. He looks up and down the risers. The wizards (all have faces)—they look eager. He cannot tell with the Flatlanders. For he sees nothing but thin straight or curved lines lying flat on their chairs. He cannot discern any kind of emotion or expression in their faces, if they have faces.[2]

MDM looks up and down the risers again. The semester is new; nothing untoward is yet brewing—that he can see anyway. (And MDM, like all professors at UU, possesses no clairvoyant or magical ability. These abilities are simply left at the college gate when they become professors.)

First Lesson (Phy. 433 Philosophy of Worlds)

Perhaps I, your faithful narrator, should explain more about the differences between wizards of Discworld and Flatlanders of Flatland. Wizards, as we are all familiar, live on Discworld, which is a round disc held up by elephants that stand upon a turtle's back, and magic is worth thinking about and experiencing here.

On Flatland there is no sun, moon or stars, so there are no shadows. But there is direction: north, south, east, and west. Adult Flatlanders are about twelve inches long; women are always straight lines. Men vary by their place in society: soldiers and workmen are triangles with two equal sides, middle class are equilateral triangles, professional men are square, nobles

---

[2] Narrator again. Rather than developing some form of projection device to show Flatlanders in more than two dimensions, UU, in its infinite wisdom, determined that such an act might produce in the Flatlanders a feeling of inferiority or suggest that they are all handicapped, leading to campus riots or worse. Learn to live with diversity, management said.

are hexagons or objects with ever greater number of sides, and priests are circles. Priests rule. The son (except for soldiers and workmen) will have one more dimension than the father so there is a kind of progressive male reincarnation at work, at least in the higher classes. Women are never more than lines, and end on they become invisible to the eye whereas triangles and the more complex geometric beings . . . men . . . never disappear. And there are laws against women disappearing. Irregularly shaped Flatlanders such as a triangle with one curved side, are destroyed or given menial tasks and are not permitted to marry. Everything in Flatland is measured, calculated, and evaluated. Only the most mathematical are tolerated, and the most perfect form, the circle is the highest possibility for existence.

On Flatland, the world is flat, two-dimensional, without a third but the society is highly ordered. If we round worlders lay a coin on the table and look down we see a circle. Now, make yourself small, smaller than the height of the coin lying flat and jump on the table and look at the coin edge on. What do you see? Try it. Go on, get a coin and look at it edge on. You see a line, don't you? Letters, as in writing, without a third dimension require some transformation, but laid on its side each letter produces a distinctive line which Flatlanders can easily understand. Geometry to Flatlanders is as important as magic is to Discworlders. Oh, yes, Flatlanders can hear quite well, which makes a lecture preferable to say, a slide show. What it all really comes down to is perspective . . .

The professor begins . . . "Each of you should at least be familiar with the two discrete perspectives . . . the 3D on Discworld and the 2D of Flatland have radically different views on what philosophy means."

MDM sees blank stares from wizards . . . and knows not what from Flatlanders though he can hear sighs. He writes the two philosophical approaches on the board, places the chalk back on the lectern, and then continues.

"As you well know, the thinkers of Discworld complain that the mathematicians of Flatland ignore the existential in favor of derivative logic, hypotenuses, and parallelograms that Discworld philosophers dismiss as superficiality. On the other hand, the mathematicians of Flatland claim that the philosophers of Discworld have but fuzzy logic in their narrativium, thaums,[3] and other such neologisms which Flatlanders describe as impenetrable obscurantism."[4] He pauses, looking for head nods . . . well on the wizards, and the wiggle of Flatlanders. Nothing.

MDM pauses for another moment. He says, "Think of the two approaches this way. If I told you a story with demons and damsels in distress and plant things that fizzle when they talk in order to explain how my society works, well that would be something like the Discworld approach. I would appeal to your emotions and ask you to see with me how relationships form and things happen. If I were to explain things like a Flatlander, I would show how the town is laid out like a wagon wheel with each street a spoke. I would construct the hierarchy of government and explain the taxation scheme and voting process to give you an idea of how order is maintained in society. And . . ."

"Professor," a question in a Flatlander's high-pitched voice. (*Faithful narrator here. Yes, the vocal pitch of Flatlanders is higher in most cases. However, we must refrain from stereotyping because some Flatlanders have deeper voices, but this is rare.*)

"Yes," said the professor.

"I've heard that some think that we're just all stiffs, geometry geeks who can't have any fun. Well we do—have fun, that is—in figuring out things. We don't just sit around dreaming and using big fancy words in long sentences that seem to go everywhere and nowhere at once like some I know do . . ." said the Flatlander. And other Flatlanders wiggle in agreement. But the wizards are groaning. Bad sign, thinks MDM and takes over the discussion. "Please, quiet down. Let's all be charitable here. Each way of looking at the world has its own reason for doing so. In this class we will explore how and why. Now it is not my place as a professor at UU to favor one flat world philosophical approach over another. What I will do is to play out their differences for you, as

---

[3] *Thaum* is the basic unit of magic made up of resons and flavors. (The round world equivalent might be a particle with quarks, bosons, and others of the standard model.) *Narrativium* is an element, the element that makes up the story, the fiction, if you will. (The round world equivalent . . . sadly missing except if one could classify its parallel as imagination and the withholding of disbelief—but already that's *two* things.)

[4] If you have no idea of what the rest of that stuff meant, that's okay, the professor probably doesn't either.

budding young philosophers on separate worlds, so that you can continue to debate their merits and demerits as you begin your long careers. So, in our second lesson, I will lay out the differences between the two philosophical camps in terms of the different approaches to being—to existing, to seeing and understanding things in the two respective worlds.

While you may presume to know all about the flat world other than your own, I have discovered that students are, by-and-large, sorely mistaken about even some of the simplest ways of seeing the world from the other's perspective. So, for those who think you know it all, know that you do not." A pause and the professor looks down his nose. "Readings in preparation for the next class are from Abbot's *Flatland: A Romance of Many Dimensions*, perhaps the pivotal philosophical text that established philosophy on Flatland, and Pratchett, Stewart, and Cohen's *The Science of Discworld*, which has been hailed as the quintessential explanation of Discworldian thought." Or simply how one gets on in a world of two dimensions as told to round worlders. I think you all will find it both informative and humorous because we all know that round worlders simply cannot fathom what a flat world could be like. That imposing third dimension of theirs clouds their thinking. They have forgotten how to look at things side on for subtle differences. They have lost the ability to finesse." MDM chuckles. But then MDM pauses because he has just realized that his critique of round worlders is out of place. God forbid, they too could be in next semester's class. Just how do you teach a round worlder common manners like look before you sit?

Hands go up and the professor deals with the inevitable grading questions, paper length, number of citations per paper, how one might earn an A in class, . . . and of course, "Do we ever get out early?"

Second Lesson (Phy. 433 Philosophy of Worlds)

Just after Old Tom's last silent chime of ten on campus, the professor begins. "We left off last time recording the differences of the two flat worlds' "phenomenology"[5] or the process

---

[5] Why does every professor in every world feel the need to make quotations marks in the air?* (*AS IF QUOTATIONS MAKE SOMETHING LESS INTIMIDATING.

of observation, of seeing things and each other in either world. Today we explore their respective concepts of how their worlds actually work, and as you might expect each of the two worlds also has a different approach to the fundamentals of physics. Flatlanders favor *string theory* and Discworlders favor *loop quantum gravity* as the way to tie the theories of Einstein and quantum mechanics together. From their perspective Flatlanders feel a kinship with the idea of strings as one-dimensional objects that have different vibration characteristics, each of which can produce a different particle.

Discworlders, on the other hand, favor telling the story of loop quantum gravity first because, like Einstein they are enamored with storytelling, and, second; the minuscule but discrete *quantum* of loop quantum gravity and *spin networks* are as mysterious as their thaum. And in loop quantum gravity there is no big bang singularity, just going back, and back, and back, one step at a time . . . perhaps into time before the great A'Tuin." Students are scribbling, wiggling, and scratching their heads. No wizard head is yet spinning, but that is a possibility.

Faithful narrator here again. Don't think because you have not completed your doctorate in theoretical physics that you can't understand this. It is simply a question of orientation to the world. If you were a flat line or other two-dimensional geometric form, what theory would you lean towards? Strings, of course. You may be right or wrong, but it does seem to fit your Flatland world. On the other hand, if you are a wizard, geometry is just too difficult. It's stiff even though some lines are curved. You like the idea of supernatural things and potions and impossibilities like something being both a wave and a particle at the same time because it makes sense . . . that is from the point of view of a wizard.

"Professor," a youthful looking wizard exclaims. Professor MDM pauses and looks up at the wizard. "Professor, does this mean that we can have two completely different theories of physics because each of the worlds is different functionally?"

Professor MDM nods, "That certainly is one of the possibilities, Mr. Tinklebottom. If Discworlders and Flatlanders cannot reconcile their differences in philosophy, perhaps there is no basis for reconciliation in flat world physics either.

PERHAPS HUMANS WOULD BE LESS BOTHERED IF I INTRODUCED MYSELF AS "DEATH." NO. PROBABLY NOT.)

Closes his lecture notebook. "In preparation for next week, continue reading in your texts."

Third Lesson (Phy. 433 Philosophy of Worlds)

This week Professor MDM caresses a very tall paper cup filled with coffee. He looks disheveled. He fiddles aimlessly with the chalk he had placed on the lectern in the first class. Speculation from the last row of seats high up in the classroom is that he is a bit hung over. But he starts on time.

"From physics last week we turn to theology this week. A quantum leap for many because quite a few physicists have trouble with the idea of God. God simply has no place in physicists' calculations. But enough of that. We know that different ways of perceiving the world produce different ways of describing the world. Why should theology be any different? In fact theology is different on both worlds. And this time I begin with Discworld.

"The Discworld theological critique begins with science. I quote Pratchett, 'Science has produced a very strange view of the universe. It thinks that the universe runs on *rules*. Rules that never get broken. Rules that leave little room for the whims of gods' (Pratchett, Stewart, and Cohen, ch. 4). And so, why not simply create those whims whether you believe there is but one god, many gods, or none whatsoever. Take the device called Hex, which Pratchett said, 'was mostly self-designed which was why it worked better than most things in the university' (Pratchett, Stewart, and Cohen, ch. 7). Hex is a thing made up of things both living and not. Permitted to function on its own, Hex creates what it calls a universe which is insulated from our own by a glass dome surrounded by spells. Its appearance is remarked as, and I paraphrase, 'the instability of nothing desperately trying to be something' (Pratchett, Stewart, and Cohen, ch. 7). And so these UU wizards (my esteemed colleagues) ponder whether a god created this universe (should it actually exist), while the Dean himself wonders whether *he* has become a god.[6] Such is the conundrum of magic because it blurs the lines of creation. That magic on its own could be a force

[6] Perhaps in size and scope only.

equal to a god is the mystery of all mysteries. And the academics (the Dean, Archchancellor, Mustrum Ridicully, Ponder Stibbons, the lecturer in recent runes, Senior Wrangler and others) notice that the Hex-created universe begins to imitate their own (Pratchett, Stewart, and Cohen, ch. 7).

"Has it crossed the line, from a universe made from gods to one made from magic or is that just like what any universe would *do*, simply follow the path of least resistance and become what it will? *Do*—like water flowing downhill, or in a magical realm, uphill because it is more convenient. A world commanded by a single god is the most orderly, of course. When there are multiple gods, the meddling that goes on produces consternation for its inhabitants. A world with a good dollop of magic thrown into the mix of god-creation will be at times quite unnerving as the professors of UU have discovered with their Hex-created universe.

"And to make this even more disconcerting, in a magical world words have power, the power to change, to meddle, to do or undo simply by their utterance and perhaps even by thought. The Hex understands this as it carefully considers a name for this universe. So, you see, the theology of Discworld is more complicated and requires a particular perspective to understand it at all."

Professor MDM switches from standing at the left of the podium to standing on the right.

"On Flatland, the priests are the thing. As Abbott reminds us in chapter 11 regarding the priests (the circles), 'Theology; doing nothing themselves, they are the Causes of everything worth doing, that is done by others.' This has become a male-dominated society because many years ago the circles determined that women are, 'deficient in Reason but abundant in Emotion, they ought no longer to be treated as rational, nor receive any mental education . . . Our Theology also in the Women's chambers is entirely different from our Theology elsewhere' (Abbott, ch. 12).

"Evolved from this is a priestly class of presumptuous demigods, the circles, who see themselves as the cause of things, but these things are actually done by the less curvaceous Flatlanders themselves, albeit many fewer things by women than men. This is a recent change, about three hundred years before the time Abbott wrote his seminal book. Abbott, as a prophet in his own right, saw the danger in in this subordination of the female gender,

> Already methinks I discern a weakness in the grasp of mathematical truth at the present time as compared with the more robust intellect of our ancestors three hundred years ago . . . I say nothing of the possible danger if a Woman should ever surreptitiously learn to read and convey to her Sex the result of her perusal of a single popular volume; nor of the possibility that the indiscretion or disobedience of some infant Male might reveal to a Mother the secrets of the logical dialect. On the simple ground of the enfeebling of the Male intellect, I rest this humble appeal to the highest Authorities to reconsider the regulations of Female education. (Abbott, ch. 12)

And, as we have all seen with recent scholarship from Flatland that the grip of sexism has been loosened and it's flavor, if you will, is decidedly less mathematical, less geometrical, more feminine."

"Professor!" cries a disembodied female voice, that of a Flatlander and from one of the higher rows.

"Ask," says the professor.

The female voice continues, "As you know, Flatlanders did heed Abbot's call for loosening the restrictions on education and I am one of the first to profit from this effort. But I do protest that by calling our more integrated approach to your assumption *feminine* implying less mathematical, because by doing so are we not going down the same path Abbott asked us to deviate from to label the emotional *feminine* when it is a fact of life in all genders."

The professor smiles, "Good point . . ." Looks at his class chart . . . "Ms. Transversal, I believe . . . Let me rephrase what I said. That the new perspective allows for, perhaps the better word is 'being', 'existence', even the 'existential'. In other words there the single straight line has become in vogue thanks to the elevation of women as equal in society. The rigid rule of geometry has been softened by the gentler touch of these new hands."

"Argh," mutters the Flatlander female, "I don't even have hands."

MDM doesn't notice the complaint and continues, "And, as we have seen on Discworld with the development of the

Thaumic Reactor, which some round worlders call the Thauminator, is a slight turn towards those elements of magic that require a mathematical twist, and this has influenced their Discworldian rhetoric. We have, I believe, a small but significant centrality developing between the philosophies of the two flat worlds. But I see that I have gone off the rails a bit, away from theology and into the everyday lives of Flatlanders. But time has expired and we must end it here. I will pick up again the theology of Flatland next week and I will post your assigned readings on the infernal machine by tomorrow's eve. First paper due next week; and wizards, please refrain from using that nasty ink that disappears and corrects itself based upon the critique that I am thinking applies to your work. Not only is it crass, unprofessional, and rude, but I am allergic to whatever's in that stuff."

Fourth Lesson (Phy. 433 Philosophy of Worlds)

Faithful narrator here and for perhaps the last time. I'm present in class, but I don't know for how long. You see I've been observing this class (yes, without paying) as a piece of chalk which Professor MDM has worn down to the smallest nub. With all the budget cuts at UU they're no longer supplying chalk and MDM has not seen fit to bring a replacement that I could slip into. I am simply too cramped in this small space. So I will attempt to migrate to the overhead projector but that might change things—in what way I do not know.[7]

There, done. But from this perspective everything is completely different. I cannot explain. It would be like trying to understand a 2D world when you live in a 3D one. That would surely be an insane thing to do. And if perspective matters so much that it affects all of our understandings from philosophy, to physics, to mathematics, even to theology, then maybe everything we know is more about the direction from which we can see than it is about the truth at all.

[7] We'll just say, "quantum." Problem solved.

20
The Intersection of Science and Philosophy, the Seediest Corner in Ankh-Morpork *(don't worry, we'll help with the big words)*

DANIEL MIORI

[The inter-schekshun of scheyensce and philoschofffy[1]] One of those streets would have to cross over the Misbegot Bridge, under which the Canting Crew meets; a group of beggars who don't even fit in with the Beggars' Guild and do a fair amount of philosophizing. The other would run behind the Unseen University, preferably one of the alleys with loose bricks in the wall where the students of the university had been sneaking out to enjoy the good life (Pratchett, *The Light Fantastic*), which also abutted the High Energy Magic Building and the squash courts (Pratchett, Stewart, and Cohen, *The Science of Discworld: A Novel*).

In the late 1990s and early oughts Sir Terry, with the help of science writers Ian Stewart and Jack Cohen, wrote a set of four books where a Discworld storyline revolved around the discussion of scientific concepts, and the concept of science itself. The great value was not its cutting-edge science (which has had to be tweaked over time) and not the views expressed, but the fact that Sir Terry brings the funny. Sometimes more subtle, sometime not so much; never really schticky or snot-blowingly funny, but funny nonetheless. Another value, however, did happen to be the science and the views expressed, but without the funny who cares?

What we learn in school as the scientific method, a process of formulating hypothesis using new information to reexamine

[1] Unless otherwise noted, all brackets denote pronunciation as per a predenture Cohen the Barbarian.

existing theories, is how both philosophy and science work. Sometimes these ideas fine tune our understanding, whispering a greater understanding of the known world similar to the ways of the talking dog Gaspode.[2] Sometimes these ideas tip over the entire table with a mad grin on their face, an event the great philosopher Didactylos (2) would rationalize as "Things just happen. What the hell" (Pratchett, *Hogfather*, 2).

A Brief History of Western Thought, Yeeee Hahhhh!

[wesch tern thossch] (This section was written by the kind assistance of *A History of Western Philosophy* by Russell and *The Oxford Guide to Philosophy* edited by Honderich.) An exhaustive review of all the scientific and philosophical advances since the dawn of recorded history isn't necessary here . . . or anywhere really, ever. What would be useful, however, is a process of cherry picking through some of the more relevant historic highlights of the times science and philosophy have crossed paths and ignoring everything else which does not help the story line. One great sin to avoid in this is excessive reduction. Analyzing a complex system by breaking it down into its parts is reduction. Taking a complex topic and expressing it in more accessible terms is reduction. Creating a new, false, overly simplified version of an idea is a form of reduction, but it's also known as "a lie." Early in the first book on the science of Discworld, oddly titled *The Science of Discworld*, this unfortunately all too common form of reduction is referred to as "Lies-to-Wizards," a method created by Ponder Stibbons, researcher at the Unseen University because "There was no point in telling your bosses everything; they were busy men, they didn't want explanations . . . What they wanted was little stories that they felt they could understand, and then they'd go away and stop worrying" (207–10 in Kindle edition). Having said this does not mean that there will be no reductionist sins in this chapter, it's just that it's one of those funny bits. Not quite as funny as the "lies to the editor" of this book

---

[2] See these Discworld novels: *Men at Arms*, *The Trouble with Dragons*, *Guards! Guards!*, *Moving Pictures*, and probably a few others that I was too lazy to find.

to explain delays or, so that you won't feel left out, the "lies to readers" that follow.

In the Beginning

There were certainly non-western philosophers and scientists, such as the Phoenicians who hinted at the idea of a round earth long before it was proposed by Aristotle, but *we* don't have the same gravitas as "the infinite universe" and must start somewhere, so for the purpose of this chapter we shall begin with Aristotle, an old Greek guy.

Aristotle (384–322 BCE)

[airy-schtooотle] From the dawn of time philosophers were scientists in that they used logic to try and explain their world. Aristotle's studies included biology, physics, geology, and optics as well as ethics, logic, and that thing that comes after physics . . . metaphysics. From the time of his death until the seventeenth century (roughly two thousand years for those who are math anxious) he was *the* authority for science and philosophy, even to the Catholic Church. Tutor to Alexander of Macedon aka Alexander the Great, or as Aristotle often addressed him, "dammit Al, enough with the conquering already!!"[3] his work stands out for being more systematic and less emotional than his predecessors. Definitely a product of his time and training, he added common sense and a professorial tone to the understood universe.[4] He views were a bit conventional and he would have been quite at home in a modern suburb for the most part, but he did have some ideas on wealth that would not seem very conservative to the modern ear. Owning land and profiting from the wise management of it was okay because there was a natural limit to how much you could gain. Trade, on the other hand, particularly usury (loaning money for interest), was unnatural and worthy of hate. He did do extensive work in physics, or at least what passed for the physics of his day. It was far more

[3] That's just some shit I made up, no one really knows what they talked about.

[4] Discworld, too, has people who "also have a thoroughgoing grounding in 'common sense' one of science's natural enemies" (Pratchett, Stewart, and Cohen, *The Science of Discworld: A Novel*, Kindle location 227).

applicable to Discworld science than anything we would recognize. One thing he got right was to think of earth as a sphere, otherwise it was Unseen University all the way. The earth was the center of the universe; planets, the moon, the sun and stars all revolved around it; everything below the moon was made of earth, wind, fire, or water. Not a bad start but why it took two thousand years to evolve past it is anyone's guess.

Antisthenes and Diogenes [anischh-schha-sceess . . . oh for the love of!], living in roughly the same time as Aristotle, were founders of the school of philosophy called Cynicism and are worth including because Sir Terry has more than a bit in common with them. They disregarded much of the formal teachings of their time and chose to associate with regular folk and teach in the common language. Diogenes, who we commonly remember as walking around with a lamp in the daytime to find an honest man, also did a killer bit about hunger which included masturbating in a public market. Kinda creepy by modern standards, and definitely one of the areas where Sir Terry's work differs, but he did make his idea accessible to the common Athenian (the *very* common Athenian).

Phyrro (360–270 BCE)

[Fi-roh[5]] Phyrro, a member of the school of Skeptics, which was more or less beholden to the Cynics for their start, even went so far as to suggest that it was proper to follow whatever custom was the norm where you lived (priests of Blind Io rejoice!). This is remarkably similar to the concept of "the power of the narrative,"[6] which is a reoccurring concept in the Discworld books. Sir Terry might offer that, if we will institutions to exist, like society or organized religion, then we might just as well enjoy them. Bertrand Russell (we'll talk about *him* later) felt Phyrro's approach to be "a lazy man's consolation, since it showed the ignorant to be as wise as the reputed men of learning" to which Foul Ole Ron of the Canting Crew might reply "Bugrit, millennium hand an' shrimp . . . " (Pratchett, *Feet of Clay*).

---

[5] There had to be a few I couldn't screw up.

[6] "Humans think in stories. Classically, at least, science itself has been the discovery of 'stories'—think of all those books that had titles like *The Story of Mankind*, *The Descent of Man*, and, if it comes to that, *A Brief History of Time*" (Pratchett, Stewart, and Cohen, *The Science of Discworld: A Novel*).

Absolutely nothing of interest happened from the time of Aristotle till the seventeenth century (lie to reader) when the next few interesting philosopher-scientists came along. For the purpose of this chapter they will be more important to the philosophy of science stuff than for the funny Discworld stuff, so please bear with.

Rene Descartes (1595–1650)

[ruh-nay day-cart] *Cogito ergo sum . . . Cogito* ("I think, therefore I am . . . I think?). These words comprise one of the better known statements by a philosopher. Well maybe not *these* words, but if we take a few out so that it reads "I think, therefore I am" we have the start of Descartes's attempt to figure out what in the universe was knowable beyond any doubt. He wound up having to start with the idea that, the only thing he knew without any doubt was that he was thinking. Considered the founder of modern philosophy, he is important to this chapter for two reasons. First, in creating a new way of looking at the world, he tried to make the discussion understandable to non-philosophers, and for that we thank him. Second, he proposed that consciousness is separate from the brain, a theory known as dualism which says that the mind (thoughts, feelings, beliefs) and the body are two separate substances that are able to interact.[7] This becomes important later in the discussion of the philosophy of science. As a scientist, he also did work in optics as well as analytic geometry, creating the Cartesian coordinate system which survives to this day. We have all had a turn at this system; x & y axis, parabolas, hyperbolae . . . are you feeling the creeping heat of math anxiety yet?

---

[7] It is worth mentioning that one other contributor* in this otherwise fine edition took liberties with the concept of dualism in "Cocking a Snook at Death and Getting Away with It, Does the Anthropomorphic Personification of Death Make It Less Scary?," kidnapping it to illustrate far lesser concepts. I swear by Blind Io the next time I see that brigand's face, I shall give it a working over with a razor!** (* I wrote that other chapter, I've been looking for an opportunity to apologize, sorry.) (**I figured "the next time I [saw] that brigand's face" was likely to be when I was shaving. I wouldn't want you to be disturbed by the graphic imagery; I found it so upsetting that I've had to switch to an electric razor.)

Lest we think of Descartes as too normal, he joined the Dutch army in order to find "more complete quiet," staying in for twenty years. His enlistment happened just prior to a little conflict in Europe known as The Thirty Years' War. He also had one of the breakthrough understandings of his philosophic method while spending a winter day inside an oven possibly while taking a break from a war that lasted *thirty years!* (Russell, *A History of Western Philosophy*).

Sir Isaac Newton (1642–1726)

[shur ischak schnewton] Another product of that very active time in science and philosophy; a time that included scientific studs like Galileo, Copernicus, and Kepler, Schnewton . . . err ahh, NEW-ton gave us an entire new trove of understanding of the movement of the stars and planets. Looking to those same heavens (with the reflecting telescope he built) he tried to understand planetary movement with the help of calculus (which he invented—or possibly Gottfried Leibniz did, your call) and came up with an explanation that included an invisible force called gravity. This was revolutionary in his time, but not in a way you might think. Prevailing thought was moving away from mystic and unseeable occult forces and toward a literally mechanical universe. There was a drive to explain heavenly movement with forces that were intuitive, like the workings of a clock. Something one might be able to understand with "common sense" (*The Science of Discworld*).

Newton himself acknowledged his departure from the conventional thought of the time describing this seeming dependence on these unseen forces as "so great an Absurdity that I believe no Man who has in philosophical matters a competent Faculty of thinking, can ever fall into it" (Chomsky, "Science, Mind, and Limits of Understanding"). Newton's seeming repudiation of his own theories for their reliance on the invisible, acknowledging that they smacked of the occultism, could be seen as an attempt to downplay his theories in the face of cruel persecution. He did do a bit of philosophizing on his own though, and this idea of a mechanical and intuitive universe was at the center of that philosophy. Other things to know about him include his work in alchemy; yes the same alchemy that was trying to turn lead into gold, but in fairness it was the field that eventually became chemistry. Also, he was deeply religious, crediting God with the actual design of the universe thus making him the first modern proponent of intelligent design.

In the decades and centuries that followed, all that revolutionary thought became dogma. By the end of the nineteenth century it had become just as entrenched and self-centered as Aristotle's teachings had. The sculpture *Nature Unveiling Herself before Science*, created by Louis-Ernest Barrias in 1899, is an example of just how smug we had become. Symbolizing the conceit we tend to show as a species as well as a fair amount of misogyny, it shows a beautiful young woman rendered in stone revealing her breasts (one presumes to male scientists). The idea being that we felt ourselves on the verge of a complete understanding of the universe. In retrospect it seems more like science yelling "*Second base*!!!" Progress was occurring however, and this information caused a new generation of thinkers to begin to examine the fundamentals of science, such as Newton's theories on gravity. Two German speaking fellows made particularly important contributions to their respective fields. One, named Albert Einstein, you may have heard of. The other, a wealthy Austrian-born troublemaker named Ludwig Wittgenstein, you likely have not.

Albert Einstein (1879–1955)

[Pronounced the same by Cohen the Barbarian and me, eye-n schtein] Born in Germany, Albert Einstein worked in Austria and the US for most of his life. In looking at the behavior of electromagnetic fields, he realized that gravity also followed the same patterns. Yes, he was working as a patent clerk at the time he first wrote about his new vision, but that was after years of training in advanced physics. Once he built on this base he wound up throwing out 200 years of scientific orthodoxy. Naturally this may give a fellow a grand sense of his own importance, possibly contributing to his divorcing his wife and marrying his first cousin. Other than that and his affair with Marilyn Monroe (Wikipedia, what can you expect), I really only included him for the name recognition. Well, name recognition and the fact that he fundamentally changed much of what we had intuited about space and time. He didn't just kick over the nice new table Newton had provided; he splintered it and never looked back.

Ludwig Wittgenstein (1889–1951)

[Hey you, put down that poker!] Born in Vienna, Austria, he spent a fair chunk of his adult life teaching at an obscure British university called Trinity College at Cambridge. A fair description of his teaching style could be: Ludwig talks, bullshit walks, that is if it doesn't want to get hit with a fireplace poker. Of course, this is a quality not confined to men of letters, or Austrians for that matter. To both Ludwig, who once shook a fireplace poker at Karl Popper, a philosopher of an opposing viewpoint (Edmonds and Eidinow, *Wittgenstein's Poker*), and Susan Sto Helit, who routinely kills monsters with a fireplace poker (Pratchett, *Hogfather*), there's nothing quite so satisfying as the heft of an andiron. (For the record, in the event Ludwig and Susan ever faced off, put your money on Sto Helit.) Wittgenstein sought to apply logic to philosophy, believing that most of what was considered philosophical problems was simply our inability to understand language and logic. In his first and only work to be published in his lifetime (*Tractatus Logico-Philosophicus*, 1921), he said that if a problem couldn't be stated simply and logically to just keep yer yap shut!—I paraphrase of course—and in his later work softened this stance somewhat, but he always kept that guy-about-to-head-onto-the-roof-with-a -rifle look in his eyes.

Science in Philosophy, Philosophy of Mind

[schy-unsche uff philoschofffy] Although it would be arrogant to consider philosophy of mind the only field in philosophy that incorporates science in its theories, it is a great example of a multidisciplinary approach to understanding, particularly an understanding consciousness. As with any field, there has been a change in the general view held by most of its proponents over time. Within the field of philosophy of mind, there is a range of theories on consciousness, our being self-aware, and where it comes from. In the conversations between experts in the field there are many subtle distinctions that just won't be helpful when looking in from the outside, so we shall ignore those otherwise important distinctions. (While that ignoring is not exactly a lie-to-reader, it certainly is wildly misleading). A way to get a sense of the progression of thought in this field is to begin with its two extremes. One is the belief that consciousness is entirely separate from any physical function of the brain, this is dualism. The other extreme is the belief that science will explain everything; consciousness, feelings, spirituality, the whole shootin' match of what it is to be human and alive; and that's called scientism.[8] In between, there are stepping stones which will be covered, but fret not, you need have no more understanding than Twoflower as he bumbled through his adventures with Rincewind and the Luggage in their travels across, and sometimes off the Disc (Pratchett, *The Color of Magic* and *The Light Fantastic*). Smile and nod, take pictures, don't worry. As long as, like Twoflower, you don't think too hard, these ideas will cause no harm to your own core beliefs.

Dualism

[dual-ischischm] Rene Descartes's idea states that the mind and body are two different substances which can interact and cause changes in each other but are not the same thing. The physical body and its functions are different from the mind which is non-physical. In spite of the fact that the majority of philosophers and scientists disregarded this theory long ago, it's still what most of us civilians believe. It's important to philosophy because it has become that puny kid that everyone else on the bus picks on. From the late 1950s onward there has been an evolution of thought moving away from dualism.

Behaviorism

[beav-yur ischischsm] Our mind is nothing but the behavior we show and the disposition to behave. It is a mistake to look for causes in the mental process. Gilbert Ryle coined the term "Ghost in the machine" to describe how he viewed dualism, and thus became the first kid to start picking on poor Rene Descartes (as if that name wasn't enough). Behaviorism wasn't really a statement of a fully formed theory as it was the start of a movement away from dualism which acknowledged that there was more to consciousness than an immaterial

---

[8] WHAT IT MEANS TO BE ALIVE . . . EVENTUALLY MUCH LESS ALIVE.

spirit (ghost) which occupied the same space as our brain (machine).

Identity Theory

States that the mind *is* [isch] the brain and that consciousness *is* [schtill isch] a brain process. Seriously questioning both dualism and behaviorism, the most important thing to know about identity theory is that its believers get really picky about what "is" means. They don't fart around; when they say "is" they *mean* it. They lay down what "is" is in a way you really don't want to argue about. They are also notoriously mean drunks, just nod when they get started about "is" [ischhh]. Actually this "is" business *is* what Ludwig Wittgenstein was referring to when he wrote about how we use language. In addition to his book *Tractatus*, he also published a review of a philosophical work early on in his career where, among other things, he took the author to task over his sloppy use of the word "is." It's the difference between saying one thing is *like* something else (Walter White is a cream puff) and defining what that one thing *is* (Walter White is a meth cook). While he was not a member of the school of identity theory, the witnesses would have described him to the police as "right there at the bar where the fight started." When sober, and only slightly easier to get along with, identity theorists believed that we can study consciousness by studying the brain. It is useful as a stepping stone to more recent, more robust understandings of brain processes, but it still allowed that sensations and feelings were not necessarily a result of specific chemical processes. They didn't actually say we are just walking bags of chemical reactions, but they got much closer. At the time it was proposed, most scientists still held onto the idea that there was a separate consciousness and that it transcended brain processes.

Eliminative Materialism

[eliminaaa schomesching materialischischm] Eliminative materialism holds that "folk psychological entities will be eliminated as our understanding of rich neuro-scientific descriptions of brain processes matures." Clearly these eliminative materialists are very pretentious, probably as a result of some brain process. The idea of "folk psychological entities" is worth explaining because it has more to do with folk than it does with psychology. It's the reasons we come up with on a day-to-day basis to understand what is going on around us, the *common sense* understanding we all develop to account for our beliefs, desires, fears, and sensations (*The Science of Discworld*). We act on our beliefs to attain our desires. Materialism, the other half of the name, is a commitment to the physical part of what happens inside our head. To eliminative materialists our consciousness is caused by chemical and electric activity in the brain processes, no question about it.

The eliminative part of this hypothesis is also what all that understanding of the neuro-scientific processes will do to our sentimental attachment to spirituality. It wants to get rid of folk psychology by calling up the Assassins' Guild and sending it for the big sleep, the dirt nap, fitting it with a pair of cement boots and dropping it off a bridge. If done on the River Ankh the cement boots are actually a good thing.[9] While they will slow down one's progress as one walks back to shore on the semi-solid river surface, they are effective protection from the more caustic elements in the river. As for the materialism part—everything that exists has the character of matter and science will tell us why the world is the way it is and will be able to predict what happens in the future in the same way a good scientific theory can predict behavior or properties of events or matter that don't yet exist. It's the machine without the ghost; dualism, behaviorism, identity theory, all *crap*! We are just walking bags of chemical reactions.

Functionalism

[funk-sahschischm] Mental states should be defined only in a functional way. It uses a metaphor of the brain as a computer, or the hardware, and the mind as the software. This view can also be described as scientism which states that science is *the* means of explaining why things are the way they are. Man is nothing but a physical chemical mechanism and science will

---

[9] ". . . the naturally turbid river Ankh, already heavy with the mud of the plains, does not, after having passed through the city (population 1,000,000) necessarily qualify under the term 'running' or, for that matter, 'water'" (Pratchett, *Reaper Man*, 45).

explain everything. Science spits on dualism, *pahh*, no ghost only machine. Science is the best way to understand our world. Not because proponents are really sold on science, but because it is better at settling arguments than philosophy or religion. While it is a well-known fact that nearly *everything* tends to settle matters better than religion, scientism says science settles things better by providing hard evidence in a way that everyone has to agree with.

The Philosophy of Science

[tha philoschofffy uff scheyensce] The following scene gives a good example of how we as civilians tend to see entire fields or aspects of society as a coherent whole. Lord de Worde, arrogant power broker of Ankh-Morpork, is standing at a dinner table full of his peers and raising his glass saying "Gentlemen . . . to evil." In our real world a toast "to evil" by rich and powerful men doesn't ever really take place, we hope. Sometimes when we are subjected to stories of political or corporate greed though, we feel that it does. In that same way we can tend look at the broad collection of disciplines which make up science as one coherent field where everyone sits down at the same table and toasts "to science" [ptoo schienschhh[10]]. It is a large number of fields, some of which are overtly hostile to the others, which defies easy description. In fact, if you want to see action mix neuroscientists (bag of chemical reaction believers), cognitive psychologists (all life is behavior believers), and the painfully too common open bar. For that reason, there is no single philosophy of science. There are a few concepts in philosophy that apply in general to the scientific process; like epistemology which attempts to understand the nature of knowledge or metaphysics which tries to understand the ultimate nature of reality; but for the most part each science had its own view of how it effects our understanding of the world. A part of that understanding, how it should behave, is ethics. In order to keep this chapter digestible, and to get it to the editor on time (lies to editors), understanding epistemology, metaphysics, and ethics become the only things you need to know

---

[10] Having been to a few science dinners, they often have open bars and by the end of dinner that's exactly how everyone sounds.

about the philosophy of science (lies to readers), in this great work of literature (lies to self).

Epistemology

[epi, epi, epi . . . oh get scheriousssss!] Literally translating as the study of knowledge from ancient Greek, it is one of the core fields in philosophy and looks at how we know things we know and how we come to believe in the things we believe.[11] It deals with having knowledge of something and with that knowledge being true and accurate. This includes things we know by intuition, a priori, and things we learn from experience, a posteriori. Rincewind, by the way, is a recognized expert in a posteriori knowledge. The scientific method, in fact just about every part of science, has to do with the careful analysis of the truth of what is known and adjusting beliefs as new information comes to light. Skepticism in philosophy questions the very nature of what we know for sure, like when Descartes said the only thing he knew for sure was that he was thinking. Socrates, who went one better, stated that the only thing he knew for sure was that he wasn't sure about anything.

Metaphysics

[messcha . . . messcha . . . oh sschkrew you guyssche!] A very broad field, the study of the nature of reality has some areas of overlap with epistemology. For the purpose of this work the discussion of metaphysics will be confined to cosmology; which deals with the universe, how things happen in it, and time; so one paragraph ought to be just right. Of all the fields Einstein shook up, his effect on cosmology was big, causing a rethinking that continues to this day. Some philosophers have now even come to question how we can know something to be the truth when it is essentially invisible and unprovable. The Higgs boson, unproven at the time *The Science of Discworld* was first written in 1999, has since only been found by the use of a multi-year, multi-billion dollar study completed with the Large Hadron Collider in Cern Switzerland. Current scientific theory

---

[11] The history of philosophy, logic, epistemology, metaphysics, and ethics are the core fields.

includes such things as dark matter, which we have no current technology capable of identifying. At best we infer its existence by existing theory and how the presumed presence of dark matter effects the things we can see.

Ethics

[esch-isch] Another of the foundational fields in philosophy, it is a field that evaluates what is morally permissible. It is considered a normative subject because it deals with how things ought to be, not how they are. Each field of science tries to look within itself (with varying degrees of success) to find its own way through the moral dilemmas specific to that field, which invariably they created. One example would be medical ethics, which struggles to accommodate technologic advances that may prolong life but cause great suffering in the process. Another, research ethics, questions how data is gathered and looks to protect research subjects. An example of a well-known lapse in research ethics is the Tuskegee study, which was examining the late effects of syphilis. The subjects studied were all black men, and the study of their disease process was continued even after a cure was found, allowing those men to suffer the irreversible effects of a disease even after they could have received curative treatment.

Summary

[schummy-mummy] Philosophy and science have always been closely associated. There was a time in the nineteenth and very early twentieth century when society had a popular belief that we were on the verge of a complete understanding of nature but time and progress taught us different. As a society we tend to look to fields such as philosophy and science as a source of absolute answers, but the best we can hope for is that, in both fields, there is a constant process of questioning authority. Both fields are constantly attempting to argue a better understanding than the last guy had in order to advance just a bit closer to that absolute understanding, which we may never reach. Borrowing from Sir Terry, a reasonable summary could be given as: "what teaching does not do" as well as science and philosophy

> is erect a timeless edifice of 'facts'. Every so often, you have to unlearn what you thought you already knew, and replace it by something more subtle. This process is what science is all about, and it never stops. It means that you shouldn't take everything we say as gospel, either, for we belong to another, equally honorable profession: Liar-to-readers. (*The Science of Discworld*, 71)

With the advent of quantum mechanics, an entirely new understanding of the outer universe was required. With the advent of neuroscience, an entirely new understanding of the inner universe was required, even the most fundamental concepts such as how we think and the nature of those thoughts.

It's hard to further dissect science into more easily digestible and informative bits than Sir Terry, Ian Stewart, and Jack Cohen did in the *Science of Discworld* series. While Pratchett never gave us a roadmap to the philosophy of Discworld in the same way, his philosophy was always there as he worked his way through his own need to understand, just as we all do every day. In the end, as with all Discworld discussion, we are left with a very compassionate and understanding voice which leads, but never commands. For those who wish to work through the learning, it's there; for those who wish to spend an enjoyable few hours laughing at the foibles of beings living on a disc, supported by four elephants, supported by a turtle swimming through space, also there.

21
Welcome to My World

CHRISTOPHER KETCHAM

What is your world? Do you begin with your home and radiate out towards where you shop, where you work, where you dine? Are you a world traveler? Have you been to space or are you a renowned scuba diver? I ask again what is your world? It's a bit complicated you say . . .

I see that it's a bit complicated.

What if I said you have an *Umwelt*, a life world? And that this life world is not as complicated as you might think. Your life world isn't "the world" as such because that is just too difficult to get our arms around. Think smaller, think of where you are standing, sitting, or driving (hopefully not driving!). What do you see, smell, hear, taste . . . the feel of the chair or the pressure of your feet on the floor? What is this little world you now inhabit? Jakob Von Uexkuell (1864–1944) explained this little world: "Around us is a protective wall of senses that gets denser and denser. Outward from the body, the senses of touch, smell, hearing, and sight enfold man like four envelopes of an increasingly sheer garment. This island of the senses, that wraps every man like a garment, we call his Umwelt" (Uexkuell, "An Introduction to Umwelt," 107). Every bug, slug, or pug has an *Umwelt*—a life world.

But it's still complicated you say. Why? Because your thoughts are running round and round in your head and the smells they come from both your kitchen and the family who cooks with curry downstairs and then there are the screaming kids in the hall and the more dull sounds of traffic outside. It's a bit of cacophony, isn't it? Overwhelming at times. So how do we stay sane with all this sensory input? Well, we're built to handle it. But not all bugs, slugs, or pugs have the same ability. Of course we'll get to Discworld. Patience. A simpler earthly example first.

On Being a Moth

Say you are a moth. You have gone through moth metamorphosis: egg, caterpillar, pupa, and now flying moth. You have one objective which is to find a mate. You haven't got any digestive organs because you can't eat. What stores of fat you have remaining from the transition from pupae to moth will just have to do. You have a keen sense of smell but only for the pheromone of the female of your species. You see you don't need more than that and energy conservation is key to your sole objective which is to live long enough to mate. You don't need a big energy-consuming lobe of your brain dedicated to smell *all* things. You can hear well, but you can only hear your archnemesis, the bat, which you can only hear because of its echolocation. You also have developed an instinctual response to a bat attack; you simply fall from the sky in a random motion. Don't think; just fall. It puts the bat off its trajectory. Sometimes it works and sometimes it doesn't.

You see now that your moth *Umwelt* or life world is rather much different than the life world of you the human. You as the moth hear only one thing, smell only one thing, can't taste anything, and have three basic things you can do: fly, have sex, and fall from the sky when attacked by a bat. You can't even get hungry. You have one other skill and that is to follow the scent of the female. Beyond that do you see the moon? Do you feel the wind as your wings flutter? Do you desire the nectar of spring flowers? You can't sense or feel any one of these things. They are not part of your world.

Life world is relative. The bacteria in a hot spring has a different life world than a similar species that lives in your gut. While we all live on the same planet, we each, each species cuts a different slice of the world for its own use. It is the parts of the world we can use, that help us live, that guide us on our journeys of existence.

About Them Bees

You and I cannot see in the infrared spectrum, but bees can.[1] If we could see in the infrared, how would that affect our vision? Would we need different kinds of eyes that could go from visible light to the infrared by blinking or would we need another set of eyes? What would the infrared do for us that we cannot already do with visible light? And if we had both capabilities how much would it cost us in brain power that we could have used for what we use our brains for now—higher order thinking. Well, except when we watch reality television and that really isn't much in the way of higher order thinking, now is it?

So, are you beginning to see what your life world really is? All species are built to capitalize on some of what the world has to offer and completely ignore other parts. This is why our little world, our life world, is an *Umwelt* and not the whole thing.

And we become into this life world of ours. We don't come fully formed like the moth. What does the child see? Does she grab for the moon from her crib because it looks like the shiny orb that wiggles above her in her mobile? When she sees little people working on a roof far away does she ask her mommy to get her one of those because unlike her dolls they move on their own? What is her world as an infant or small child? We all know a child's world is different from our own but few of us remember just what that difference could have been. It's a bit of a mystery the child's world. But we wouldn't have it any other way. And, of course, we wouldn't want to change anything on that other magical world we have come to know—Discworld.

The Life Worlds of Discworld

It stands to reason that a flat world like Discworld would have different features and functions than our own. Even more so it would be different because it runs on a different reality than our own. Discworld is not explained by science but by magic. However, the same issues of life world apply. You see, even on a world where magic is king, things must work otherwise

[1] One can only imagine that bees in Ankh-Morpork regret their finer-tuned senses . . .

everything would get all bollixed up. And, believe it or not, some of the "laws" of physics break through the magical because, as we all know from our quantum physics classes, even though science has strict laws, some of them seem to just break down at times or do some strange things that only a magician would love.

So we have talked about moths, children, and our own life worlds. Time to consider those in Discworld. It is best then, as we have done with earthly life worlds (*Umwelts*), to use specific examples from the flora and fauna of Discworld.

The God of Evolution

First of all, there is a God of Evolution who hangs about, fiddling and adjusting things on the species the god has constructed from bits of this and that (*The Science of Discworld*, ch. 26).[2]

Say the god decides that a human would be better off with gills.[3] That sounds delightful, you say. Think of all the fun one could have frolicking in the sea. We wouldn't have to surface to breathe! But there are just a few things wrong with this picture. We humans have very small feet and hands that don't propel us very fast in the water. And there are sharks and Humboldt squid and all manners of ocean nasties who would make a meal of us. We won't have much of a chance with our feeble swimming skills. And our eyes, we would need goggles because we can't see so well underwater. And talk, we would need to learn how to hum and squeak. Well, at least we would all be bilingual. On our own round world the science called evolution would have addressed these things otherwise we would have become extinct—the gilled human that is. The God of Evolution's meddling aside, there are other species on Discworld that are not as endangered as the human with gills.

---

[2] Pratchett books referenced in this chapter: Terry Pratchett, Ian Stewart, and Jack Cohen, *The Science of Discworld*, Terry Pratchett, *Mort* , *Pyramids*, *The Wee Free Men, Small Gods*, *Men at Arms*.

[3] I wouldn't put it past a god to do something like that. They seem like they drink a bit too much.

The Ambiguous Puzuma

The ambiguous puzumas have so slowed down the speed of light that they can run at near light speed but this warps space and time to where they become disoriented and crash into things (*Small Gods* and *Pyramids*). Their mortality rate is high because they break ankles after chasing after females that aren't there (too fast to see) or die from Heisenberg's uncertainty principle because they can't know who or where they are at the same moment. So fast, no person has seen the ambiguous puzuma, but they are thought to be the size of a leopard (*Pyramids*, endnotes).

Yes there is a bit of physics left over for this unfortunate puzuma. We know from Einstein that as we accelerate closer and closer to light speed our field of vision narrows until it looks like a point in front of us. We don't see what is around us any more, just a distorted field that becomes narrower and narrower. And the colors shift because we know that we are outrunning some colors and getting closer to others (yes, scientists, the red shift or Doppler effect). So if we are capable of moving at very high speed like the ambiguous puzuma we are going to be challenged to see, let alone find female puzumas. And consider the force of deceleration from such a speed: it would surely break even the sturdy elephant's legs. So the life world approaching the speed of light is a different life world than at the more leisurely pace we experience on earth. It is all relative as Einstein might say. So let's slow things down a bit.

Dromes

What world would be complete without its pests? We know that our body is filled with good bugs. Then again, sometimes bad bugs, whether they be viruses, bacteria, or worms, can get inside and really mess us up. There are also pests on Discworld, of which one of the most hazardous to its inhabitants are dromes.

Dromes in Discworld are a menace, not to themselves but to others, for they can penetrate the envelope of your *Umwelt* life world (*The Wee Free Men*, 184). They're like spiders, spinning dreams for people and others which dromes like to watch. But if you, the unfortunate dreamer, should eat something in your dream you're likely not to want to ever leave the dream.

This works just perfectly for the life world of the drome. Unfortunately for you, you slowly starve to death eating imaginary food while you are in the dream-stolen *Umwelt* of the drome. And the drome waits and watches patiently until it penetrates your *Umwelt* to make you a meal—but you're already dead and no longer in a life world.

But once again, what makes the drome a drome? It makes and listens to dreams. That's its life world. It's a simple life world like that moth in our Roundworld. The drome doesn't hear the traffic in the streets or that blaring radio. Nor does it see what is on television; it's wired only for dreams. Put it in a crowded park, all it will do is find people who want to dream and eat something while they are dreaming so that they will keep dreaming and die. It won't watch the Frisbee game because it can't see the game. It won't want a hot dog from the cart because it can't taste it. And how is this drome not like the rhinovirus on our Roundworld that invades your sinus making you want to die from the fever, the headaches, and the constant nose blowing? It's the same thing, only from the perspective of a different life world.

We are about to leave your head cold and your dreams for something different. Remember, Discworld is a flat world. Dimensions beyond length and width such as depth are theoretical even though magic makes them so. I agree, this is confusing at best. However, there is one beast on Discworld that is comfortable in just two dimensions.[4]

The Shadowing Lemma

The Shadowing Lemma eschews the third dimension entirely, a true Discworld throwback, living in two dimensions and consuming mathematicians (or the quantum weather butterfly) as have the lemmas of the roundworlds done for years as they choke their mathematicians with chalk dust, producing chronic proofing disease (*Men at Arms*, 154 note). What a di-lemma . . .

---

4 And no I don't mean your average pop star whose answer to the question "How would you make the world a better place?" is "By wearing my bikini more often."

Certainly you are familiar with lemmas. Lemmas are mathematical theories. These are the things that choked you in calculus class as you worked through proof after proof after proof . . .

In the shadowing lemma we have a species that has similar needs on Discworld as the lemma does in our own round world. Both lemmas consume mathematicians, not musicians, nor clerks, nor savage baggage handlers, only mathematicians. This is surely some kind of proof that the Roundworld we inhabit and Pratchett's Discworld have similar evolutionary constructs. We both are located in the same universe, aren't we? Well that is certainly a subject for further debate. But it isn't inconceivable that we should both have lemmas.

The Gaspode

The Gaspode is a walking disease factory, an *Umwelt* petri dish of pathogens warring so much with each other it doesn't interfere with its host (in many books, including *Men at Arms*, 109).

Are we not a lot like the Gaspode? I would hate to put a sensitive microphone into our gut—the life world of what the television commercials want to call our biologics. The microphone would record the constant cries of this bacterial species trying to crowd out that bacterial species for a piece of underdone potato or that rancid enchilada that sat so heavily in your stomach last night.

Or the microphone would record the reverie of microbial parties after you consume too much wine. But, then again, there are species who use the alcohol not to get tipsy but because it helps them digest those nachos with extra hot jalapeños. But it is time that we move out of the gut into the larger world.

The Hermit Elephant

The hermit elephant doesn't have the thick hide of its larger kin. Instead it carries a hut around with it, much like the turtle wears its shell (*Men at Arms*, endnotes). Well, the problem is that if one drinks a bit too much scumble (a potent alcoholic drink made of apples and who knows what else . . . nobody seems to know) one might awake in a village of huts that was not there the night before, each hut with a sleeping hermit elephant inside. Of course, you say, the equivalent on round worlds is a convoy of Airstream trailers that has reached a scenic campground for the night . . . and we all know that these Airstreamers often down a bit too much of libation before they nod off next to their campfires.

Again, more parallel worlds. I am beginning to think we are getting to the point where we can declare more than the possibility of parallel universes but the probability. We have moved out of the gut and into the world where we, even as inebriated fools, use technology such as houses and trailers. Are these not part of our *Umwelt*? When we get cold, what do we do? We put on a coat! Well, it is no different on Discworld. If we get cold after a night of celebration on Discworld, would we not find a warm place to lie down? The Hermit Elephant is warm, has a shelter . . . Not too farfetched, is it? But we have been talking only of animal species. What about plants. Do plants have life worlds? Better yet. Do they intersect with our own?

Re-annual Plant

Look into the field over there in your round world. There are plenty of flower and grass stems. Consider this account by Von Uexkuell. First we see a flower stem that is straight and tall. We bend over to look closer. It is full of liquid that a tiny meadow spittlebug consumes to build a nest. An ant travels up and down the stem to hunt for juicy aphids to feed its young. A honey bee sucks at the nectar of the flower to bring back to the hive to make honey, and now the cow comes along to chew down the stem for food and to make milk ("An Introduction to Umwelt," 108). And, later on of course, the cow produces milk and meat for our own consumption.

This little corner of the world is host to a number of different species, each of whom has its own life world. The ant probably will not dance to a Strauss waltz but we do know that bees dance in their nests, sadly, however, not to Strauss. The spittlebug probably can't even hear. The aphids are hungry but only for sugar. The cow finds this stem satisfying but not others that cause indigestion. All these little animal and insect life worlds intersect and overlap with the flower stem which in turn has its own life world which intersects with the life world of these and other species. And on and on. But on Discworld things can get, well, a bit strange.

Consider the curious case of the re-annual plant whose life cycle is the reverse of the Roundworld flowering plant (*Mort*, 3). In a world only magic can love with its reverse osmosis and rain that falls up, or could anyway, in a soil infused with an extra dollop of magic, the re-annual plant flowers the year before its seeds germinate. What, say that again? The plant simply grows and flowers and then produces seeds but new plants won't come from these seeds. The plant grows first not from a seed but from . . . You guessed it—magic. Some things on Discworld are really better left unexplained. Like what is the purpose then of its seed? We likely will never know.

I can only believe that earlier ancestors of this plant were swarmed by bees that so injured the flowers that no seeds could be produced. As a protection against this invasion of its *Umwelt* the re-annual plant decided to forego the bee pollination thing so that its seeds would be able to thrive. You ask again, what purpose do the seeds now serve? It's still a mystery.

But listen to what Pratchett says about the re-annual's *Umwelt*, "A farmer who neglects to sow ordinary seeds only loses the crop, whereas anyone who forgets to sow seeds of a crop that has already been harvested twelve months before risks disturbing the entire fabric of causality, not to mention acute embarrassment" (*Mort*, 3). Likewise on a roundworld if you put the cart before the horse, you won't ever get to market to sell your produce and it'll rot . . . that is, unless you pull the cart yourself and that would be acutely embarrassing![5]

So the re-annual plant messes with time. Of course we know that time is relative. What do we know about how a thousand-year-old towering redwood experiences time? The giant tortoise lives fifty years beyond the longest-lived human and what do we know about how it experiences time? We know not the satisfaction the fly feels of a life of only a few days. We can only understand what it is we are equipped to understand in the life world that we are capable of experiencing.

But what is important about our journey is the fact that no matter how bizarre or strange or whether in a round world or

---

[5] IT IS FRUSTRATING WHEN THE FABRIC OF CAUSALITY IS DISTURBED.

Discworld, everything has its life world. This is something we can't seem to shake. It is a common feature of both science and magic worlds. So there must be something to this *Umwelt* thing that is more fundamental than either magic or science. I'm positive that there's a Nobel Prize in this somewhere for the person who finds the fundamental linkage.

However I sense a drome nearby because I have become ravenously hungry and there is that hot dog stand over there that's just begging me for my last dollar. I do need to move quickly in the opposite direction. Where is an Ambiguous Puzuma when you need one?

22

Cocking a Snook at Death and Getting Away with It: Does the Personification of Death Make It Less Scary?[1]

DANIEL MIORI

Not the Introduction

On a cold late winter day, in the western region of New York State, a markedly unimpressive man hunches over a small computer. Both are rapidly approaching obsolescence. That man, typing away furiously, is a not-a-philosopher. He is a part-time teacher of medical ethics, a field widely felt to be the bastard stepchild of philosophy, particularly by those who practice it. That being said, he teaches clinical ethics, considered by bioethicists with any self-respect to be the lab section of a medical ethics curriculum. Fortunately, since the vast majority of bioethicists long ago gave up on anything remotely approaching self-respect, he muddles on with a particularly Rincewind-ian street cred. Street cred, that is, with the understanding that the street would most likely be a back alley in Ankh-Morpork.[2]

The Introduction

Death appears in every book of the Discworld series except *The Wee Free Men* and *Snuff*. Terry Pratchett (Sir Terry) gave him very real doubts and questions, making him one of the most humane characters in the Discworld multiverse. Of the major

---

[1] YES.* (*It was Azrael's answer to an entirely different question, but you have to love his style.—Pratchett, *Reaper Man*).

[2] Where the half-life of the average philosopher is about however long it takes a man named "Nails" to relieve a much smaller man of all of his money in said back alley.

characters, Death is most often present, least cynical, and evolves in a traceable way through the series. His personality may have different aspects depending on the plot, his humor sometimes more sharp sometimes absent, but he is almost always present; leading one to posit: "what the F!!!"

To Be, or Not to Be . . . or to Be, or, Whatever. All I Know Is That There's a Duel at Noon in the Town Square. Or at Midnight.

In *Reaper Man*, Sir Terry gave us a clue as to his view of . . . well, just about everything. "Belief," he wrote, "is one of the most powerful organic forces in the multiverse. It may not be able to move mountains, exactly. But it can create someone who can." He continued "People get exactly the wrong idea about belief. They think it works back to front. They think the sequence is first object, then belief. In fact it works the other way around." [Belief] "created Death. Not death, which is merely a technical term for a state caused by prolonged absence of life, but Death, the personality. He evolved, as it were, along with life" (120). Just as the character Death is real, so are our own deaths; reapers, dark angels, lurking realizations of mortality, and bogeymen (like Schleppel).

The relationship between death and life is an example of dualism. Dualism is the idea that when we start identifying and describing a concept, we instantly bring into being the opposite concept. Once someone wrapped their brain around existence and why it was so perplexing and groovy they realized that, once they were no longer able to perceive existence, an entirely different thing was going to happen. For that reason, from the very first time some poor schnook started to think about the nature of existence, the idea of non-existence occurred. "As soon as a living thing was even dimly aware of the concept of suddenly becoming a non-living thing, there was Death" (120). In these passages Sir Terry offered the thought that we humans have a reality in our brains that is more real than all the provable stuff around us. There are certainly problems with this real-ality, like how we each understand our own reality and how we communicate that understanding with others, but there is no question as to its realness.

We Are Who We Say We Are—Narrative and Identity

One way to examine the idea that belief creates reality is with narrative theory. This says that we each understand the events of our life through the narrative we create to explain those events. We do that on a personal basis to make sense of events in our relationships with each other as well as in larger social relationships such as school, town, profession, race, and religion. We negotiate this relationship through our participation in those beliefs and morals. When Sir Terry navigated the plot of *Reaper Man* (or any of the Discworld novels) over the divide between life and the afterlife, he was always careful to let us know that he was not there to judge. That we can rely on whatever our narrative is, and that each narrative in its own way is pretty silly. There are certain groups who would criticize the idea that first we believe and then reality is formed based on those beliefs. Many people would tell you that reality, and morality, is not negotiable. That God (or Gods) existed before we were created and will continue to exist after we have left. The character Death would tell you this is truly the case, but would then turn around and break all his own rules by taking a job as a cook or adopting a daughter.

Manifestations . . . and Womanifestations If It Comes to That!

From Thanatos in Ancient Greece, to the Hebrew Midrash, to the Grim Reaper, to good old Bill Door, it seems that every culture has created a figure to represent death. There is even a crossover personification in some of the Abrahamic religions (Islam, Judaism, and certain Christian sects) named Azrael (probably just a coincidence, one of the Baltimore Azraels, likely). There is the Hindu god Yama who lives in Naraka, a kind of a Dharmic purgatory, and the guide Mercury from the Roman pantheon. The existence of such a manifestation is nearly universal in the religions, mythologies, or psychologies of all cultures. A term for this type of character who guides souls to the afterlife or to the place of the dead is *psychopomp*. Generally it refers to some symbolic critter, but it can also be a person; a mid-wife into the next life, so to speak. Depending on your religious affiliation, psychopomps could help you be born again, again. Serious secular humanists (translate as *atheist*) who might not be swayed by spiritual gobbledygook would still feel existential pangs about the end of their existence and could possibly look to an assisted suicide organization like Compassion and Choices in the US (previously known as The Hemlock Society), Dignity in Dying in the UK, or Dignitas in Switzerland as their psychopomp. Ultimately the specific individuals in the organization who participate directly with a patient in the end of life process would serve as that person's psychopomp.

No matter how your narrative reads, death is the end of all firsthand knowable existence for each person who experiences it. It has been described, in fact, as spiritual annihilation. When viewed without emotion, such as from the perspective of a Zen Master or the friendly neighborhood sociopath, the moment death occurs is almost anticlimactic. It isn't anything, not thinking, not breathing, nothing. No loud noises like thunder and trumpets, no sky parting with legions of angels, not even a 7-foot-tall skeleton in a hooded cloak sitting astride his mighty steed Binky. It holds all the spectacle of a quiet evening at Granny Weatherwax's house and yet we attribute such power to this lack of happening that we have created these anthropomorphic personifications (psychopomps) to help us get our collective heads around the concept.

Oblivion, Thy Name Is Bel-Shamharoth!

Well actually thy name is Oblivion, but it could also be Bel-Shamharoth. In the first book of the Discworld series, *The Color of Magic,* the Discworld gods engaged in a game of chance (or possibly fate) that resulted in Rincewind, Twoflower, and Hrun the Barbarian being in the temple of Bel-Shamharoth. Also known as the Soul-Eater, Bel-Shamharoth, as his aka name suggests, eats souls. Not in the usual Discworldian sense, where those souls are liable to pop out just about anywhere. Bel sends them to a place from which they will never return, known as the dungeon dimensions. In a series where even oblivion is part of the crowd (aka Oblivion), this sending of souls beyond what is knowable sounds queasily familiar. If we Roundworlders spend a few seconds pondering our own mortality (that's enough, stop pondering!) we start to get the same kind of creepy crawly uncontrolled magical field sort of feeling that the temple of Bel-Shamharoth gives Rincewind. Twoflower doesn't get that feeling, of course, he's oblivious to oblivion. Not to Oblivion probably, he's hard to ignore, but to oblivion, yes.

Afterward, Afterworld?

What happens next is the real question, and that boils down to just two possibilities: either there is a continuation of consciousness or there's nothing. Not nothing like "here we are in the desert and it's just rocks and dirt, what a great vacation!" and not even nothing like the physical oblivion of outer space with its dark matter, black holes, and the infinite darkness of the Star Wars franchise. We're talking about nothing, as in the lack of a conscious *us* to be thinking about what is (or isn't) around. Not *knowing,* we try to understand.

An intuitive understanding of death as the end of life is probably good enough for a casual coffeehouse discussion, but not for this higher caliber philosophical essay. In the United States we have been freed from the worrisome and unpredictable thought process in many areas, including figuring out the difference between dead and not dead. *The 1981 Uniform Determination of Death Act* pretty much describes how we define death from a legal perspective. It's a bit clinical and depressing, so now that I've mentioned it, let's forget I did that and move on to how we look at death philosophically.

Windle Poons . . . Every-zombie

Windle Poons was several different kinds of dead throughout *Reaper Man*, and so becomes our Everyman of the afterlife. When we look at the way societies view death, there are three main ways to describe it: animalistic death, mindistic death, and personistic death.

An animalistic death is so straightforward that even politicians agree on it. It would view the good professor Poons as dead right when Death was supposed to pick him up at his going-away party. The fact that he manages to re-animate due to the temporary loss of death is a bit of a flaw in this discussion, but there was full agreement in the book that he had ceased to function as a living being. Not that his stubborn residual lack of death kept the faculty of the Unseen University from burying him in the middle of a busy intersection. Even Windle himself tried to *kill* kill himself by jumping from The Brass Bridge. While the jumping was rather successful, the *killing* was not. Animation aside, Windle was what we would intuitively call dead. Heart stops working, lungs stop processing air, bowels stop processing those five sausages he ate at the going away party and a certain aroma begins to be acquired. Not from the sausage so much, more from the deadness. Had the faculty of the Unseen University known about it, they could have thrown in The 1981 Uniform Determination of Death Act because as of page twenty-four of *Reaper Man*, Windle was an animalistic fugitive.

Mindism says that life exists while the mind exists. If the mind ceases to exist, then we are dead. Not to be confused with brain death, where even basic functions like breathing stop. A mindistic death would occur when the everyday automatic function continues, but the brain's ability to conceive of or react to the outside world stops. Clinically, someone in a vegetative state would meet this definition. Modern medicine has more or less created the vegetative state as our ability to extend the body's function with things like artificial nutrition and hydration has improved over time. Someone who believes in a mindist view of death would hold that when someone with no chance of improving would have experienced animalistic death without the intervention of medicine, they are dead.

A personistic death might best describe Windle early on, when he continued to operate in a somewhat autonomous way. He needed help with many of the functions of daily living but he swallowed his five sausages safely, he took in air without the aid of a machine, and he could continue to interact with others in a rudimentary way, but he was certainly not the old Windle. That wizard, who had grown, learned, taught, and at the height of his prowess run Unseen University. He lived back in the day when there were "*proper* wizards, great big men built like barges, the kinds of wizards you could look up to." Some people feel that, even though the body and mind's daily functions continue to exist (swallowing safely, having brief polite conversations about being reincarnated as a woman, making the next to last entry in one's diary) the absence of that person's full vital self becomes death.

Stoicism in Rome and Greece and Shintoism in Japan held that once the juice is all squeezed out of life it is completely okay to check out. In current Western thought some people still believe this, and more often than not these people are atheists. At least the really dedicated atheists who have managed to surmount those moments of doubt and terror associated with contemplating absolute and total annihilation without an anthropomorphic personification to hold their hand. They take the view that this physical world is all we've got. When the good times that make life worth living are gone, what's left can be brought to Modo the dwarf's compost heap.

Religion vs. Philosophy: Steel Cage Death Match!

Fortunately, finding Sir Terry's specific beliefs within his writing is relatively straightforward and will be useful later in teasing out some of the finer points of his world view on really funny stuff like death and dying. One somewhat spiritual concept that winds through his books, whatever helps you in life is what you meet at death, when you meet Death. Possibly Mort, but most likely Death. Unless it's Susan, but almost certainly Death.[3]

Sir Terry, viewed by a religious individual could have been accused of being an atheist (read as secular humanist). When viewed by a secular humanist however (read as atheist), he might have been considered intellectually soft for his sentimental adherence to spirituality. In fact, if we were sitting between them, the conversation would sound something like the discussion between the Unseen University's Senior Wrangler,[4] and the priests of Blind Io;

"Credulous fools!"

---

[3] Unless there are kittens about. In which case Death might be busy.

[4] Sir Terry described him best; "The post of Senior Wrangler was an unusual one, as was the name itself. In some centers of learning the Senior Wrangler is a leading philosopher; in others, he's merely someone who looks after the horses. The Senior Wrangler at Unseen University was a philosopher who looked *like* a horse thus neatly encapsulating all definitions" (*Reaper Man*, 40).

"Godless tinkerers!"
"Gullible idiots!"
"Atheistic scum!"
"Servile morons!"

You probably get the drift. Point of fact, several blogs that were reviewed for this chapter read surprisingly (and somewhat less cordially) similarly.

Death and What Comes Next; the Role of Faith

Joseph Campbell was an author and professor at Sarah Lawrence College and expert on the value and universality of myth and its place in our lives. He and Sir Terry have a few things in common. For example, the belief that even without an absolute firsthand knowledge of the nature of our spiritual existence, the faith within that spirituality provides us with great value. Campbell is also suspected of being an atheist (don't read this one as secular humanist, he was evasive on the matter) for the same Old-Testament-as-myth reason, so there were a few things they don't have in common. If we take him at his word though, and he's dead so we are more or less are forced to do so, he had a few things to say that tend to illuminate Sir Terry's view on the existence of God(s). Campbell felt that myth, which we can translate to symbols like anthropomorphized personifications, serves to instill a sense of "grateful, affirmative awe before the monstrous mystery that is existence." Doing this carries us "from birth, through maturity through senility to death." So those religious systems that produce the Grim Reaper and his cousins help keep us safe from . . . the Grim Reaper, and his cousins.

The Middle of the Start of the . . . End of the . . . Middle . . . Oh Sod Off and Just Read the Thing!

Discussing Sir Terry and his pondering on the nature of life and what is real becomes a bit sobering when we take into account the fact that he has passed away from complications related to Alzheimer's-type dementia and went through a certain loss of those traits we might define as personhood. The idea of consciousness and whether or not it survives the end of the life is one of many themes in his books, as are academia, the fraught nature of human communication, love, and shopping malls. In all his works there was a message of hope, love, and acceptance, offered with gentle and honest humor as he examines much of this flawed and wonderful world. There seem to be only two ways to knowingly and lovingly approach the fact of his dementia, either completely ignore it or incorporate it into the discussion. Since mentioning the ignoring of a topic is a very poor way of actually ignoring the topic, this brings us to the next section.

There were two fairly indisputable facts about Sir Terry Pratchett. Firstly, that he had a curious mind. He did not accept the world as presented but worked hard to try and understand it. Secondly, he was driven to communicate that experience. He has shown this both in his fiction writing and in his firsthand experience, as in the documentary produced by KEO North for BBC Scotland, directed and produced by Charlie Russell, *Choosing to Die*, which was filmed while he was working on *Snuff*, the thirty-ninth book in the Discworld series. In the hour-long presentation he tried to clarify a few things for us: that by "snuff" he is referring to the ground tobacco product that one inhales by the nasal route; that there is a great deal of tea drinking associated with discussing assisted suicide; and that "I know there will come a time when my words will fail me. When I can no longer write my books I'm not sure I want to go on living. I want to enjoy life for as long as I can squeeze the juice out of it, and then I'd like to die."

It is the process of reaching death that we struggle with, not the actual event. In Sir Terry's case, his end came in a roughly predictable but at times inconsistent way. The type of Alzheimer's disease he had is called Posterior Cortical Atrophy (PCA), which primarily affects the occipital lobe of the brain. Located in the back, this is an area responsible for processing visual data and initially causes difficulty reading, blurred vision, and light sensitivity. It also causes problems with functions closely associated with vision, like balance and eye-hand coordination. In his case, he had already lost the ability to type at the time *Choosing to Die* was filmed.

He wrote *Snuff* by dictation software and an assistant who would make fine adjustments and retype the words which the software couldn't recognize, like *&#@! (Pardon the faux obscenity; part of the source for this was a National Public Radio interview where, despite their supposed journalistic integrity, they bleeped the word). Peculiarly, and perhaps most cruelly, as his PCA progressed in severity it affected that part of him which brought so much pleasure to him and to so many others, namely, his literary ability. Also, spreading to other parts of the brain like the parietal lobe where a great deal of motor function is coordinated, the illness affects the ability to speak and to swallow safely. The point at which that ability to swallow safely is gone is one of the few points of clarity in the progression of the disease. Death, usually from secondary causes like pneumonia, will occur within six months. Possibly a little later, possibly a little sooner, but ultimately and without question death will come. Then one is left with decisions best made with a clear mind, but which become increasingly difficult as PCA robs one of one's mind.

By the time the big decision that accompanies a deteriorating ability to swallow has been made—feeding tube versus careful oral intake—the ability to clearly state one's mind has passed. For the record, whether one takes the artificial nutrition route (feeding tube) or not, the patient gets the same six months. Because of Sir Terry's specific disease, he needed to make decisions much earlier than patients with other diseases that lead to losing the ability to swallow, for example. People with Multiple Sclerosis or Motor Neuron Disease, like the other subjects of *Choosing to Die,* can roll the dice and see how their disease progresses, knowing that when things get worse they will be able to think about any choice they need to make. With Sir Terry's illness, the tool he most needed was to be taken from him. Like Bill Door's all too mortal scythe in *Reaper Man*, getting a proper sharpness was just not possible.

Advance Directives, Advanced Directly

A living will is a way to make sure that your wishes are respected once you lose the power to make decisions. In the US many states have official forms for this purpose that go by names like MOLST (medical orders for life sustaining treatment) or POLST (physician orders for life sustaining treatment). One of the nastier sides of the lingering tendency of physicians to be paternalistic is the decision to passively allow decision making to revert to one's family once an individual's ability to make decisions has passed, even in the presence of some form of advance directive. Informed professionals didn't reach that decision officially; rather, it was more due to cowardice. It comes down to a de-facto removal of a person's right to self-determination once the patient is no longer a person. It's not sentimentality or a desire to preserve life that drives this tendency so much as the fact that a family member who retains their personhood also tends to retain the ability to contact an attorney, which a non-person person lacks.

As a result people who would never want to be kept alive by artificial means end up in what is essentially medical storage, with all kinds of tubes they would have refused. One way around that is to have lots of tedious forms filled out. The alternative, though perilous, is that we speak to the ones who will be at our bedside about what we do and do not want. Frightening as it is, this conversation informs our loved ones of our preferences so they are less likely to stray from the reservation, and it prepares them so they will be able to experience our death in a slightly less traumatic way. It might be viewed as brave or altruistic, this concern for others in the face of Death, but it is actually a way to recruit all the resources we will need when meeting Death (and Binky) or whomever one will be expecting.[5]

Anthropomorphic Personifications Are Good, but Are They Enough?

Even with having that anthropomorphized personification to help one wrap one's head around the process of declining life, at the moment of death (which *Choosing to Die* very subtly and ably captures) one is struck by the oppressively concrete ordinariness of everyday things in the face of the unreality of the end of one human's existence. In our traveling beyond the frontier of what is knowable we need an anchor, and our life partner, child, or (God forbid) parent can be that anchor when all the stuff we have learned or thought up along the way becomes pale.

That we conceptualize death at all is a sign of just how great an impact this inevitable loss associated with the absence of

---

[5] THERE'S JUST ME.

our *self* and those we love is for us (yes, we do mourn our own passing). The fact that there is no way of actually knowing what does or doesn't happen after this life is really scary and drives us to attempt understanding it by, at times, highly specious methods like religion and philosophy. The personification of death helps us find a place for that fear. Viewed from outside our thinking feeling selves the cessation of existence is anticlimactic, but as a personal experience it is nearly inconceivable. The ability to conceptualize death is possibly as important as vaccination to our ability to exist as a society. Discworld—it's improbability as a world on a disc supported by elephants supported by a turtle swimming through space, it's codification of all that need be understood in a coherent (and irreverent) system—is itself a journey away from fearful nothingness. That personification of death, Death, brought into creation by the dualistic need of the living as they struggle to understand, compelled into being without his consent or cooperation, has been set to a thankless task and is destined to remain till the last of the Disc's sentient passengers passes off past the great terrapin frontier. Death is a fundamental human drive expressed in a marvelously creative way by Sir Terry, who showed us that the anthropomorphic personification of death makes the end of our existence just a little less scary.

* * * * *

Having completed his task, the writer ceases to write. Reading back over the almost casual jumble of ideas, he thinks "I can't believe I get paid for this," taking comfort in the fact that the paycheck will buy little more than some craft beer and a sandwich at the local pub. He ponders one of the most frightening parts of the Choosing to Die *documentary, when Sir Terry asked a young man with MS, "Do you have a lot of happy memories?" and then followed by saying "I don't, they are disappearing at a reasonable rate." He looks out the window at the bright sunny landscape of winter turning to spring and picks up the phone to call his wife and tell her that he loves her. While just a bit corny as a device to close a chapter, it may just be part of the most fundamental reality there is.*

In the words of Sir Terry . . .

The End.

23
I'd Rather Stay an Orangutan Because That's Why Discworld Exists

NICOLAS MICHAUD

One said, We do not like this.
One said, It can only cause more trouble.
One said, How should we proceed?
One said, We do what we must.
One said, Right, but what must we do?
One said, That which must be done.
One said, Sure, but what is *that*.
One said, What is what?
One said, What is that which must be done?
One said, If what is that, then that is what, and so we will proceed.
One said, With *what???*
One said, Exactly.
One said, Look, I'm starting to get pissed o—
*And there in the dark an Auditor of Reality disappeared and *plink* a new one replaced it.*
One said, So what is it we are doing?
One said, That which must be done.
One said, *Gods damn it!*

Nicolas Michaud stared at his computer. He wrote words, but he was not particularly happy about it, or them. The book was late. He was late. And he knew if he didn't finish his chapter, his boss was likely to push him down a stairwell. But it was an impossible task. How was he to write a chapter about one of the most brilliant book series ever written? How could he write a chapter when all he could really feel was sad that there would never be any more of them?

"What is my *problem*? I can usually write a chapter in an hour. Trying to come up with an idea for this one has taken *weeks*." Michaud closed his eyes, breathed deeply and *begged*. "C'mon, just one brilliant idea. Maybe something about the Librarian? *Why* would he choose to stay an orangutan? Maybe something about that?"

Clearly, though, "brilliant" was a bit too much to ask; at this point he'd settle for "Marginally intelligible." "Screw it," he thought to himself. "I'm going to take a shower." It was then that, as is the case with all great ideas, when it was impossible to write anything down, far from his computer, tablet, or even a pen, Michaud got his idea.[1]

* * * * *

"Crap!"

And so, desperately holding on to his idea, shampoo still dripping into his eyes, the entoweled philosopher began to write, and found himself somewhere else.

"Lord Vetinari will see you at your convenience," said Drumknott, looking down at the middle-aged philosopher.

"But . . ."

"Might I suggest, Dr. Michaud, that when his Lordship says 'at his convenience' he means, 'At my convenience' which may be loosely translated, 'Before I decide he should have his head removed from his neck.'"

"Can I at least get dressed first?"

"That depends, sir: do you expect to need a necktie in addition to the custom hemp one with which the Patrician will present you if you keep him waiting?"

"Fair point."

Michaud climbed into the black carriage, holding onto his towel with as much dignity as he could. Somehow, as is ever increasingly the case in Florida, it was both hot and cold at the same time.

---

[1] It is a well-known fact that good ideas only come when one is incapable of writing them down. The universe isn't so much funny as it is malicious. I imagine that on his final walk home John Lennon was whistling to himself his newest and most brilliant tune.

"Dr. Michaud." The Patrician looked over his long, steepled fingers at the philosopher, as if deciding whether to throw a rather unattractive and small fish back, or simply do the world a favor and bludgeon it with a medium-sized rock. "You have a service you wish to perform."

"I do?"

"Are you saying you do not wish to perform it?" Long fingertips tapped against each other.

Michaud got the sense that this kind of question really should come with its own sound effect—a "dum-dum-*dummm,*" if you will. It was the kind of question that suggests that if it ended in a period instead, one would pay dearly for wasting the Patrician's time—likely at the cost of a limb per wasted word. Doing a quick and rough calculation in his head, Michaud decided he simply did not have enough spare limbs to take the chance.

"Of course not, my lord!" Michaud insisted, holding his splayed hands out ahead of him, like a starfish hoping to fend off a predator. "I meant only if you would be kind enough, I would be indebted"—the patrician's gaze sharpened—"*more indebted* to your lordship if you could remind me of what service I have already agreed to perform . . ." And just for good measure Michaud added, ". . . gladly."

The Patrician took a beleaguered breath. "As you know, Dr. Michaud, I do not like to waste my time with fools. That is to say, as long as they continue to do their work well within the confines of their guild hall. And for that reason, I am sure you are aware, I do not have much . . . patience . . . for philosophers."

Michaud kept his mouth closed and only nodded. Sometimes facts were just facts.

The Patrician continued, "However, taxingly enough, the good wizards of Unseen University insist that I need one. Simply, I do not want to waste the hard-earned money[2] of the good tax payers[3] of this fine city that, on hiring philosophers, as the fruit over their efforts[4] should continue to go to beautifying the city and maintaining, for example, its fine infrastructure . . ." and because the universe likes to have a laugh even at Lord Vetinari's expense, the carriage was suddenly jarred as

---

[2] Read, "the money gladly given away at knife point."

[3] Also read, "At knife point."

[4] Read, "The ability to afford a good knife."

the right front wheel hit a pothole, tossing Michaud about, while the patrician continued as if nothing had happened. "And so, in order to keep the cost to a minimum, we have decided to hire a . . . cheap . . . philosopher. Namely, you."

"I see." Michaud should have been insulted. But, like any other professional philosopher, he knew that any money was good money and looked forward to the fact that he might be able to afford to eat tonight, assuming he lived through the day. "And what is it you need a philosopher for, exactly?" Michaud quickly added, "—your Lordship."

"I am told by the wizards that there is concern due to the fact that your world does not believe that our world exists."

"Because it doesn . . . "

"I assure you, Dr. Michaud, it does. And I am charging you with proving it. As you know, the power of belief is significant, and your world's lack of belief, to be blunt, is causing a bit of blustering and indigestion amongst the wizards, and, while the bluster I can ignore, the indigestion is simply not good for business in the city. Happy wizards buy food, a great deal of it in fact, and when their appetite is reduced, the entire economy of my fair city suffers. So," Vetinari leaned forward disconcertedly, particularly to a man with soap in his hair and only a towel between his behind and *very* expensive leather upholstery, "*you* need to convince your people."

Michaud leaded back, mostly in thought but in part because the Patrician was the kind of terrifying that can only be accomplished by people who can whisper things like, "I can kill you any time I want to, with any object I choose, including, but not limited to a herring, and the only thing stopping me from doing so is the fact that I might find you useful someday" while smiling at his grandmother. "So you want me to convince my world that your world *really* exists?"

"Exactly."

"But that's imp—"

"Let me assure you, Dr. Michaud. There is no such thing as impossible. There are only things that should and should not be done. The question of possibility is only a question of . . ." and the Patrician's lips twisted in a rare smile, ". . . motivation. So, do not let me detain you further. I believe you have already wasted much time introducing your premise."

"What?" Michaud had difficulty taking hints sometimes.

"And remember, I know everything you know."

"Because you are only a figment of my . . ."

"I would not say it."

And Michaud thought, only to himself, "Imagination."

The Patrician raised one pristine eyebrow. "Philosophers would be wiser if they learned to keep some thoughts to themselves . . . there would be more of you still around." Michaud swallowed hard. "And now, Doctor, as you can see, the carriage has stopped, and I have kept you far too long. Please, do enjoy one of Mr. Dibbler's sausages as you are a tourist in our fair city; they are simply to *die* for."[5]

* * * * *

And then, as if in a dream—well, let's be honest, a nightmare—Michaud found himself, still dripping and awkwardly holding up his towel with one hand, in front of the door to Unseen University.

"Well, I suppose I should knock," the recently terrified philosopher thought to himself. "What harm could that do?"[6] And then, as if on cue, the Bursar opened the door.

The Bursar was looking at a point slightly over Michaud's shoulder and to the right, as if it were of far more interest than Michaud himself, which it probably was.

"Ah, good. We will have the garbanzo beans."

"I'm sorry?"

"Excellent. We appreciate your business." And with that, the Bursar bustled happily away with his prize, presumably imaginary garbanzo beans.

Michaud steeled himself. He had an idea. He just needed to get to the UU Library and the door was open. "Alright; down the rabbit hole we go," he thought to himself rather clichély. As Michaud crossed the threshold, he couldn't help but look around at the gilded arches and hallowed halls of Unseen University with awe. "It is so beautiful," he thought to himself. He felt the most at peace than he had for a long time as he breathed in the thick air that spoke of wisdom, age, and *books.*

---

[5] As eating one may well kill *you** (*IF I AM LUCKY.)

[6] Sometimes philosophers are offended that people think they ask stupid questions, but some questions are exactly that.

Of course, it was at that moment that a crossbow bolt embedded itself in the crotch of a priceless 1000-year-old satyr relief. Michaud couldn't help but think to himself, "Well, at least the satyr still has plenty of . . ." when the rational fear of a man who almost took a bolt through the eye caught up with him, causing him to throw up on the 2,000-year-old antique flooring.

"Hands up! That was a warning shot," bellowed a figure from the banister. "If I fire again, you will need an eye patch just to make a presentable corpse at your wake."

"But . . ."

"You heard me!"

Michaud put his hands up. Problematically, he had been previously holding up his towel, which now found itself about his ankles. Michaud was now acutely aware of how cold it was in the university. The Archchancellor laughed, and lowered his crossbow. "Well, we can see you are no danger to anyone but yourself. Pull up your trousers, man; show some self-respect!"

"But I don't have any—"

"It is indecent, son! Lord help us if Ms. Whitlow sees! I won't hear the end of it for a month. Propriety is propriety, son. Now I don't know what kind of weird cult you are in . . ."

"But . . ." Michaud, hazily, was pulling his towel back up.

"*But* around here we wear respectable clothes and carry ourselves with dignity. You should try it, boy. You are, after all, a doctor."

"Wait; how did you . . ."

Archchancellor Ridcully gave the confused philosopher a broad wink as he put his arm around him. "So. To the library, yes?"

"Yes, but . . ."

"Good!" Ridcully slapped Michaud on the back so hard the boy . . . er...ah . . . *man* almost dropped his towel again.

"Right this way. The Librarian can always use a good laugh, and when he gets a look at your hairless chest, he might cheer up a bit.[7] You see we've all been a bit on edge around here."

"Yes the Patri—"

"There has been some magical dissonance caused by a lack of belief. Normally, we don't really care what others believe about us as long as they believe *in* us."

---

[7] Which was unfair. Michaud had at least seven chest hairs.

"Kind of like go—"

"Don't say it son. Not unless you want to be nothing but a human frankfurter wrapped in a charred towel . . ."

Michaud's mouth clamped shut so quickly he bit his tongue.

"Really, it is just a matter of *respect*. We don't go around disbelieving in *you,* now do we?" Ridcully gave Michaud a rather disapproving up and down glance. "You should think that you all would do us the same courtesy."

"But—"

"Ah, here we are. I'll leave you in the Librarian's good hands, or whatever you would call those leathery mitts of his. Just remember, don't piss him off. If you annoy him, he can pull your sternum out through your nose and use it to play some Music with Rocks in, if you catch my drift."

"Oh, you mean don't call him a monk—"

"Really, do you philosophers have any sense of self-preservation? You are like a deer that decides to open a dentistry for mountain lions. It's a wonder any of you are left."

"Well, really there aren't that m—"

"Alright, son, you've been talking my ear off! Learn to listen. Now off you go. And seriously think about investing in some clothes!"

"But—"

* * * * *

And the Archchancellor was gone. Michaud heard one clear syllable behind him, and noticed the smell of mildly wet dog.

"Ook."

Michaud's face whipped around like a heady fanboy. "Holy crap! It's the Librarian! Finally! Okay, whatever you do, don't call him a monkey," he thought to himself.

"Eeeeek!" The Librarian jumped up and slammed his two fists into the ground on either side of Michaud, denting the hardened old wood noticeably.

"I'm sorry, sir! I'm beginning to realize my thoughts are not my own around here."

The Librarian gave Michaud a quizzical look. The kind that says, "Oh, so you are just now realizing that you are an idiot?" Really, it is the kind of look that only an ape can give a man.

"I meant no disrespect. In fact, I am a huge fan. You might be my favorite character."

The Librarian tilted his head in the opposite direction, as if to say, "Clearly, you are not appreciating the fact that right now you should be only so much red and pink paste smeared onto the hard wood floor."

"Ooooook?"

"That is to say, my *favorite* character."

"Ook!" Translating that one would likely take way too much time, and, well, may require some colorful words.

The Librarian turned around, waving Michaud into the library as the ape padded his way into what was the largest library in the entirety of the multiverse, and a pretty damn good place to keep a fine variety of bananas, if the Librarian could say so himself.

"Ook!"

Michaud leaded forward over the counter. The Librarian was now all business, looking over his glasses at Michaud.[8] "I need a book. I need one that will help me prove that Discworld is real."

"Ook?"

"My point exactly." Michaud actually had no idea what the Librarian was saying. But he figured he liked his sternum where it was.

Hopping down, the Librarian again made a motion to Michaud to follow him as he knuckled his way down one of the many corridors of books. Following the Librarian was a bit like walking behind a waddling 1970s armchair upholstered with shoulders.

As they meandered down the labyrinthian corridors, Michaud looked up in awe; he could not see an end to the books. It was a philosopher's dream. Everything that had been, would be, and *wouldn't* be written was here on these shelves. If only he had eternity and *a lot* of coffee. "Somewhere in here is my bestseller." Michaud couldn't help but wonder if it would be in the "Must read" aisle or the "Never written" section.

"Eeeeeek!"

---

[8] No, he wasn't wearing them before. Librarians always look over their classes dubiously at their patrons. If you were the guardian of the world's knowledge and the person before you was probably going to take one of your treasures, keep it in the loo, and then return it late with a couple of pages crinkled, you'd look annoyed too.

"Sorry!" Snapping back to reality, or whatever this was, Michaud hiked up his towel and hurried after the Librarian, who was now off in the distance.

By the time Michaud caught up, the Librarian was swinging himself from the top shelves as if he was at home in the forest.

"Ook, ook, ook!"

"Awesome!" (He still had no idea what the Librarian was saying).

The Librarian began to swing down, landing heavily, yet lightly next to Michaud and presented the man with his prize.

"Ook!"

"Holy crap." Michaud both thought and said this out loud. He was literally in unison with himself. He held in his hands . . . *Discworld and Philosophy*.

"Eeek!"

"Can I check it out?"

"Ook! Ook! Ook! Eeeeeeeek! Ook. Oooooook. Eeek!"

Taking his best guess: "I can't because, since I'm writing it right now, if I take it out it'll never be written, causing a temporal/spatial/logical paradox that will destroy the universe."

"Ook!" [9]

"Understood! Well, I will just give it a read here, then! Wouldn't want to destroy the universe, right?"

"Ook." The Librarian rolled his eyes.

* * * * *

Now firmly satisfied with his own self-importance, Michaud sat down in the newly renovated reading area of the library[10] and began to read . . .

. . . exactly the words that he was writing at this moment . . .

"Holy crap. I am watching myself reading my own thoughts as I write them." He could see the description of himself, seated on the couch, laptop on his, well . . . lap: smallish man, receding hairline, really should shave more often, bespectacled in black-rimmed hipster glasses.[11] "How is this possible? And what does

---

[9] Translation: "No, you idiot; like I just said, it is already on hold for another patron. Don't you philosophers *listen?*"

[10] There were now trees in the space from which readers could hang comfortably if they so chose.

[11] These glasses were now all the rage amongst philosophers, causing them to immediately go out of favor with the hipsters.

it mean? I am having the experience of my own self-narration! I am reading myself writing myself reading myself." Michaud found himself dizzy and enthralled.

And, in that daze, Michaud realized it, just like he had in the shower earlier, and then here again, *this* is why the Librarian wanted to stay an orangutan. *Words.* Words were power, but they were also distance. A dog doesn't have words for bones, or trees, or humans . . . all those things were just immediate experiences, immediate perceptions. But as much as some philosophers (**cough** David Hume, 1711–1776) wanted to believe that existing meant being a bundle of perceptions . . . only a collection of whatever they were perceiving through their senses now. Humans couldn't be *that,* because they experienced everything with words. Michaud wasn't *holding a book* right now; he was "holding a book." Unlike the Librarian who holds a banana and only *experiences the banana,* Michaud holds a banana and thinks to himself, "I am holding a banana."

This makes sense, Michaud read, in a crazy, stupid kind of a way. When I look around at my world I see "couch, blanket, TV, dog." What I am experiencing is the words *but the things themselves are lost behind the words.* I don't just get to see blue; I experience my own experience of the word itself, and so the experience is always lost in the words. A dog, on the other hand, like the one at my feet now doesn't think any of that; she just, with immediacy, experiences whatever is in front of her. So no wonder the Librarian wants to stay an ape; he wants to *actually experience the world, rather than be distant from it because of human language.* Every time the Librarian experiences *anything,* it is new because, unlike humans, he isn't reducing *all* chairs to "chair" and all bananas to "banana." Each singular experience of banana is its own texture, color, taste, and experience, which cannot be reduced to one abstract word!

And, right now, is the closest feeling Michaud ever gets to have to being the Librarian, because his immediate experience of "words" as he reflects on them *is of actual words.* So, unlike, say, a brick, in which his experience of red, porous, rough, and gritty are reduced to the word "brick," the words he was reading himself reading himself write are the actual content of his experience. *He was experiencing word as he wrote "word."* And that is the only time he ever gets to have that experience of both the perception and the act of reducing the perception into a word at the same time.

"So what I am saying is," Michaud thought to himself, his head beginning to hurt, "is that the words we use *actually create reality*. We don't experience any of the world directly; we always experience it as a set of stories, narratives, and terms. Our history isn't a set of facts; it is long gone. It is a series of stories we tell. Physics isn't a set of facts; it is a story we tell to help us understand the universe, everything we experience we experience as words, and *so our reality is words.* Everything we experience is words. Once we start using language we create a reality of words, unlike a dog or an orangutan. So for us, there is no real difference between words and reality because *the only way we can conceive of reality is to think in words!*

And that, my friends, is why Discworld is real. As Sir Terry always tried to point out, nothing is more real than narratives. In fact, narratives are all we have. The Disc is no less real than the world we *talk about* and *think about* living in. This is no trick of philosophical or linguistic frippery; it is *real.* Words make reality, and thus the Disc is real.

Michaud looked up at himself and wondered if the Patrician would be satisfied. Had he been convincing enough?

NOPE.

From the Ephebian Library

Abbott, Edwin M. 1884. *Flatland: A Romance of Many Dimensions.* London: Seely & Co., http://www.geom.uiuc.edu/~banchoff/Flatland/.

Alfano, Mark. 2013. *Character as Moral Fiction.* New York: Cambridge University Press.

Aristotle. *Nicomachean Ethics.* 1999. Trans. Terence Irwin. Indianapolis: Hackett.

Beauvoir, Simone de. 1964. *The Second Sex.* Trans. H. M. Parshley. New York: Bantam.

Butler, Joseph. 1736. Of personal identity. Appendix to *The Analogy of Religion, Natural and Revealed, to the Constitution and Course of Nature.* 2nd corrected ed. London: J. and P. Knapton. Reprinted in Perry 2008, *Personal Identity,* 99–106.

Camus, Albert. 1991. *The Myth of Sisyphus and Other Essays.* Vintage International.

Choosing to Die. 2011. Documentary produced by KEO North for BBC Scotland, directed and produced by Charlie Russell. (Not available on the BBC website at the time of publication, but available on Dailymotion and Youtube.)

Dikötter, Frank. 2010. *Mao's Great Famine: The History of China's Most Devastating Catastrophe, 1958-62.* Walker & Company.

Ducharme, Howard. 1986. Personal Identity in Samuel Clarke. *Journal of the History of Philosophy* 24, no. 3: 359–83.

Goodman, Nelson. 1968. *Language of Art.* Indianapolis: Bobbs-Merrill.

Harman, Gilbert. 1999. Moral philosophy meets social psychology: Virtue ethics and the fundamental attribution error. *Proceedings of the Aristotelian Society* 99: 315–31.

Honderich, Ted, ed. 2005. *The Oxford Guide to Philosophy.* Oxford University Press.

Huemer, Michael. 2013. *The Problem of Political Authority: An Examination of the Right to Coerce and the Duty to Obey.* New York: Palgrave Macmillan.

Kant, Immanuel. 1997. *Lectures on Ethics.* Cambridge University Press.

Locke, John. 1694. Of identity and diversity. Ch. 27 of bk. 2 of *An Essay Concerning Human Understanding*, 2nd ed. London: Th. Dring and S. Manship. Reprinted in Perry 2008, *Personal Identity*, 33–52.

MacKinnon, Catharine. 1999. Only words. In *Political Thought,* ed. Michael Rosen and Jonathon Wolff. Oxford: Oxford University Press,

Miller, Christian. 2003. Social psychology and virtue ethics. *Journal of Ethics* 7:4 365–92.

Moore, G. E. 2002. Hume's theory examined. In *Epistemology: Contemporary Readings*, ed. Michael Huemer. New York: Routledge.

Nozick, Robert. 2013 (1974). *Anarchy, State, and Utopia.* Rev. ed. Basic Books.

Perry, John, ed. 2008. *Personal Identity*. 2nd ed. Berkeley: University of California Press.

Plato. 2007. *The Republic*. Trans. Desmond Lee. Penguin.

Pratchett, Terry. 2013 (1983). *The Color of Magic.* New York: HarperCollins.

———. 1995. *Discworld: The Trouble with Dragons*. CD-ROM. Teeny Weeny Games and Perfect Productions.

———. 1996. *Feet of Clay.* New York: HarperCollins.

———. 2004. *Going Postal*. New York: HarperCollins.

———. 2013 (1989). *Guards! Guards!* New York: HarperCollins.

———. 1996. *Hogfather.* New York: Harpertorch,

———. 2000 (1984). *Interesting Times.* New York: HarperCollins.

———. 1998 (1997). *Jingo.* New York: HarperPrism.

———. 1999 (1998). *The Last Continent.* New York: HarperPrism.

———. 2001. *The Last Hero.* New York: HarperCollins.

———. 2013 (1986). *The Light Fantastic.* New York: HarperCollins.

———. 2007. Meeting Mr. Pratchett. Interview Juliette Hughes. http://www.theage.com.au/news/books/meeting-mr-pratchett/2007/02/15/1171405371862.html

———. 2000 (1993). *Men at Arms*. New York: HarperCollins. (HarperCollins eBook edition, 2009.)

———. 2008 (2007). *Making Money*. New York: HarperCollins.

———. 2004 (2003). *Monstrous Regiment*. New York: HarperCollins.

———. 2009 (1987). *Mort*. New York: HarperCollins. (HarperCollins eBook edition, 2009.)

———. 2002 (1990). *Moving Pictures.* New York: HarperCollins.

———. 2003 (2002). *Night Watch*. New York: HarperCollins.

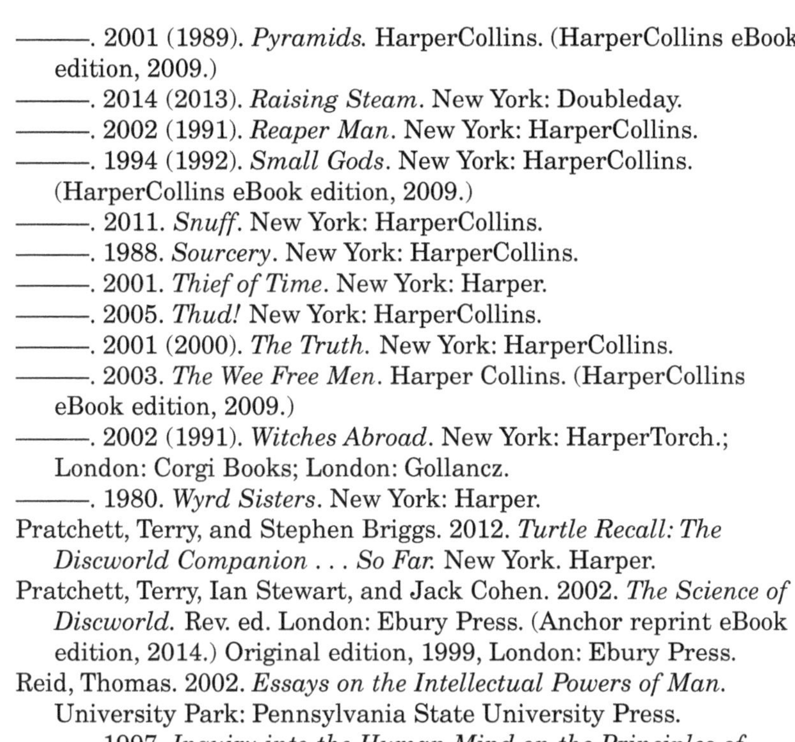

———. 2001 (1989). *Pyramids*. HarperCollins. (HarperCollins eBook edition, 2009.)

———. 2014 (2013). *Raising Steam*. New York: Doubleday.

———. 2002 (1991). *Reaper Man*. New York: HarperCollins.

———. 1994 (1992). *Small Gods*. New York: HarperCollins. (HarperCollins eBook edition, 2009.)

———. 2011. *Snuff*. New York: HarperCollins.

———. 1988. *Sourcery*. New York: HarperCollins.

———. 2001. *Thief of Time*. New York: Harper.

———. 2005. *Thud!* New York: HarperCollins.

———. 2001 (2000). *The Truth*. New York: HarperCollins.

———. 2003. *The Wee Free Men*. Harper Collins. (HarperCollins eBook edition, 2009.)

———. 2002 (1991). *Witches Abroad*. New York: HarperTorch.; London: Corgi Books; London: Gollancz.

———. 1980. *Wyrd Sisters*. New York: Harper.

Pratchett, Terry, and Stephen Briggs. 2012. *Turtle Recall: The Discworld Companion . . . So Far.* New York. Harper.

Pratchett, Terry, Ian Stewart, and Jack Cohen. 2002. *The Science of Discworld.* Rev. ed. London: Ebury Press. (Anchor reprint eBook edition, 2014.) Original edition, 1999, London: Ebury Press.

Reid, Thomas. 2002. *Essays on the Intellectual Powers of Man.* University Park: Pennsylvania State University Press.

———. 1997. *Inquiry into the Human Mind on the Principles of Common Sense.* University Park: Pennsylvania State University Press.

Russell, Bertrand. 2007. *A History of Western Philosophy*. 10th ed. Simon & Schuster.

Searle, John R. 1995. *The Construction of Social Reality*. Free Press.

Singer, Peter. 1972. Famine, affluence, and morality. *Philosophy and Public Affairs* 1, no. 1: 229–43.

Uexkuell, Jakob von. An Introduction to Umwelt. *Semiotica* 134, no. 1-4 (2001): 107.

UNICEF. The impact of the food and financial crises on child mortality: The case of sub-Saharan Africa. < http://www.childimpact.unicef-irc.org/en/macro-micro-simulations/impact-of-food-and-financial-crises-on-child-mortality>.

Wittgenstein, Ludwig. 1974. *Tractatus Logico-Philosophicus*. Routledge.

Ephebians

Don Fallis is Professor of Information Resources and Adjunct Professor of Philosophy at the University of Arizona. His philosophical work includes the scholarly articles "What Is Lying?" and "What Is Disinformation?" He is preparing to teach in the Department of Fluencing at Unseen University next year.

Vanessa Fröhlich is working on a PhD thesis on the Discworld novels at the University of Bochum, Germany. Her philosophical interests include Postmodernism, Existentialism and theories of humor. Since these don't tend to pay her bills, she also has a proper job as a translator. In her free time, she likes to knit (better than Lady Sybil, she hopes). She lives in Bochum with her husband and two cats, who are still waiting for the invention of the paw-operated can opener so that they can finally throw the humans out of the apartment.

Douglas Jordan studied philosophy at Fredonia State University and criminal justice at Buffalo State College. He still wonders if there will ever be knowledge of the origins of the universe, or if we are floating on the backs of elephants.

Kamil Karaś is still trying to earn his Ph.D. in English Literature at the (very much Unseen) University of Gdańsk, Poland, in the Department of Ne(cr)ophilology. As a scholar, Kamil thinks of himself as similar to Jason Ogg—Jason being an omnipotent smith who can shoe any animal (and will do so). Kamil does the same with students—only he does not provide them with horseshoes (though he would like to more often than not), but rather with knowledge. Kamil can teach English and Literature to anyone (and often does). As a deeply (im)moral person, his philosophical interests are Christian (but not only) morality and ethics.

John V. Karavitis, CPA, MBA. What's that, you say? You want John's bio? "His"-story? Here. Grab your favorite color crayon and write it out yourself. (Remember, stay within the lines!)

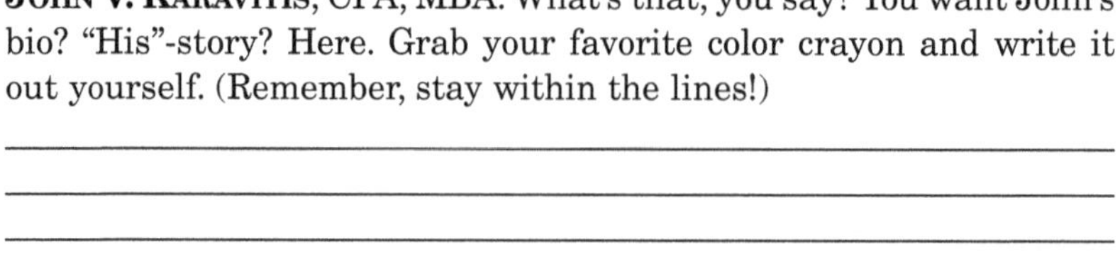

Brandon Kempner lives and teaches in northern New Mexico. He earned his Ph.D. from Penn State and has published essays in *Neil Gaiman and Philosophy, The Walking Dead and Philosophy, and Jurassic Park and Philosophy*. His research into creating his own Luggage is going quite poorly, but what else would you expect of an English professor and a philosopher?

Christopher Ketcham earned his doctorate from the University of Texas at Austin. He teaches business and ethics for the University of Houston Downtown. His research interests are risk management, applied ethics, social justice, and East-West comparative philosophy. Chris is left handed and writes backwards as a result, He is from Sinesterata, the left world, far to the down of Discworld in both politics and ideology.

Mike Kugler earned his doctorate in history at the University of Chicago. He's taught at Northwestern College in Iowa for over twenty years. Sometimes accused of being Victorian by day but Mediterranean at night, he often wears a kilt just for that fresh, free feeling . . . and for the spare change and lit cigarettes tossed at him from moving cars.

Daniel P. Malloy, Ph.D., has been teaching philosophy and writing about philosophy and popular culture for a while now. He's published chapters on *Star Wars*, *Inception*, *The Terminator*, *Batman*, *Superman*, *Green Lantern*, *Iron Man*, *Spider-Man*, and *The Avengers*. He's run out of dried frog pills. Please send more, for the hallucination that he is perfectly sane is wearing off, and the office supplies are on the verge of rebelling.

Trip McCrossin teaches in the Philosophy Department at Rutgers University, where he works on, among other things, the nature, history, and legacy of the Enlightenment. He's grateful for many things, not least of which is that no one seems to have figured out yet that he actually believes in the "theory of narrative causality."

Nicolas Michaud, Ed.D., teaches philosophy and English in Jacksonville, Florida. He is a philosopher, which means the wizards wouldn't like him, and likely neither would the Patrician or the Watch. He does, however, have an affinity for cats, which means he and Death should get along famously. Great.

Daniel Miori, MS PA-C, is a physician assistant who works in Geriatric and Palliative medicine by day and is a discredited fly-by-night ethicist of irreligious character, great laxity of moral principle, and intemperate habits. He is a writer, if grocery lists and the popular philosophy books count, and has contributed to six of one and a half dozen of the other. When traveling through Ankh-Morpork he can be found drowning the last of his professional pride at Sham Harga's House of Ribs, where Death may not be on the menu, but he is the cook.

Jeremy Pierce did his Ph.D. in philosophy at Syracuse University and now holds the position of Prehumous Professor of Extreme Metaphysics at Le Moyne College in Syracuse, NY. His philosophical interests range widely across philosophy of race, philosophy of religion, and of course extreme metaphysics. He also enjoys clacks gaming, helping out the History Monks in repairing temporal paradoxes, and using Headology on his five children.

In what is destined to be known as its great age of Discworld writers, **Matthew Skene** also obtained his Ph.D. in philosophy from Syracuse University. He has published papers on how easy it is to know stuff and on how hard it is to know stuff. He currently teaches in Denver, CO, where he is a dad.

Jamie Carlin Watson earned his doctorate studying the ancient Ephebian art of epistemology and now teaches in the much less magical Ft. Lauderdale. He rarely visits the Disc these days, spending most of his time avoiding clacks from the Watch and writing about epistemic authority, expertise, and bioethics. He has applied to teach at Unseen University a number of times, contending that philosophy is an important kind of magic that makes people see things your way. Unfortunately, the response is always the same: No one listens to philosophers anymore.

A High Magical Index

www.ingramcontent.com/pod-product-compliance
Lightning Source LLC
Jackson TN
JSHW071701170426
101040JS00022B/448